The Invisible Cut gets inside the editor's head more than anything I've ever read. O'Steen provides a fascinating window into the editorial process through the use of frame grabs and film analysis. This honest and unique book defines the language of film in the special way editors must understand. *The Invisible Cut* will be enlightening to filmmakers or anyone who loves the art of film.
 — Carol Littleton, film editor, *E. T. The Extra-Terrestrial, Beloved, Body Heat,* and *The Anniversary Party*

With this meticulous book, Bobbie O'Steen has dissected the fine art of cinema's surgeons and created an invaluable guide for anyone seriously interested in the mysteries of film.
 — Lawrence Kasdan, writer/director, *Body Heat, The Big Chill,* and *Grand Canyon*

Normally I don't like to read books about editing in my spare time, since it's a bit like bringing the office home, but unlike most film technique books, Bobbie O'Steen's book is both entertaining and instructive. *The Invisible Cut* is original and captures a complete picture of what we do. Great required reading for any filmmaking class.
 — Chris Lebenzon, film editor, *Sweeney Todd, Charlie and The Chocolate Factory, Enemy of the State,* and *Top Gun*

This book is a terrific demystification of a poorly understood art. Without burying the reader in "geek" or "tech" talk, Bobbie O'Steen, drawing on a distinguished editing heritage, introduces us to no-nonsense, easy-to-comprehend principles of the mysterious art of editing.
 — John Badham, director, *Saturday Night Fever, WarGames,* and professor, Film & Media, Chapman University

The Invisible Cut is a wonderful book for both filmgoers and filmmakers — explaining and illustrating how editors apply their magic and the world that editors live and work in. Bobbie O'Steen clearly explains the politics of the editing room, the screening room, and the studios. It would have made everything easier if I had had this book to read at the start of my career.
 — Alan Heim, film editor, *All That Jazz, Network,* and *The Notebook*

This is the first book about the craft of editing that demystifies the process: that clarifies precisely what a film editor does with film, how he does it, and why. It's a straightforward, engaging exposition of the editorial process from the first day of shooting until the movie is in the theater. All this, using as examples some of the best films ever made. I wish I'd had Bobbie's book when first starting out. It would have saved me a lot of time and trouble, because it explains certain truths about editing that one comes to grasp only after editing for many years. Highly recommended!
 — Joe Hutshing, film editor, *Jerry Maguire, JFK, Almost Famous,* and *Born On The Fourth of July*

I wish *The Invisible Cut* had been available to me when I made my first cuts as an editor. It would have guided my choices, reinforcing them with purpose and focus. With personal accounts from editors who made the cuts, accompanied by perfect frame grabs, O'Steen's book explains an intuitive and abstract art that is the film editor's craft.
 — William Hoy, film editor, *We Were Soldiers, Fantastic 4, 300, Watchmen*

The Invisible Cut is an impressive book. Bobbie O'Steen has a unique perspective and an uncanny insight into the complicated mind of the editor. I found that a bit unnerving, as if she could read my thoughts when I wake up at 4 a.m. obsessing about a sequence I'm grappling with. I found her book very educational and entertaining.
 — Michael Tronick, film editor, *Scent of a Woman, R*
 and *Hairspray*

The Invisible Cut is the essential book of editing for students and professionals alike. Its use of frame clips brings to life what other authors only write about. O'Steen has created one of the truest books about film editing ever written. I wish I'd had this book when I began my editing career. It should be mandatory reading for all film schools.

> — Randy Roberts, President, American Cinema Editors and producer, *Law & Order SVU*

The Invisible Cut has taught me the ins and outs of the final — and often least understood — stage of producing a film. Perhaps most importantly, it has taught me how to apply tricks of the editor's trade to my own craft. Whether you're a writer, director, actor, DP — or even a novelist or playwright — exploring how film editors shape raw material into a final, emotional whole offers valuable lessons in scene construction, pacing, shot composition, and even dialogue-writing. Whatever your particular craft, Bobbie O'Steen's book is a terrific resource for anyone who spends their life making movies or telling stories.

> — Chad Gervich, TV writer/producer, and author of *Small Screen, Big Picture: A Writer's Guide to the TV Business*

Using scripts and frame shots from classic films, Bobbie O'Steen takes you inside the world of editing — turning it inside out to show you most everything you need to know about the process. An excellent book for both filmmakers and film fans.

> — Matthew Terry, filmmaker, screenwriter, teacher, and columnist for *www.hollywoodlitsales.com*

Bobbie O'Steen's new book makes visible some of the secrets of a mysterious art. With great clarity it reveals the craft of the editorial magician. It is a fine follow-up to her earlier book on the invisible art.

> — Ray Zone, 3D filmmaker; columnist, *Editors Guild Magazine*

THE INVISIBLE CUT

HOW EDITORS MAKE MOVIE MAGIC

BOBBIE O'STEEN

Published by Michael Wiese Productions
3940 Laurel Canyon Blvd. # 1111
Studio City, CA 91604
tel. 818.379.8799
fax 818.986.3408
mw@mwp.com
www.mwp.com

Cover Design: MWP
Book Layout: Gina Mansfield Design
Editor: Linda Norlen

Printed by Sheridan Books, Inc., Chelsea, Michigan
Manufactured in the United States of America

Library of Congress Cataloging-in-Publication Data

O'Steen, Bobbie, 1952–
 The invisible cut : how editors make movie magic / by   Bobbie O'Steen.
     p. cm.
 Includes bibliographical references.
 ISBN 978-1-932907-53-7
 1. Motion pictures--Editing. I. Title.
 TR899.O88 2009
 778.5'35--dc22

                              2008038628

TABLE OF CONTENTS

FOREWORD

What does a film editor really do? He decides what you see on the screen and for how long you see it. But that makes his work sound too simple. Whenever the editor chooses a shot, even if it only subtly changes a point of view or the timing of an actor's response, he will create an impact on the scene and even the entire movie. And every time he decides precisely where to start that shot and where to end it, he is contributing to an overall rhythm and pace that must pull the audience in and tell the story in the most satisfying way. In fact he is constantly taking the audience's pulse. No matter how moved or excited they are, no matter how much fun they may be having, the editor has to always be aware that he might lose their involvement.

Editing is hard to analyze and evaluate. Only a movie's director, cinematographer, and editor really know the quality of the original footage, and how much control the editor had over the final cut. Many editors have actually done their best work with mediocre films, because they salvaged a movie that otherwise would not have been viable. Not only is the art and craft of editing elusive; in many cases, so are the editors themselves. For the most part they are insightful and visual, but not very verbal. Because they're primarily led by their instincts, when they're asked to explain why they made a particular cut, they may simply say, "It just felt right."

I developed an understanding of those mysterious editors by being immersed in their world. My father, Richard Meyer, was a film editor and so was my husband of twenty-three years, the late Sam O'Steen. These two men couldn't have been more different in personalities, but they both shared a passion for their work. They thought that editing movies was an endlessly intriguing challenge, and each would lie in bed at night, turning possibilities over in his mind, trying to solve the puzzles that could make a movie reach its greatest potential. They would never be completely satisfied; if they happened to see their work years later, they'd be convinced they could have done a better job, always holding onto the hope for more. Editing permeated their lives to the extent that they would even see life around them in edits, especially when someone told a joke or made a speech that went on too long.

Working as a story editor, a screenwriter, and film editor gave me my own perspective on the moviemaking process. I am also known to my family as "the interrogator," which certainly helped when I wrote *Cut to the Chase*, based on interviews I did with my husband about his work. In those interviews he said, *"When people notice editing, it's probably bad. You're trying to tell a story. It's not about somebody showing off. I prefer not to be seen in my films."*[1] It's not easy to describe something that is intended to be invisible, but in that book I was able to get Sam to explain his process of cutting a movie. This book goes beyond any one editor's experience; it is meant to give the reader an even deeper and more visually exciting understanding of editing.

The first section of this book will explain the whys and hows of cutting movies. However, an editor would be the first one to say that his work can never be fully explained without "show-and-tell." For that reason, I've dedicated the second section of the book to thirteen scenes from nine different movies and used "frame grabs," individual frames from the scenes themselves, to explain the choices the editor made. (These movies are referred to at various points throughout the book with asterisks.) They were selected not only because they represent different types of scenes, such as suspense and comedy; they also come from movies that are memorable markers in movie history. Three of these movies have personal significance for me as well, since my father edited one of them (*Butch Cassidy and the Sundance Kid*) and my husband edited two of them (*The Graduate* and *Chinatown*).

My use of masculine pronouns to refer to editors and other members of the moviemaking team is meant to be a neutral choice. There are at least as many talented women in film as there are men. In fact, the two editors I chose to interview for this book are women: the film editor Carol Littleton and the music editor Suzana Peric. I would also like to note that most of the editors in the early days of silent movies were women, at the time when editing was thought to resemble a craft such as knitting. When sound was introduced the job was considered to be more "technical" and eventually men came to dominate the field. However, as editors went from being considered hired hands to key collaborators, women kept their foothold.

INTRODUCTION:
THE SEDUCTIVE MAGICIAN

Movies take us on a journey like no other. When we watch a movie, we let ourselves forget we're seeing pieces of film joined together — and that we're being completely manipulated. The director, along with the screenwriter, cast, and crew, all help set up the illusion, but ultimately the editor must pull the rabbit out of the hat and make us believe in movie magic. He's the seducer who not only anticipates our needs and feelings, but makes us want things we're not even aware of. He's the deceiver who tricks us into believing we're experiencing real time instead of movie time and convinces us we're in a familiar three-dimensional space, even though film is actually in two dimensions. Like the magician who uses the sweep of his cape to distract the audience from the setup of a trick, the editor uses the movement on the screen as his sleight-of-hand, so the audience won't notice that moviemaking really is quite problematic.

The editor and director know they've pulled off their act when they're sitting in the middle of the theater observing the body language of the audience all around them. Moviegoers may lean forward or backward in their seats, widen their eyes, or look away. They may gasp, scream, cough, clear their throats, laugh, be silent — or for a moment even stop breathing. The editor will notice how engrossed the audience is, but he'll be more consumed by the times when he feels he's lost them. When the audience is bored, annoyed, or confused, the magic bubble bursts, and no one knows those moments more acutely or feels more responsible for them than the editor.

An editor has to be born with a strong sense of rhythm and an instinct for what looks good. He has to have a keen memory so that he can replay in his head all the film he's seen, then visualize the sequence of cuts he'll put together. He has to have a gut feeling for what works, be able to sense what's in the audience's hearts and minds. Only then will his cuts become those invisible transitions that grab viewers by the seat of their pants and keep them there.

Digital technology has opened up mind-boggling possibilities for filmmakers and only time will tell how endless they may be. Audiences have also changed; along with a greater ability to absorb information than ever before, they now have a shorter attention span. But they still have the same need: to be told a story in the most interesting and involving way. The editor has evolved, too, and is allowed and even expected to break rules more often. However, he still has to learn the basic concepts and techniques of editing first, which he'll only really master through trial and error. When he has done so, he'll have the confidence to take chances and try some pretty crazy things — and it's amazing how many times they actually work!

All told, editing is a quirky combination of truth, trickery, and luck. When the editor reaps the best of all three, he can create movie magic

CHAPTER 1

SETTING THE STAGE

There are two stages of filmmaking that predate the "first cut" (when the editor puts the movie into the first complete chronology of scenes before fine-tuning begins). Both include the editor to various degrees.

PREPRODUCTION

In the stages when the director is rehearsing, doing script revisions, location scouting, casting — or even making costume, set design, and makeup decisions — the editor may or may not be a part of them. Because he's not considered essential to these stages, the role the editor plays varies tremendously. It depends on his interest in being involved, but more significantly on the egos and personalities of both the director and editor, and how that combination affects the depth of their relationship.

SHOOTING

The energy, sometimes even chaos, on the set, contrasts sharply with the controlled quiet of the cutting room. Some editors prefer to stay in their environment, in some cases just to keep their objectivity. There are also others who find that, by occasionally being on the set and observing the choices made, they have a better understanding of what the director wants. The confidence of the director is a real factor here. Some directors, especially first-timers, feel they need the technical expertise of the editor along with that of the cinematographer. In that case the editor may suggest shots, but he has to be careful not to step on the cinematographer's toes.

Even with an experienced director, it's common for the editor to be called on the set when there's a sticky logistical problem. When shooting a complex action or group scene, filmmakers may need to ask the editor if the shots are "blocked out" (that is, the camera and actors positioned) well enough to get "coverage" (the necessary camera setups and angles) for a scene. The editor, or his assistant, may also be called in for a matching issue. For instance, he may be asked to bring film clips to show what position an actor was in or what he was wearing. Also, if the production is short on time and money, the director may ask the editor if certain coverage is really necessary.

Regardless, it's unusual for the editor to sit on the set all the time, if only because he needs to be cutting while the rest of the crew is shooting. The director will usually expect to see most of the movie in a first cut after completing "principal photography" (the shooting that involves the entire cast and original crew). "Second unit photography" (shot by a secondary crew that doesn't require the director or principal actors) may occur before or after principal photography. If the movie is a huge production that has two or more units shooting and an enormous amount of film, the first cut may not be expected to be done by the time filming is completed. However, this is the exception rather than the rule. The director should see the film cut before he releases the crew and cast, in order to know if he needs to reshoot anything. In fact, that extra time is usually built into the initial schedule. Logistics and cast availability can become an expensive problem if the reshoots have to be done later.

If a production company is shooting on location, the editor may not be in the same city, but usually he travels with the company unless the budget is very small. During the shoot the editor's assistants will prepare the "dailies" (the film shot the previous day to screen for the director and often for the cast and crew). Traditionally, dailies were in a film format, but now, depending on the movie's budget and the ever-changing technology, they can also be shown on high-definition tape or in a digital format. In fact, the director and editor may sometimes just watch the previous day's footage together on a computer.

The degree of input the director has when the editor is putting the film together also varies widely. But at the very least the director almost always gives his opinions during dailies. He may select certain shots, and he may want to start a scene from a particular angle. He many prefer specific "takes" (units of film shot from the same angle), a decision which might be based on an actor's performance. How much cut film the director sees during shooting varies, depending on the number of problems or concerns about the movie — or the director's confidence in the editor. The maximum input would be the director working with the editor on weekends and during downtime on the set and telling him where to cut. This is rare, and might mean the director has very little faith in the editor, a very big ego, or both. If he knows a great deal about the mechanics of editing, and he has specifically planned his shots to cut together a certain way, he may be more involved. But if the director values the editor's talent, usually he'll want to begin by seeing how the editor works with the material. The director will also be able to keep a certain degree of objectivity if he steps back and lets the editor wrestle with the film.

CHAPTER 2

PULLING OFF THE ACT

THE FIRST CUT

The logistics of making movies are overwhelming and, in fact, each stage of the process will leave behind problems. Whatever the case, only a percentage of the filmmakers' intentions end up on film, and miracles are not made in the cutting room. Even though an editor can make the most out of a bad script or terrible dailies, he cannot make a good movie out of such material. The editor has to bear the repercussions of this cold reality when he assembles everything. That's the negative part. But this first cut is also the time of greatest potential for the editor, because he will be in the freshest and most open-minded state when he approaches the movie. Still, it's a frightening first step when the editor plunges in to find out what he's really got to work with.

Before the editor even touches the film, though, he has to prepare himself. Initially, he should read the script many times and become as familiar as he can with what the director and writer envisioned. Once he's internalized the material, he must think about each scene and its context in the whole movie. He should see the script as the blueprint with his editing as the final step of the movie. He is, after all, the last storyteller in the filmmaking process. When at last the filmed scene is sitting in front of him, he should ask himself such questions as:

> > What is the scene about? What is its overall function? Where is this scene in the trajectory of the story and in the development of the characters?

> > Is the audience supposed to identify with a particular character or are we supposed to hate him? Should that character be dominant or play a secondary role? Should the emphasis or sympathy shift to another character during the course of the scene?

> > Are there details that need to be emphasized to reveal character or plot?

> > Is there a surprise or shock that has to be set up?

> > What are the dramatic arcs or climaxes in the scene, and if there is more than one, which is the most powerful?

> > How well does that scene play within the context of the whole movie?

Each editor has a different way of looking at the raw footage. Some editors say that initially they watch it as if they were the audience, while other editors immediately start cutting in their heads as they view the dailies. Regardless, the editor should run the film as many times as he needs to absorb it, logging notes about which angles and takes he and the director like best, along with special moments and particular lines of dialogue.

Then comes the physical part. The editor sits at the computer. He's absorbed the film and the comments about it, and now he realizes he is about to face a stream of constant decisions. He has three to make right away: what angle and take to use, where to start each shot and where it should end. It seems so simple, until he realizes how nearly limitless his choices are. The good news is that the first cut already dramatically reduces the number of potential choices, but the number of decisions may still feel overwhelming.

The key advice here is that the editor should relax and let the material lead him. He has to trust his instincts and try to see the movie as a whole. Just as an artist does when he makes sculpture out of a piece of clay, he has to first create a basic shape and worry about polishing it later. He should not be overwhelmed by the whole movie, but just take it scene by scene. He shouldn't count frames, or inch backward and forward over the cuts. This is not math or mechanics. He should just let the cuts be and not get tripped up by subtleties or details, such as an action that doesn't match up perfectly from shot to shot or a line that can't be heard clearly. If he over analyzes and second-guesses this early in editing, he may become lost and confused at a very crucial stage.

If the editor finds himself stuck, struggling with a scene and unable to fix it, he should put that scene aside and let it rest. This is also true if he runs a scene and hates what he did. If he lets even a few days pass, he'll be amazed at how much more objective he'll be about what needs to be done to fix the problem. Showing it to others, especially assistants or apprentices, can also be helpful, although too many opinions at this stage can be dangerous. The editor should trust that once the film takes shape, it will become more obvious to him where the pacing is too slow, what should be eliminated or moved, and what the problems are.

There are also no hard-and-fast rules that dictate how the editor should approach the material. It depends on the editor, the input he gets from the director, and the needs of the particular scene. An editor might first use the best "master shot" (the all-inclusive shot that establishes characters and their setting), and then run different angles after that, trading them into the shot where necessary. Some editors may choose a different starting point, maybe even a close-up, and build from there. No matter what, the editor should try to put in a version of everything the director shot from the script, unless it's horrible. This doesn't mean he must use every angle, since that would bog the movie down. But a first go-through will be longer than the final movie will be. The basic rule of thumb is that the first cut is 10% to 15% longer than the final cut. As the cutting progresses, the film will take on a life of its own, because every movie has its own rhythm, based on the type of story being told, the actors' performances, and the director's style.

THE EDITOR AND DIRECTOR GO TO WORK

After the first cut, the director may move right into the cutting room — or, more likely, take a short vacation. If the director has not seen the entire movie before the company "wraps" (finishes shooting), he will at least have seen most of the edited film, and certainly any problematic material that may need to be reshot. After the director's hiatus, he and the film editor often screen the movie in a small theater to simulate the real viewing experience, rather than watching it on a computer. When the editor and director see this initial assemblage of the movie, it's their golden moment of objectivity. It's the closest they will both ever be to the heart, mind, and body of the audience. Once they start picking at it, they'll both lose that precious distance. Although the director is usually nervous about seeing the first cut, at least he's not yet susceptible to outside pressure and too many opinions. The downside is that the editor has to help the director deal with the fact that only some of his expectations are captured on film.

In those months when the director and editor are fine-tuning, they will pay a lot of attention to details, but they should always remember their first impressions of the overall movie. They must also remain faithful to their initial concerns, such as whether the main character is likable enough, which characters need to be more developed, what part of the story is confusing, and whether the story is saying what they want it to say. As the director and editor continue to discuss the movie, the editor will become more in tune with the director's intentions, and he should honor them but also try to surprise the director by going beyond those expectations. Sometimes he will even need to play the devil's advocate and subvert the director's expectation. There will be an exchange back and forth between the director and editor working together and the editor working alone. They may run a scene and discuss it at length, and the editor may do some cutting while the director is present. However, he will often want to be alone to struggle with the film after getting the director's input, especially if it is problematic. Then the editor can totally concentrate, while giving the director some distance before he returns to look at it again. During this process they may juggle a scene or "sequence" (a series of scenes connected by story, time, or place), "lift" scenes (remove them from the edited movie), alter their length, and change takes and angles. They may also undo many of those changes, and then make them again!

This is the time when the editor's patience, flexibility, and sense of humor will be tested. If the director asks him to do something he's strongly opposed to, he can voice his objections, but he should still try it. No matter what, the editor should not fall into the trap of thinking he's right just because he has more technical knowledge or is more familiar with all the film. Being a collaborator is an essential part of the editor's role. Besides, he'll never know for sure that something doesn't work until he tries it.

CHAPTER 3

MASTERING THE MAGIC

Although it's often necessary to be flexible when working with the director, here is some advice to keep you, the editor, on track as you master the art of editing:

Concentration is the name of the game.
Because you have to be totally immersed in the film when you cut it, getting organized is a necessary first step to keeping your head clear.

Tell the story and get the good stuff.
This may seem obvious, but if you keep that line in the back of your mind like a mantra, it will help you stay on course. Think of it like telling a good joke, where your timing must be just right and you must know when to wrap it up.

Every story has a beginning, a middle, and an end. Know what's expected in each section.
Beginning: Open with impact: You've got about ten minutes before the audience judges you.

Middle: You must keep the audience caring while you keep the story moving.

End: No matter how much the audience has liked the movie so far, if the ending doesn't work, you're dead. You must find a delicate balance with the ending; you should try to make it believable and emotionally satisfying without its being overly predictable.

Movie first, scene second, moment third.
That should be the order of importance whenever a cut is made. Each has to be justified by how well it serves the movie. You can't hold onto a scene or moment just because you or the director falls in love with a showy piece or something that has personal meaning. The editor should be less susceptible to such ego-driven choices.

As long as it's working, don't cut.
Appreciate the values on screen, trust the moment.

Always cut for a reason.
Cut for new information or emotion. Editors have a tendency to over-cut, often to get noticed.

The moment you peak — cut!
Don't be on the nose, be barely ahead of the audience. Always leave them wanting more.

Never cut for a line, only for a reaction.
If the audience knows what the character is saying, and they're not going to get more information from seeing that character, cut to someone else who reveals more.

What moves and makes noise attracts attention.
Keep this in mind whenever you need to use sleight-of-hand to distract the audience.

Avoid boring the audience.
It's the editor's worst sin. Not only will moviegoers' minds wander, but so will their eyes. As a result, they'll notice more mistakes and problems.

Avoid repetition.
Not only with storytelling, but also with visuals. If you have to cut back to the same shot again for some reason, make it shorter every time, since you're not giving the audience new information.

Avoid confusion.

This is especially true about the audience's sense of placement. Try to establish the geography of the actors or objects as quickly as possible and then if new actors enter, reestablish them in relation to the other actors.

Look at the movie as a series of arcs.

Both in individual scenes and in the movie overall, you start at one level, build to a climax, then have to lower intensity and start all over again, because there's nowhere else to go. If you stay at one level, the movie won't sustain interest, even if it's all noise and drama. What makes a film interesting is how you structure the highs and lows.

Trust the quiet moments.

Silence and stillness are usually more powerful than their opposites. Editing is often about pausing, watching, and waiting. In the quiet of a dialogue scene, you can create as much suspense as you can in a car chase.

Cut in motion, whenever possible.

Individual shots and entire scenes should, if possible, begin and end with continuous motion, because those transitions makes the cuts appear seamless and keep the momentum going.

Initially, cut longer rather than shorter.

It's easier to trim down than to add more.

Keep tracking the emotional impact.

Cut for the actors' eyes or for any other subtle expression that reveals the heart. The slightest change in expression can show depth of feeling.

Figure out how to correct what's wrong without hurting what's good.

A change has a domino effect on the value and impact of the film around it.

Don't presume anything until it's all put together.

A scene that may have been powerful on its own can fail to work with what comes before or after it. A more subtle version — or no scene at all — may make the movie play better.

Never say never and never give up.

You should try everything, even making cuts that, logically, should not work. There are so many happy accidents and welcome surprises. Besides, you can always undo what you've tried.

Surprise them.
Keeping the audience on edge and off center sustains interest.

Rules are meant to be broken.
Eventually knowledge and experience will help you know how far to push the limits and give you the nerve to follow through on whatever bold choice you make. After all, only after Picasso had the skill and training to depict the human body realistically did he have the guts to paint it all cockeyed!

If you want to shake up the audience, do it for a reason.
A cut that's meant to be obvious and have visual punch should still serve a purpose.

Editing is about thinking, not cutting.
Don't jump the gun; sit back and ponder your choices before you act.

The best cut is the one you never see.
The invisible one that pulls the audience along without their knowing it.

The art of editing is the art of trickery.
Don't remind the audience of the mechanics of moviemaking. Make them believe in the magic.

CHAPTER 4

MAKING THE INVISIBLE CUT

An editor's most basic job is to keep the audience unaware that they're being manipulated by the cuts — unless the editor is intentionally trying to shake up the audience. More often, though, an editor wants to make those cuts seem invisible by having the shots flow together in a smooth, continuous motion. One would think this would be achieved by making a "matched cut," where the action of the previous shot matches up perfectly with the subsequent shot. But often that is not the case.

Say the editor has to cut from a shot of an actor walking through a door to a subsequent shot showing the actor from the other side of that door. It may seem easy to cut around as the actor continues to come through, but it's not, even for the most experienced editor. The editor may find out through trial and error that the cut appears smoother if it's not a matched cut. It could be a "jump cut" (a section of film taken out of the beginning, middle, or end of a shot) where, for example, the swing of a door is visually discontinuous from one shot to the next. Whether or not the jump cut is smooth may depend on the way the audience's eyes follow the motion and angle of the door, but the effect is also the result of what the audience is thinking and feeling.

What if the actor opens the door, which reveals his long-lost love, and the next shot shows his reaction from the other side of the door? In this case, the most important factor would be the quality and timing of the actor's reaction. Because the audience can only focus on one thing at a time, that moment is what they will zero in on. They won't even notice if the door swings in a continuous arc from one shot to the next. That is why the editor must always cut for impact first. If the movie is working and the audience is involved, they won't care about a mismatched door swing or any other detail. Probably only the director and editor will notice.

PROBLEM SOLVING

An editor faces a great many hurdles in creating those invisible cuts. So much goes wrong or has to be compromised during shooting that an editor must use sleight-of-hand to distract the audience from that reality.

Let's revisit the door-opening transition, but in this instance the actor is opening a front door to enter a house. The exterior of the house would probably have been shot at a totally different time and place from the interior of the house — the former on location, the latter on a sound stage. So what are the odds that the lighting, the speed of the actor's walk, the mood of the actor, the angle of his arm as he turns the doorknob, or even the way he wears his shirt, will perfectly match from one day of shooting to another?

Because the audience must not be aware of any of these mismatches, the editor must both finesse the cut and control the focus so that those inconsistencies are not noticed. There are also many other potential flaws in this seemingly simple transition. What if a camera move or stage move is not well executed, or the editor has to eliminate a poor performance or a flawed piece of dialogue? Actually, it's highly unlikely that the movie will be shot and ultimately edited exactly as the screenplay was written. An editor might have to eliminate part of a scene, take it out entirely, or even change its order — all the while keeping the audience from being aware that he has performed such "surgery."

There are, in fact, some classic ways an editor uses sleight-of-hand to finesse these new and unplanned transitions:

> "Wiping the frame": cutting to a shot where something or someone moves across the screen, often in front of the subject, filling the screen.

> Using a "cutaway," which is also known as "cutting to the kitchen sink," that is, cutting to something that is not related to the action within the frame but is somehow connected to the scene, such as a secondary action or observer.

> Cutting to a close-up or an "insert," which is a close shot of an object or specific piece of action. A close-up can even be "stolen" from another part of the movie for this purpose, because the background will be less noticeable and a subtle facial expression can always be reinterpreted in the new location. In general, inserts and close-ups are effective bridges that can be used to remove unnecessary or problematic footage, because they usually have a less obvious physical context and are more flexible in terms of where they can be placed.

CHAPTER 5

CHEATING TIME

The editor also uses sleight-of-hand to shorten or stretch out the duration of what is happening on screen. When he does it skillfully, it's amazing how irrelevant real time can be.

Here are some examples:

CONDENSING TIME

The audience is bored.
Watching an event such as a baseball game may be interesting in real life but will slow a story down. The editor has to find the highlights of the game and bridge the time gaps by cutting to interesting shots of the crowd, the coach, the scoreboard, etc. The audience will accept the time jumps gratefully.

The audience is anxious to discover something.
If an actor sees something significant off screen — an envelope containing crucial information, for example — the editor may want to cut to what the actor is looking at and hold on that shot until the man enters the frame to retrieve it. This shortening of time not only puts emphasis on what's important, but also satisfies the audience's curiosity more quickly than staying with the actor's actual movements.

The audience knows what's going to happen.

An example would be an actor running up the stairs. If the editor changes angles just when the actor reaches the stairs, he can eliminate some of the bottom steps, because the audience already knows where the actor is going.

EXTENDING TIME

The audience wants to milk the suspense.

Say a bomb is about to go off. The editor extends the time and creates tension by cutting back and forth. That is, he "cross-cuts" or "inter-cuts" between the main elements of a scene to establish the parallel action and eventually build to a climax. In this case the elements are the ticking bomb and the main characters trying to escape or defuse it. The editor can also cut to other elements, such as additional threats or hurdles that heighten the drama. With suspenseful and escalating cross-cutting, a bomb that is set to go off in thirty seconds can end up taking two minutes of movie time and no one will blink! The audience will actually appreciate that the editor has thrown real-time logic out the window, because they're not only enjoying the thrill ride, they're also trying to buy time for the characters they're emotionally invested in.

The audience needs more information.

Say there's a sign above the door that the audience should read. If the first shot shows the actor coming out of the door but does not show the sign clearly, the editor may repeat part of the actor's exit in the more distant shot.

CHAPTER 6

CHEATING MOVES

A cut can seem invisible when an editor manipulates time. He can also create a seamless transition by making an "action cut," using body motion as a bridge when cutting to a change in camera angles. Here are two classic examples:

STANDING UP

An editor may have to cut from a close shot of an actor, to show him standing up in a more distant shot. Generally he will cut right after the actor shows the intention to stand. This is because the audience will lose interest once the actor's face begins to leave the frame.

SITTING DOWN

What holds true of the previous cut is also the case here — in reverse. That is, when an actor is shown from a distance, first standing and then starting to sit down, the editor should try not to interrupt the flow of movement. He will usually want to cut to the closer shot slightly ahead of the completed action, just as the actor's butt touches the seat of the chair. Even if the actor is sitting behind a desk or something else that obscures him, the editor can still time the shot by getting a feel of the actor's rhythm. If the actor is using a prop (for example, if he's drinking or smoking in the close-up), then the editor might delay cutting until the hand just enters the frame.

Sometimes these rules do not apply. For instance, the editor may cut at the peak of that sitting or standing motion, even if it involves using an awkward shot.

ENTERING AND EXITING

Entrance/exit cuts are other ways an editor can use body motion to create an invisible cut. If, for example, an actor walks from the left side of the screen across to the right side, the audience will focus on his face, especially his eyes. As he keeps walking and his face starts to leave the right edge of the frame, the audience's eyes will start to swing to the center. This is because the audience is already anticipating the next shot. When the editor cuts and the actor enters from the left edge of the frame, they will look to the left and not notice the cut; the action will seem continuous and the cut invisible.

As a result, the rule of thumb for when an actor exits, say, from the right side, is that in the next shot he will enter from the opposite side, in this case from the left. Here are the exceptions when an actor would exit and enter again from the same side of the screen:

> The actor is shot from front to back and in the next shot from back to front or vice versa.

> The actor changes direction within the shot and then exits from the same side as he entered.

> The actor suggests a change in direction, and the editor cuts to something else before the actor reenters the frame.

When an actor exits, the editor should usually try to avoid completely emptying the frame because that dead visual time kills the momentum. Also, when matching the walking action from one shot to the next, the editor should cut out at the peak of the actor's energy, which is often the moment his foot touches the ground. When the actor reenters the frame, editors often like to have the same foot come down to the ground, but the choice ultimately depends on what feels natural, both visually and dramatically.

CHAPTER 7

KNOWING THE EYE

Like the magician, an editor has to trick the audience into seeing only what he wants them to see, while he sets up the effect he wants. He can only pull this off if he understands how the audience's eyes react to what they see on screen. This includes knowing the human eye's limitations: the fact that it can absorb only so much of a film frame.

HOW THE EYE FOCUSES

In general, the editor understands that the eye searches for the greatest intensity within the frame, whether it be motion or emotion. The eye will naturally focus on the center and foreground of the frame unless:

> The eye was focused somewhere else in the previous shot.

> There's movement away from the center and/or foreground, particularly toward the horizon.

> An actor is in dramatic close-up or just shows strong emotion, and then the focus will be on his eyes, wherever they are within the frame.

> The eye is pulled to a point somewhere else within the frame, because a person or object is much denser, brighter, bigger, or in greater focus.

HOW THE EYE BLINKS

There's another subtle window of opportunity for the editor to distract his audience: when there's a cut and a new image appears on the screen and the eye needs time to adjust and refocus. (This is similar to what happens when you read, and your eyes move from word to word or across the page.) That fuzziness in between cuts lasts three to five frames, or about one-fifth of a second, since there are twenty-four frames per second.

Interestingly enough, the amount of time it takes for the eye to adjust is also about the same as the time it takes for someone to blink. That is why a sharp sound, which usually makes the eye blink, can also smooth over a bad match or transition or just distract the audience. A prime example is the faked slap. The editor can cut out of a shot just as the actor starts to slap someone or has even barely completed the slap. He can then cut to the next shot showing that the second actor has already been slapped. If the editor plays the sound of the slap very close to the cut, the audience will blink and think they've seen the slap even though they actually haven't.

Because the eye cannot retain an image that lasts less than three frames, that number of frames also becomes the magic number to create a subliminal effect. Although the eye doesn't see it clearly, the effect does register in the mind's eye.

HOW THE EYE REACTS TO MOTION

The closeness of an image makes it appear to move faster because the information comes quickly and is simpler to absorb. The psychological intensity of a closer shot also makes the screen time seem shorter. Movement coming directly at the screen appears to be faster as well, since it has a more dramatic, possibly even threatening impact than horizontal movement or movement away from the screen. Diagonal movement has its own special effect, since it leads the eye specifically to whatever edge and/or corner of the frame it eventually moves out of — and the eye will anticipate the next shot by focusing on the opposite edge or corner.

CHAPTER 8

KNOWING THE CAMERA

COVERING THE SCENE

An editor has to rely on the director and cinematographer to shoot the right coverage for a scene — that is, all the necessary camera setups and angles — but then it's up to the editor to create an involving, understandable narrative with the footage he's given. A scene may start with an all-inclusive master shot or a close-up and usually, as the scene builds, it may be broken up into closer angles. But there are no hard-and-fast rules. Whatever the choices are, the editor has to understand the impact of those different angles, as well as camera moves and lenses, so he can use the shots in the most effective way.

The editor also has to adjust to whatever approach the director uses to cover a scene. For example, if the director uses a locked-down camera with the whole scene played out in one shot, the editor will have a very narrow choice of options. The editor will also be somewhat limited if the director decides to play the scenes out in long, elaborate shots and resist cutting whenever possible, which may be the case in a crucial dialogue scene. On the other hand, the director may also use the opposite approach and shoot a lot of short, varied angles, especially if he wants to create a dizzying, exciting action scene.

In terms of planning, he may "camera cut" (preconceive the exact choice and sequence of shots). This may be the case if the scene is logistically very complicated and needs a "storyboard" (shots sketched in sequence as a blueprint for coverage). A director might also lean toward the camera-cutting approach if he has an especially good grasp of the mechanics of camera coverage and editing, and/or has severe time and budget constraints. But if a director chooses to pre-plan every shot — giving the editor virtually no options or leftover film and himself no opportunity for a second guess in the cutting room — he's probably being foolish. (Unless he's an Alfred Hitchcock, whose uncanny way of working I will discuss later.)

KNOWING "THE LINE"

One of the editor's key responsibilities is to keep the audience from getting confused, and that means making sure they always know where the actors are in relation to each other. He has to make sure that the film he cuts together honors what's called the "stage line." This is an imaginary line that cuts through the middle of a shot, and the camera must stay on one side of that line, within that 180-degree space. If the camera crosses it, the viewpoint will be reversed and the audience will become disoriented.

To illustrate: a shot establishes a boy and girl seated across from each other. The stage line cuts through the middle of the table and both of the actors. If the camera shoots a close-up of the boy, then mistakenly crosses the line when it shoots the girl, and then those two shots are cut together, the two actors will be looking in the same direction and not at each other. In Figure 1 the boy and girl are actually looking at each other, which is what the camera would see if camera angles 1 and 2 or 3 and 4 were cut together. But if camera angles 1 and 4 were cut together, the boy and girl would both appear to be looking to the right, and from angles 2 to 3 to the left, not at one another. What this classic example shows is that actual reality has no bearing on screen reality.

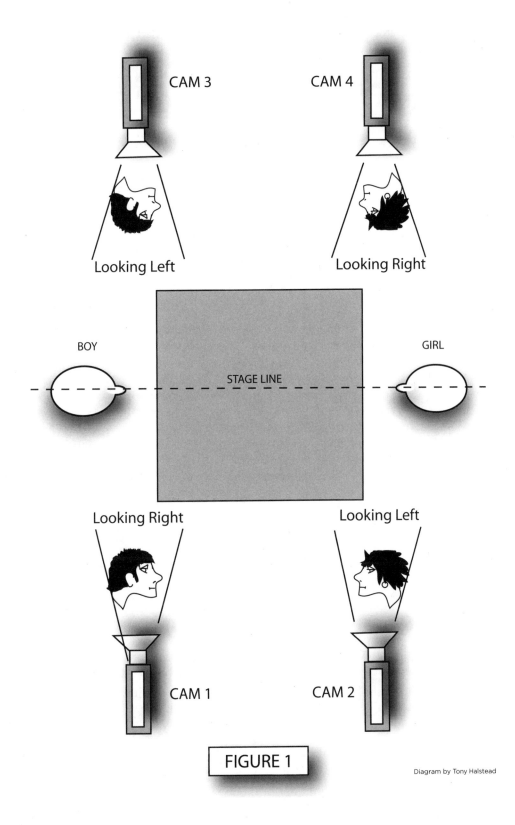

CAM 3

CAM 4

Looking Left

Looking Right

BOY

GIRL

STAGE LINE

Looking Right

Looking Left

CAM 1

CAM 2

FIGURE 1

Diagram by Tony Halstead

Inevitably, it can get much more complicated than that. For instance, if there were three people sitting around a table, three stage lines would run through each pair of actors. If the only film available to the editor were single shots of each of the actors, the best he could hope for would be that two of the three pairs of actors would be looking in the direction they should, which is the case in Figure 2. That is, two of three lines would not be crossed if he cut from cameras 1 to 2 or 2 to 3. All the other angle combinations would cross more lines and at best only one pair of actors would be looking in the correct direction.

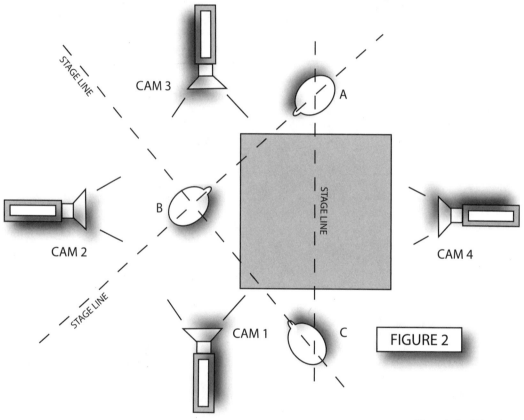

Diagram by Tony Halstead

Ideally the editor would not get stuck with angles he couldn't use, but he has to recognize such mistakes and avoid footage that will disorient his audience. In reality, a smart director would not corner himself into these kinds of problematic setups, where he would be dodging every line. He would do this by moving actors, moving the camera, and grouping actors in various ways. Close-ups can also be used as a bridge for the editor to wipe the stage line slate clean, since they often don't have a specific geography of their own.

The movie *Twelve Angry Men** is a classic example of how filmmakers brilliantly maneuvered their way around potential crossing-the-line traps, because virtually the whole movie is a group shot of twelve jurors seated around a table. I will show examples below with diagrams and frame grabs from two scenes, and I will refer to them again as I deconstruct this movie in Chapter 13.

The way the editor, Carl Lerner, takes on the dreaded group scene is to initially establish where all the jurors are seated. He does this by cutting to shots which angle down at the jurors from all four corners of the table. After the first high shot (shown in *frame grab #1-3*), the editor cuts to another shot (seen in *frame grab #1-4*) that crosses the line completely and reverses everyone's direction, so the audience sees two clearly opposing angles. The same is true of another pair of shots (*frame grabs #1-8* and *#1-9*) which then completes the coverage of all four corners of the table, illustrated in **Diagram 1**.

frame grab 1-3

frame grab 1-4

frame grab 1-8

frame grab 1-9

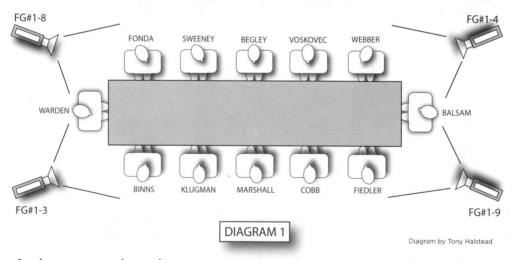

DIAGRAM 1

Diagram by Tony Halstead

In the next two shots, the actors are positioned a certain way so that when the editor cuts from one group (*frame grab #1-10*) to the next (*frame grab #1-11*), only

frame grab 1-10

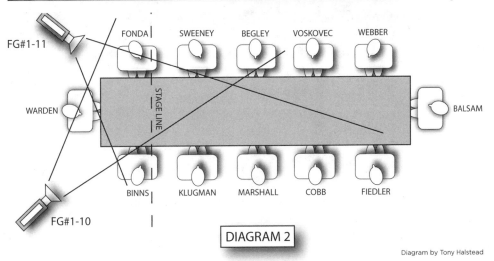

frame grab 1-11

DIAGRAM 2

Diagram by Tony Halstead

actors Fonda and Binns appear both times. Thus he has to honor only one stage line, as shown in **Diagram 2**.

frame grab 1-14

frame grab 1-15

frame grab 1-16

Frame grab #1-14 is the same angle as *frame grab #1-10* but now the interaction shifts between two other actors, Warden and Fonda, and a new stage line is established, as seen in **Diagram 3**. When the editor cuts to the next two shots (shown in *frame grabs #1-15* and *#1-16*), only those two actors appear and they continue to stay on the left and right sides of the screen, respectively. If the camera had crossed that line from *frame grab #14* to *frame grab #15*, the actors' positions would have been flipped and the audience would have become confused.

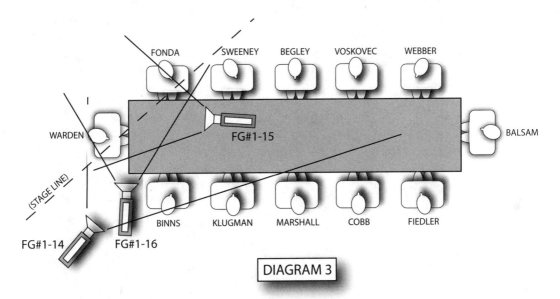

DIAGRAM 3

Diagram by Tony Halstead

The editor is sometimes able to violate a stage line rule when he knows the audience is looking elsewhere. For instance, when the editor cuts from one group of jurors (*frame grab #2-5*) to a "reverse angle," the opposite perspective of a shot already taken (*frame grab #2-6*), there are six actors seen in each shot. The dramatic focus is between actors Balsam and Fonda, who remain in left-right positions from one shot to the next, honoring Stage Line A, as seen in **Diagram 4**. The positions of the jurors sitting between them are flipped from one shot to the next — their Stage Line B is crossed — but the editor knows the audience won't notice, since they're not focused on the other jurors.

frame grab 2-5

frame grab 2-6

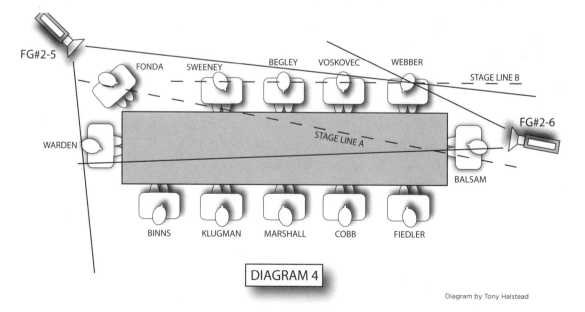

Diagram by Tony Halstead

Honoring the stage line is most important in dialogue scenes, because it's crucial that the audience knows where the actors are looking and at whom. On the other hand, if the editor is cutting an action scene, the editor will probably want to cross the line and purposely break the rules, because that visual disorientation gives the scene energy and excitement.

CAMERA ANGLES

Where the camera is placed in relation to its subject has a distinct effect on the audience's perception. Because of this, an editor has to be aware of the impact of various camera angles and how to use them most effectively to convey the story.

In terms of camera distance, there is a lot of variation in how filmmakers label different shots. This is especially true of mid-range distance shots. For example, a "medium full shot" could be sometimes called a "medium shot." For the purposes of this book, the choices will be simplified to the following:

Overview of Shot Sizes
Tight close-up: Cuts off part of chin and top of head
Close-up: Head
Close shot: Head to shoulders or breast
Medium close shot: Head to waist
Medium shot/medium full shot: Head to knees
Full shot: Whole body
Medium long shot: Middle distance showing small group or some geography
Long shot: Full geography

The long shot has enough distance to show the actors in relation to each other and their surroundings. If it's completely inclusive, it's one and the same as the master shot. The opposite extreme, the close-up, is an editor's most powerful weapon, so it should be saved for when it can be used to its maximum effect. It can show the interior life of a character or be used just for dramatic emphasis. Because close-ups have less physical context, they can also be used as setups to surprise or scare the audience, or as cutaways to fix a problem. But if a close-up isn't motivated or necessary, the audience will feel bounced around and be too aware of the cutting. If it's not clear which actor to cut to, a "two shot" (two actors within the frame), or an "over-the-shoulder shot" (shooting past an actor's shoulder or part of his head to another actor) may be preferable. Also, usually the editor should not cut to a shot that's only slightly closer or further away than the previous shot, because the change will not give the audience enough new information and it will be disorienting.

The same may happen with a slight change in the positioning of the subject in relation to its background. For example, imagine an actor standing in front of a tree. If his position changes just a little from shot to shot, the audience will be confused and wonder if the tree behind the actor moved slightly to one side. But if the audience sees the actor in profile after a straight-on shot, which is a dramatic change in angle, they will expect the tree to be in an entirely different position, and they won't be confused. In fact, the greater the change in angle, the more an editor will be able to create distraction and a smoother cut. A cut that involves no change in angle, but a change in distance — such as cutting in close from the same vantage point — can be very effective, but not naturally as smooth as a change in angles.

An editor must be aware of the psychological impact of angles. For instance, when the camera looks down on an actor, it creates a perspective that can make him appear more benign or powerless. If this angle represents the point of view of another actor looking down at him, he will appear even more victimized. An angle looking up at an actor usually implies a more menacing perspective. This angle can also have a different impact depending on the context. If the audience admires this character he may seem more heroic. All told, extreme perspectives usually have a powerful effect of some sort.

CAMERA LENSES

An editor must also know the visual and psychological impact of lenses so he can use the best one to serve the scene. The length of the lens has its own particular impact; it greatly affects the "depth of field" or the range of sharp focus. For instance, if an actor is shot with a long lens, the background will be less in focus than if he is shot with a shorter length lens. If an editor cuts between two actors who are shot with different lenses but from the same distance, the focus in the background will be somewhat different between the two shots. If done for no good reason, it will confuse the audience. However, if there are other changes between the two shots in addition to lenses — in distance or angle, assuming this is properly motivated — then the new information will be useful and not disorienting. The following two extremes illustrate the different effects.

Wide angle
Using a wide-angle lens (a lens of less than normal length) causes the background to seem to be more in focus, but the images appear to be farther from the camera and from each other. As a result, an actor or object moving toward or away from the camera will appear to change more dramatically in size and move faster than he actually does. It also has a large "field of view," the area covered by a lens,

which is useful when including a lot of visual information in confined locations. It can also magnify and distort a subject very close to the camera, possibly making it seem more threatening or disturbing.

Telephoto

Using a telephoto lens (a very long lens) makes images seem closer to the camera and to each other so that the foreground, middle ground, and background are more compressed. Because the background seems closer, when the camera is following a traveling actor or object in the foreground, their speed will seem greater than it really is. The telephoto lens has a unique versatility when multiple cameras are used, because it can capture an effective close-up from a distance, without getting in the way of the other cameras. When the camera is close it will also flatten the perspective of the subject, often making it appear more benign.

Sidney Lumet, the director of *Twelve Angry Men*, described how the psychological and visual aspects of both lenses and angles affected his choices in making his courtroom drama. (The length of a lens is measured in millimeters.)

One of the most important dramatic elements for me was the sense of entrapment these men must have felt in that room. Immediately a "lens plot" occurred to me as the picture unfolded. I wanted the room to seem smaller and smaller. That meant that I would slowly shift to longer lenses as the picture continued. Starting with the normal range (28 mm to 40 mm), we progressed to 50 mm, 75 mm, and 100 mm lenses. In addition, I shot the first third of the movie above eye level and then, by lowering the camera, shot the second third at eye level, and the last third from below eye level. In that way, toward the end, the ceiling began to appear. Not only were the walls closing in, the ceiling was as well. The sense of increasing claustrophobia did a lot to raise the tension of the last part of the movie. On the final shot, an exterior that showed the jurors leaving the courtroom, I used a wide-angle lens, wider than any lens that had been used in the entire picture. I also raised the camera to the high above-eye-level position. The intention was to literally give us all air, to let us finally breathe after two increasingly confined hours.[2]

CAMERA MOVES

An editor must understand the impact that camera moves have on the audience and the cumulative result of cutting those shots together. Here is a basic list of shots, ranging from least flexible to most flexible:

Zoom: The camera lens moves in or out with no loss of focus. (Because the zoom has an unnatural two-dimensional effect, it's difficult to cut in smoothly on a zoom. It works best when shot without any real background, with a very slow move or combined with a more flexible move like a tilt, pan, or dolly. However, the very inflexibility of the zoom lens can make it useful for the editor if he wants to create a jarring effect.)

Tilt: The camera moves up or down.

Pan: The camera moves left to right.

Swish pan: Like a basic pan but very fast with blurs between its beginning and end points.

Dolly (aka Traveling or Tracking Shot): A move from a wheeled platform or on tracks that move forward and backward.

Crane: A move from a wheeled platform with a boom, the arm on which the camera is mounted, which can raise and lower itself to many levels and swing to many angles.

Crab dolly: A move from a wheeled platform with a mounted camera and steering control, which can have a combination of moves in nearly any direction.

Steadicam: A handheld but stable camera, which is the most flexible of all.

OPTICALS

Opticals are effects that were originally created by optical printers, which used film projectors mechanically linked to a movie camera. This technique allowed filmmakers to re-photograph previously processed film to create transitions and composite effects.

To review the basics:

Dissolve: one shot gradually fades out at the same time the next shot fades in so that at midpoint each shot is equally superimposed over the other. It is often used as a transition between scenes either to slow time down or to show the passage of time, a change in place, or a connection between ideas, moods, or interior thoughts.

Fade: the outgoing shot gradually disappears into blackness or washes out to a white screen, and is called a "fade-out"; a "fade-in" is the reverse. Although both dissolves and fades can indicate a change in time or place, the fade creates a more complete, distinct break in the narrative.

Wipe: a dividing line — horizontal, vertical, diagonal, straight, jagged or even invisible — sweeps across the screen and wipes out the shot to reveal an entirely new shot. It can be used like a fade or dissolve, but it's a rather old-fashioned device.

Skip framing: By optically eliminating every second or third frame, the editor can speed up a sluggish shot, but he can only get away with it in a shot with very little motion, such as a static shot of an actor. "Double framing" has the opposite effect, slowing down the action by repeating frames two or three times. The same limitations apply.

Freeze frame: repeated printing of a frame to extend the moment and make it more dramatic.

Since the 1980s, digital compositing has, for the most part, replaced optical printing, and has vastly expanded filmmakers' options. Also, directors and editors are less dependent on transition opticals for telling a story, because today's audiences are so savvy and quick to accept plot complexities. They don't need, for example, a dissolve to tell them there's been a passage of time. With digital technology, filmmakers can also create much more elaborate transitions. One of many possibilities is to have part of an outgoing frame inserted into the first frame of the next shot, creating a kind of mosaic. Digital art can also be animated and used to create a transition from one shot to the next.

Before computer technology, simple matte shots were created by photographically combining two or more elements and masking parts of each image to avoid double-exposure. An example would be combining a studio shot of an actor in a boat with a background "stock shot" (pre-existing film from a library) of a lake. Computers made it easier to create "traveling mattes" (mattes that change), because the images that are composited could be more easily synchronized. With the advent of CGI (computer-generated imagery) opticals have become even more complex. For example, actors can be filmed at different times against any imaginable background or special effect.

In this case, when the editor initially puts the movie in a cut, the actors may just be reacting to a blue or green screen that will later be replaced by the CGI-created background. The editor probably will have to continue cutting all the way through "postproduction," the period after the movie is shot, until all the effects are completed and perfected. The editor may also have to cut in a digitally generated "character" that interacts with other live characters but may not yet be perfected or even created when the editor first puts the sequences together. He will have relatively little flexibility with such a character. He can't, for instance, choose another take or change the length of the shot, except possibly to shorten it slightly, since each frame of animation is very expensive. He may even have to mentally act out the moves of the character, to time the scene out correctly and give the optical house guidelines.

A director may want to use "previsualization" (digital graphics used to create a rough version of a sequence often with digital counterparts to the actual actors), which can then be edited, and even have music and dialogue added before the director films the final version. An editor can also add or remove elements from the frame digitally. He can cut people out of the scene, move them around, move in for a close-up; basically, he can direct the movie in three dimensions in the cutting room. These types of innovations are virtually unlimited. Although they dramatically increase the editor's options, he and the director have to decide to what degree the technology serves the movie.

CHAPTER 9

THE SOUND
AND MUSIC

SOUND

The film editor is, in a sense, both a picture and sound editor, because the two elements are completely dependent on each other, and sound is always part of the editor's decision-making process. In many ways, sound and film editing are similar: both are often the most effective when they are imperceptible, giving invisible support to the story. However, there are differences. For example, in a movie the sound is instantaneous, but the picture is slightly delayed, since it takes a few frames to absorb it. And because sounds can be heard from many directions, one sound doesn't necessarily have to replace another. Sound can also be isolated, made louder, or heard off screen, all of which makes it more flexible and versatile than the movie's images.

Sound can be "synchronized" (recorded during shooting) and "post-synchronized" (recorded afterward) and can be used to add either imaginative elements such as the sounds of a monster or realistic "foley" sounds (recorded in sync with the onscreen action such as footsteps or punches).

Film editors will add some sound effects to their first cut to punch up a scene or to just enhance the synchronized sound that already exists. The "sound designer," who is responsible for the postproduction effects, may end up keeping some of this temporary sound, but will usually end up replacing virtually all of it with elements from his own library for the "final mix," when separate tracks of dialogue, music, and sound effects are equalized and combined into one track by technicians on a soundstage.

Dialogue

Dialogue is a crucial part of the film editor's process. Dialogue will also be both synchronized and post-synchronized. Of post-synchronized, there are three kinds:

—"Looping" or "ADR": replacing dialogue by recording it on a soundstage in sync with the original picture. Looping becomes necessary because of poor sound conditions or flawed performances during shooting, or a need for additional exposition.

—"Voice over": recorded narration added to what's on screen that can be recorded later.

—"Wild track": sound recorded on the set or later, not meant to be exactly synchronized, and usually capturing ambient sounds such as crowd noise or random dialogue. It can be especially useful for the editor as background sound to connect a discontinuous cut.

Since the film editor does the initial dialogue editing, his primary goal is to make sure the dialogue is as smooth from shot to shot as he can make it, in terms of tone, volume, and background noise. He does as much as he can with what he has, sometimes even stealing bits of dialogue from different takes, because the natural sound that was captured on the set is usually best.

Overlapping Dialogue

The audience often knows what a character is going to say before he finishes speaking. They may also be eager to see the other character's reaction, in which case the editor can "overlap the dialogue," that is, continue to play the soundtrack of the previous shot until someone in the new shot starts talking. Some editors let two or three words spill over on cuts as a stylistic technique, to tie the shots together; but a significant overlap will usually happen only for a reason. The dialogue in a scene can naturally overlap if there is high energy and emotion, and that can be challenging for an editor. If there are only two actors, the filmmakers can have a camera on each actor and one track running for both of them, so they will be naturally overlapping whenever the editor cuts to each actor. What happens is often more complex. The editor may have to overlap the closer shots through editing and also use more distant, multi-actor angles where the dialogue overlaps within the shot. Creating a consistent flow and momentum in the track, while always being on the appropriate actor, can require real editing finesse.

MUSIC

Music and movies both involve sequence and rhythm, and the philosophy for editing them is similar. There has to be a justifiable reason to make a film or music cut, and once the full impact is reached, it's time for the editor to cut. The roles of the film editor and music editor also overlap, since either one of them at various times may collaborate on what music is chosen for the picture.

There are three types of music.

—"Source": a sequence of music or a song that is taken from a definable source to accompany a scene or can be heard in the background coming from, for instance, a radio or CD player.

—"Playback": pre-recorded music that accompanies any singers, musicians, or dancers performing in a movie.

—"Score": music written by a composer specifically for a movie.

The editor has to know the way music is used in different types of movies. Although it's difficult to generalize, in horror movies and some action movies, usually the music is highly synchronized, because it exists not just for emotional impact but also as an effect. Music in physical comedy is usually well synchronized, too, coming from the influence of cartoons. Music in romantic movies often has a more sweeping effect and is less specific.

The editor must also understand the psychological impact of music. It may act as a counterpoint to the mood or the content of a scene. For instance, bittersweet music accompanying a happy scene may reveal something foreboding or a sad reminder of the past. Music may also heighten emotion, such as tension or fear. A burst of music can shock or surprise, especially during or after a period of silence. It can be used as a link in time and/or space to help smooth out a jump in the storyline or for a "montage," which is a sequence of shots that compresses the narrative, usually without dialogue. The absence of music can be a significant part of the movie's score, since silence makes its own powerful statement. For instance, if the movie is playing on its own and is already as effective as it can be, then, in principle, music shouldn't be added. Music may also soften a moment that shouldn't be softened. For example, a deathbed scene may be more bearable with music, when in fact the effect that the director wants is for the scene to be unbearably painful.

If an audience hears a song or score after they've seen a movie, and it makes them vividly remember the scene that accompanied it, or if they think back on a scene and remember the feeling the score or song created, then the music has done its job.

Film editors have always cut montages to music, and since the innovative sixties and even more so since the advent of computers in the eighties, editors can easily add as much music as they want to their first cut without the expense of going on a mixing stage. Because of this, directors have come to expect that virtually the whole movie will be cut to music and that it will accompany the movie at a very early stage in the editing process. Yet music can also have a seductive effect, giving the filmmakers false confidence in the movie's quality. It can smooth over bumpy moments and give an energy boost to the pacing, so that mediocre film (extra "fat") stays in the movie when it shouldn't.

In general there are really no hard-and-fast rules about editing music. For instance, when editing a montage to a song, the preferred choice may be to have the visual cut come in on the music's "downbeat," the prominent first beat of a measure, or on a percussive word. This "hard cut" is emphatic and calls attention to itself, but sometimes that choice can be too obvious. Instead "a soft cut," letting the picture cut come in between beats or on the second or third beat of a four-beat measure, for example, can feel more fluid.

An editor should not, as a rule, cut his images exactly to the beat of the music, because it will seem as if the music is pulling the visuals along. Because of the time lag of picture to sound, there's a rule of thumb for music editing: when music is intended to be cut on a beat, it should come three frames after the picture cut.

When the editor is cutting the movie to a song, he also has to consider not only the beat, but also the lyrics and how they all relate to the mood, style, and content of the film. In the final analysis, the choices that the music and film editor make are by no means mathematical or scientific. An editor develops a visceral feeling, an instinct that tells him where to cut for the images and music to move together in a satisfying way. As film editor Carol Littleton says, "*You want it to be unpredictable; you don't just want to be a metronome. You want it to follow the phrase, you want it to follow the turn of the words of the song, or the instrumentation, you want it to fit into that glove. I always think of cutting to music, you're not forcing it, you want it to be a good fit, so which pinky you put in first, you know, it all has to be in some way harmonious.*"[3]

CHAPTER 10

THE ACT COMES TOGETHER

After the film editor puts a movie into a first cut, music and sound editors add other elements. There will be a series of what's called "temp dubs" or "scratch mixes," in which more sound and music will be added beyond what the film editor has already done.

How many screenings take place between the first cut, preview, and final mix depends on budget, time, what the director wants, what the studio demands, and the specific needs and problems with the movie. A period film or a movie heavily dependent on opticals, where much of the location sound is unusable, will require more postproduction work. Sometimes all the temp mixes will be done on a computer, but it's always preferable to do a pre-mix on a sound stage, because of the expertise of the technicians who mix and equalize all the sound elements.

SPOTTING

The sound designer will have a "spotting session" sometime before the final mix, where he'll run the movie with the director and film editor, and they will decide what existing sound needs to be fixed and what special sounds are needed. The dialogue editor will try to salvage whatever original dialogue he can. (The amount of rerecorded dialogue on a movie averages about 30%.) The music editor will also have a spotting session where the movie will be screened with the composer, director, and film editor. Because sound effects have become increasingly complex and musical, the music spotting session may include the sound designer. The music editor will add some score and songs and, in some cases, replace some of the film editor's choices, but not if they're working. Songs that accompany montages, or visual sequences like chase scenes that were specifically cut to songs, may stay in the movie. A song may be chosen as early as the script stage or at any point during the editing process or the composer will write a new song to replace the temporary version. The temp score will always be replaced by that of the composer.

PREVIEWS

While the film editor usually sits in on the spotting, recording, and scoring sessions, the editor will always sit in on the final mix. His opinions may be needed, but he is even more vital as a technical resource. For instance, he may need to pull a piece of sound, dialogue, or music from another part of the movie if the director is unhappy with what he hears on the mixing stage. Also, he may be aware of useful sound or film not yet in the final cut, since he knows more about what was shot than anyone else.

The most delicate role the editor will play is during previews when the movie is screened at a theater, and the final changes are made based on the audience's reaction. The director is really under duress at this time because the movie will now be judged by the outside world. The stress is often increased if the director is being pressured by the studio or the producer — or both — to make changes he disagrees with. The editor can be expected to magically fix problems or can be unfairly blamed for flaws that he had no control over. This is the last chance for everyone to give their input, and the editor becomes the final hope before the studio releases the movie out into the cold, cruel world.

At this late stage the relationship between the director and editor is really tested, because this is the time when the editor will most likely be put in a political squeeze between the director, producer, studio executives, and on and on. Even though the producer may have more power and may be signing his paycheck, the editor should remain loyal to the director. If the editor finds himself agreeing with others on certain points and disagreeing with the director, this is fine as long as the editor is up-front about his differences and doesn't go behind the director's back. If the editor does make changes for the producer or studio that the director doesn't want, the editor must tell the director what he's doing. The worst thing an editor can do is to deceive the director, or try to please both sides. Although all these situations are potentially precarious, and the worst sort of studio politics can certainly play out, the best defense for the editor and director is the strength of their relationship, because then it's hard for anyone to come between them.

There's an additional danger. The editor and director have been working on the movie for so long that their attention to detail and general closeness to the movie can make them lose perspective. For instance, they may not be aware that the story is confusing at a certain point, because they know it too well. Or they could just be numb to the impact of certain special moments that originally made them laugh or cry. But the shock of the preview should make them keyed up and tuned in to the audience. Both the preview cards and the post-screening discussions from a selected part of the audience can be helpful. The questions, however, can be so specific that the audience may give conflicting input — one person's favorite scene may be another's least favorite — and may focus more on particular problems than on the overall movie. Because it's so easy to get overwhelmed by all the input, it's often true that the gut reactions from the audience — in which they laugh, scream, or just fidget in their seats and show boredom — are more revealing than all the postmortems and words scribbled on cards. The director and editor should be open to suggestions, but they should never forget their reactions at that first viewing, when they assessed the movie's strengths and weaknesses and were clear on what needed to be done. The director and editor should trust themselves. Ultimately they are the most capable judges of what's best for the movie, because they've lived and breathed it. They know it better than anyone — and probably care the most.

CHAPTER 11

THE MARRIAGE OF THE EDITOR AND DIRECTOR

No other crew member will ever spend as much time alone with the director as the editor does, and the relationship between them functions much like a marriage. If the chemistry of their two personalities click, if they're both willing to listen to and respect each other's opinions, are both prepared to give and take, and most of all trust each other, then they'll have a healthy relationship.

If there's an editing issue that is really important, and the editor strongly believes his position is the right one, he should speak up and fight for it. Sometimes, though, if the director is really off base, the editor has to trust that, just by letting the director see a part of the film edited his way, the director will eventually see the error of his ways. By the same token the editor should also be willing to try something even if it seems ridiculous, even if it's upside down and backward. Refusing to try simply means his ego is getting in the way.

The marriage is tested at various times, especially when others become more involved in the movie. Even when the marriage is good, the editor must always be able to choose his battles and not fall into the trap of needing credit for an idea or being right for its own sake. And although this is a partnership, it is not an equal one, nor should it be. The movie belongs to the director, and the editor should try to make him happy and honor his vision. The editor should also be mindful of the fact that the director is the one who's ultimately on the line. If the movie bombs, the director gets hurt the most. If it's a hit, there's enough glory for everyone.

If the relationship sustains itself over more than one movie, this unique balancing act between the roles of director and editor does settle into a pattern. And like a marriage, the longer the relationship lasts and the more successful it is over time, the more there is an implicit understanding and predictability to the partnership. That comfort level is invaluable.

Carol Littleton, who worked on *Body Heat** and *The Big Chill*,* has had a very long-term relationship with the director of those movies, Lawrence Kasdan. She has the following to say about their "marriage":

CL: *I would have to say I think the world of Larry and we have a very similar film aesthetic. He doesn't even have to say anything — he'll make a move in a chair or he'll straighten up or he'll cough or something; all of that's meaning to me. I know when he's acting and reacting.*

BO [Bobbie O'Steen]: *Did you know that early on?*

CL: *Instantly. I just had a very strong sense of the kind of man Larry is, the sort of integrity he has as a filmmaker, as a person, those two are inseparable. I had respect for him the very first time we met that has grown over all these years.*

Larry has always said, "You just do it the way you feel it first and then we'll talk about it. Just go ahead, try anything you want. I want to see what you come up with." Many times when Larry was directing, we'd go to dailies and the only thing he would say is, "I think that shot should go first," and usually that's it. There'll be parts of takes and he'll say, "I really like that, I really like that."

He doesn't speak that much in dailies and he doesn't really ever tell me that much; he really wants to see how I'll do it because it gives him fresh ideas. That's not to say he doesn't have very distinct ideas about how he wants things to go…. I've worked with a lot of directors and I really try to understand what they need in an editor, because I see my job as an editor as two-fold: One is to interpret what the director wants and his unique view of the material and the other thing is that I want to tell the story in the best way possible.[4]

Another editor who developed long-term relationships with directors was **Sam O'Steen**. For thirty years O'Steen was editor to director Mike Nichols, with whom he collaborated on *The Graduate*.* O'Steen also edited four movies for Roman Polanski, one of which was *Chinatown*.* O'Steen was able to develop an understanding of each of their personalities and adapt to their different working styles.

BO [Bobbie O'Steen]: *Polanski and Nichols are very different in their strengths and styles.*

SO [Sam O'Steen]: *If you want somebody to make something funny, you get Mike to do it. If you want somebody to make something scary, you get Polanski to do it. They can't do each other's thing… Words were all important to Nichols. He would say, "I don't like how that guy says so and so." Then I'd go through all the outtakes and find a different inflection… Polanski is the best with the camera of anybody I've ever worked with. I can't even explain it, but when I look at his film, I know it's his film, that he shot it. And his film tells me where to cut, really speaks loud to me, whereas the others, it whispers to me.*

BO: *Did you cut differently for each of them?*

SO: *Well, to use sound as an example, Polanski tends to overlap a little bit, he likes the sound to go just a little over to the next cut because he feels it ties them together. Nichols doesn't like overlaps. He likes more of a punch.*

BO: *And working with the two of them in the cutting room?*

SO: *Nichols is funny. Especially on the first couple of movies, when he'd first run a cut sequence, he wouldn't like it, he'd be jumpy about it, and give me a lot of changes.*

BO: *Did you make them?*

SO: *Not if I didn't agree. On the next running I would say, "I didn't have time to get to it" and pretty soon he would relax, get used to it.*

BO: *And Polanksi?*

SO: *He'd like to run my cuts back and forth again and again.*

BO: *But he wasn't looking for matched cuts.*

SO: *No, he just wanted to see the flow, see if it worked or didn't work. But both Nichols and Polanski were always real kind to me, they would tell me, "That's great" about certain things. I would often give Nichols surprises on the first cut, and he loved that.*

BO: *Nichols said that you can look at his dailies and know what he intended, that you think very similarly. Can you elaborate on that?*

SO: *When you work with a director for years, you know what they're thinking. You may argue about what's too tight or too loose, but basically you're in sync.[5]*

CHAPTER 12

A HISTORY OF MAKING RULES AND BREAKING THEM

All editors should be movie buffs, studying filmmakers who made the rules, such as D.W. Griffith, as well as those who broke them, such as Jean-Luc Godard. This chapter will describe how different movements in moviemaking evolved and affected the styles and technique of editing. The nine movies whose scenes I will analyze in the next chapter, will be indicated here by an asterisk (*) according to the time period when they made their mark in movie history.

THE EARLY 1900S: D. W. GRIFFITH

Griffith revolutionized moviemaking in basic ways that we now take for granted. He pioneered film editing techniques that had powerful psychological impact and created an involving narrative. He used cross-cutting to create suspense between the pursuer and pursued or opposing forces. He used cutaways and varied the length and pace of shots to create the buildup to a climax. He also used close-ups, dissolves, flashbacks, and parallel action as storytelling devices that pulled the audience into the emotional lives of his characters, all of which are on full display in his first epic production, *The Birth of a Nation*.

THE TWENTIES AND THIRTIES

The Russians

Revolutionary director Sergei Eisenstein used Griffith's methods to communicate political ideology through the collision of images. His groundbreaking movie *Battleship Potemkin* displayed the full power of the montage, a word he coined. His landmark scene depicts the massacre of civilians by soldiers on the Odessa steps. It illustrates how his sequencing of an astounding number of shots — contrasting in mood, visuals, and length — created an emotional impact greater than the sum of its parts. He had been inspired by the famous filmed experiment of the Russian theorist Pudovkin, in which he paired three sets of shots: a single actor reacting first to a bowl of soup, then to a woman in a coffin, and finally to a little girl playing. The audience raved about the "range" of the actor's performances, when, in fact, the same shot of him had been used each time. The way the shots were juxtaposed had changed the meaning.

Early Sound

The powerful fusion of sound and image made movies reach their full potential and created a greater challenge for the editor, who was now considered to be more of a collaborator than just a hired hand. Filmmakers wanted sound to be used not only for dialogue and realism, but also to create new layers of meaning. In the first full-length English talkie, *Blackmail*, which Alfred Hitchcock directed, one example of his many innovations was to use distorted off-screen dialogue, repeating the word "knife" to incite panic in a girl who had just committed murder. In Fritz Lang's groundbreaking movie *M*, he played off-screen dialogue over montages to condense storytelling and repeatedly used a child murderer's whistle to haunt the audience with his lurking presence. Lang was also one of the foremost directors of the **German expressionist** movement. These movies were extremely stylized, creating a feeling of anxiety and despair through the use of oblique angles, deep shadows, distorted perspective, and claustrophobic composition, all of which would later have a powerful influence on the film noir movement.

THE FORTIES

Film Noir

These movies, which had their heyday in a cynical postwar America, were moody stories of crime and passion in which the dark subject matter was reflected in the visual style. The typical protagonist was a basically honorable but disillusioned loner who was often seduced by a heartless, sexually aggressive "femme fatale."

A prime example, from the German expatriate director Billy Wilder, is *Double Indemnity*. Even though this genre peaked in the forties, such movies continued to be made as a tribute to this style of filmmaking.

THE FIFTIES/EARLY SIXTIES

Television

Live television dramas, variety shows, and news coverage gave audiences a desire for naturalism and spontaneity in their living room. The use of close-ups had also become more prevalent because of the smallness of the screen and the need to show details more readily. *Twelve Angry Men,** which was originally made as a live television drama and then as a movie by the same director, displays this style of shooting, which was well suited for the character-driven, tense atmosphere.

Wide Screen

The competition of television prompted the need for something more dramatic to lure audiences into movie theaters. "Wide-screen projection" used a newly developed anamorphic lens, with which wide images were squeezed into a standard frame and then projected twice as wide as the original screen ratio. This screen was especially well suited for grand scale "spectaculars," because it could encompass more information and show greater contrast between foreground and background action. Often in such movies either the editing was kept to a minimum or it continued the effect of the wide screen with the use of extreme close and long shots. Anthony Mann's *El Cid* is a prime example of this genre.

Rule-Breaking Europeans

After World War II, Europe experienced unrest and a desire for change. The need to shake things up and rebel against bourgeois tradition made an impact on moviemaking as well.

Cinema verité (literally "film truth," a term coined by Jean Rouch and used to describe his *Chronique d'un Été*) was a movement that blossomed in Europe. A precursor to the modern documentary, it was inspired by more new technology: that of lightweight, handheld cameras and portable sound equipment. These gave filmmakers the freedom to observe and record real people in actual situations.

Neorealism originated in Italy and used a documentary approach to convey political ideas. Using on-location cinematography, often nonprofessionals as actors, and sometimes no script at all, the editor had more freedom to allow the story to take shape in the cutting room. Roberto Rossellini's *Open City* was a groundbreaking example from this era.

These movies also had an impact on the revolutionary **New Wave** movement, which was founded by a group of French film critics and students who became directors themselves. Directors such as Jean-Luc Godard (*Breathless*) and François Truffaut (*400 Blows*) felt that logical and conventional storytelling was unnecessary; the point was to reveal emotional and intellectual truths. Nowhere was the rule breaking more obvious than in the style of editing. Pans, tracking shots, and zooms were often provocations used to confound the audience's expectations by fracturing time and space. The jump cut was very prevalent and was used to make the audience aware that they were being manipulated by editing, unlike the traditional approach, which had been to make the cuts seem invisible. *A Hard Day's Night,*[*] whose director, Richard Lester, was inspired by the New Wave movement, used shots like zooms, swish pans, and jump cuts to create an anarchic, frenetic style.

LATE SIXTIES/SEVENTIES: AMERICA'S GOLDEN AGE

There were many other foreign directors who made their mark during the fifties and early sixties — such as Federico Fellini (*8 1/2*) and Ingmar Bergman (*Persona*) — by displaying daring visual styles and highly personal, provocative narratives. The impact of these movies on filmmakers was felt when our country was experiencing its own political and cultural revolution. The era of fifties conformity had passed, the traditional studio system was crumbling, and there was a whole generation of college-educated baby boomers who made up a new movie audience. They viewed their parents' values as hypocritical and wanted to challenge their own intellect with offbeat antiheroes, frank sexuality, and ambiguous, unconventional storytelling. This intellectual, breaking-the-rules style was absorbed into mainstream American moviemaking, which created its own hybrid style during a very inspired period of filmmaking history. American filmmakers had also developed the most advanced technical expertise of their time, which empowered them to experiment with sound, music, camerawork — and editing. The editor was considered more as an artist than just a craftsman, and his role became more prestigious. *Butch Cassidy and the Sundance Kid*[*] and *Chinatown*[*] were the movies from this era that reinvented the Western and film noir, respectively. *The Graduate*[*] had a potent anti-establishment hero and message as well as a dazzling, innovative visual style. *The French Connection,*[*] which was influenced by cinema verité, was shot partly with handheld cameras and had an edgy, improvisational shooting style.

THE EIGHTIES AND MTV

The zany visuals and musical energy that was used to drive the shooting and editing for *A Hard Day's Night** made it a prototype for the music video. These videos, which later became prevalent on the pioneering network MTV, threw out the rules for narrative logic and dramatically changed the audience's expectations. They now wanted more cutting and jump cuts and a faster, more frenetic style. The images in American movies and videos also parodied the media and culture, and the conservatism of the Reagan era. This latter approach was reflected in *Body Heat,** with its slyly humorous take on the film noir genre. *The Big Chill,** which was also from this decade, continued another trend that started in the sixties with *The Graduate.** *The Graduate* had been the first dramatic movie to use only pre-recorded songs as its score. By the time *The Big Chill* was made, the number of songs that were used was unprecedented.

THE NINETIES AND ONWARD: COMPUTERS

The star-powered, blockbuster movie was established in this decade. Not only did budgets grow much bigger, but so did the demands on the filmmakers, because of the increased pressure for a movie to succeed and be finished quickly. The computer came into the cutting room, and swiftly accommodated the needs of the time. With computers the postproduction time is compressed so that a fairly finished product — with music and sound effects — can be shown by the editor as early as the first cut. The computer has made it easier to wade through all the film, especially complicated action sequences with multiple cameras and tons of footage. An editor can also be less afraid to take chances, because he doesn't have to worry about splices, as he had to in the past. Now the editor can keep multiple versions of a scene and easily undo any cut with the click of a keystroke.

The original editing machine, the moviola, was a device used by editors to view the film while cutting. It was an intimidating piece of machinery that could easily chew up film, and that only the editor knew how to operate. But because of that, it was easier for him and the director to be left alone when they were putting the cut together. Now a studio executive or anyone else can sit at a computer and tell an editor and a director what to do. Virtually anyone connected with the movie is able to download a DVD of the edited movie, take it home, and run it. In fact, anyone can buy editing software and cut their home movies on their own computer. But even though editing has become more accessible, it's still a challenge to master the editor's invisible art. This is especially obvious when, after everyone's been hopelessly fiddling with a problematic scene, the editor comes along and "magically" makes it work.

Despite the profound ways in which technology is changing the way editors work, when all is said and done the tools are just a means to an end. And the editor's goal, which is to tell the story in the best way possible, will never change.

CHAPTER 13

ANALYZING SCENES AND THEIR FRAME GRABS

The editor has to stick to certain basic principles whenever he's telling a story, but each kind of scene requires a somewhat different approach. The thirteen scenes in this chapter represent a range of types. I will use frame grabs pulled from these scenes to illustrate why and how the editor made his choices. Most of the analysis will be based on the actual cuts — that is, the "out" frame (the last frame of one shot) and the "in" frame (the first frame of the following shot) — although some frame grabs will come from within the shot.

DIALOGUE-DRIVEN: *TWELVE ANGRY MEN*

In a dialogue scene the emphasis can be dramatic or comedic, but the scripted word always plays a major role. The mind of the editor will be fully engaged here. He has to understand the characters' motivations, the subtext in both words and silence, and the overall truths in the scene. His basic challenge is to figure out when to cut for delivery of a line and when to cut for a reaction, but a subtle variation of those choices — like taking an extra beat before an actor speaks — can dramatically affect the impact and significance of a scene in ways that can go even beyond what the screenwriter and director intended.

The editor is obligated to maintain a tight pace, because the audience has less tolerance for the more passive nature of a dialogue scene. He has to cut at the exact moment the audience has the information they need or when they want to see someone's reaction. He can overlap dialogue to speed up the pace, but the greater challenge is to know the best technique for how to cut out lines that are unnecessary, given that the scenes are so structured and anchored by words.

The editor has to be especially sensitive to what's at stake for the actor, when those stakes are heightened, and how to support those moments with the actor's performance. For example, the editor may feel that a particular moment aches for a close-up, but the actor delivered a better performance in the medium shot. The editor should also protect the actor's pacing and must be especially careful about editing out an actor's pauses. Silence is often more powerful than speaking, and certainly provides more tension. But unless there is a specific reason for the actor to pause before or after an action, the editor should avoid showing him waiting to perform or letting down.

In general, the editor can less easily bend basic rules in a dialogue scene. Because the direction the actors are looking is especially significant, crossing-the-line mistakes will be more noticeable. Large groups of actors are a headache to an editor, and not only because he has to worry about crossing stage lines and making sure all the actors are looking in the right direction. The editor also has to keep every actor "alive" so the audience isn't disoriented later in the scene when an actor suddenly appears out of nowhere. To do this, the editor has to sometimes cut to actors who are not necessarily interesting or capable.

Dinner table scenes can be especially difficult, because the editor has to watch for consistency in the actors' movements as they eat and drink. Of course, content and performance are always more important than whether an actor's fork was raised higher in the previous shot. Since inconsistencies and problems are more obvious in a dialogue scene, the use of inserts and close-ups can be especially useful as sleight-of-hand transitions. All told, because of the constraints and subtleties involved, it's safe to say that an editor will spend more time on a dialogue scene than on any other.

FRAME GRAB ILLUSTRATION: *TWELVE ANGRY MEN*

Twelve Angry Men is the ultimate example of a dialogue-driven movie because, except for the opening and closing shots, all of the scenes take place in a single room as a jury of twelve deliberates its verdict. This movie also carries the full challenges of a group scene. Having the actors spend virtually all their time sitting around a table could have been a logistical nightmare, because the director, cinematographer, and editor had to constantly make sure the audience was never confused about where the actors were in relation to one another, while keeping the movie visually dynamic. And the power of the dialogue, what it reveals, clearly motivates both the shooting and editing.

"What is the movie about?" asked director Sidney Lumet. *"It becomes the riverbed into which all subsequent decisions will be channeled."* In response to where the audience's focus should be, Lumet said: *"Listen."*[6]

THE CAST

Juror 1, the Foreman: **Martin Balsam**
Juror 2: **John Fiedler**
Juror 3: **Lee J. Cobb**
Juror 4: **E. G. Marshall**
Juror 5: **Jack Klugman**
Juror 6: **Edward Binns**
Juror 7: **Jack Warden**
Juror 8: **Henry Fonda**
Juror 9: **Joseph Sweeney**
Juror 10: **Ed Begley**
Juror 11: **George Voskovec**
Juror 12: **Robert Webber**

(Note: To avoid the confusion of identifying jurors by number, I will refer to them by the actors' last names.)

The opening scene establishes the jurors in court as they get instructions from the judge. The scene ends with a close-up of the boy who is accused of the crime. This shot dissolves into a high shot of an empty jury room. The credits roll, and the camera moves in and out and pans among the jurors as they enter the room and mill about, engaging in small talk and some discussion about the case. There is a hint that most of them consider this an open-and-shut case, or that they just want to get the process over with. The shot ends at the jurors' table.

SCENE ONE: THE FIRST VOTE

INT. JURY ROOM - DAY
Medium long shot from left end of table.

> BALSAM
> Okay fellas, can we hold it down a minute?
> Uh, fellas, say we'd like to get started.
> Gentleman at the window?

FRAME GRAB #1

CUT TO:

Medium close shot of Fonda. He's looking out the window.

FRAME GRAB #2

He turns.

> BALSAM
> (OS)
> ...we'd like to get started.

> FONDA
> Oh, I'm sorry.

Camera pans over with Fonda as he sits down among the jurors.

CUT TO:

Master shot from right end of table.

> BALSAM
> Is everyone here?

> BINNS
> (gesturing over shoulder to bathroom door)
> The old man is inside.

> BALSAM
> Oh, would you knock on the door for him?

> BINNS
>
> Uh, yeah.

Binns barely starts to get up.

FRAME GRAB #3

CUT TO:

Reverse master shot from right corner, head of table.

FRAME GRAB #4

Binns opens the bathroom door and Sweeney appears, as camera moves in slightly and pans to right, settling in at the middle of the table.

> BALSAM
>
> Say, we'd like to get started.

> SWEENEY
>
> Oh, forgive me, gentlemen. I didn't mean to
> keep you waiting.

He sits down.

> BALSAM
>
> Okay, gentlemen, if I can have your attention.

CUT TO:

Close shot of Balsam.

> BALSAM
>
> (cont'd)
> You fellows can handle this thing any way you want....
> I'm not gonna make any rules. We can discuss it first, then
> vote on it. That's of course, that's one way and, uh...

FRAME GRAB #5

CUT TO:

Master shot from center, head of table.

> ***FRAME GRAB #6***
>
> BALSAM
> (OS)
> Well, we can vote on it right now.
>
> MARSHALL
> I think it's customary to take a preliminary vote.
>
> WARDEN
> Yeah, let's vote. Maybe then we'll all...
>
> **CUT BACK TO:**

Close shot of Balsam.

> ***FRAME GRAB #7***
>
> WARDEN
> (OS)
> ...get outta here.
>
> BALSAM
> Uh huh...Okay... I think that we... 'course you all know that we
> have a first degree murder here and if we vote the accused
> guilty....
>
> **CUT BACK TO:**

Master shot through center of table.

> BALSAM
> (OS)
> ...we've got to send him to the chair. That's mandatory.
>
> MARSHALL
> I think we know that.
>
> BEGLEY
> Yeah... Let's see who's where.

> BALSAM
>> (OS)
> Okay, anyone doesn't want to vote?

CUT BACK TO:

Close shot of Balsam.

> BALSAM
> Okay, just remember that this has to be twelve to nothing either way. That's the law...

CUT TO:

Master shot from left corner, end of table.

> BALSAM
> Okay, we ready? All those voting guilty please raise your hands. One, two, three, four, five, six, seven... (pauses) eight, nine, ten, eleven.

FRAME GRAB #8

CUT TO:

Reverse master from left corner, head of table.

FRAME GRAB #9

> BALSAM
> Okay, that's eleven guilty. Those voting not guilty?

Fonda raises his hand.

> BALSAM
>> (cont'd)
> One, right. Eleven guilty. One not guilty. Well, now we know where we are.

CUT TO:

Medium shot from right corner, end of table shooting past Binns and Warden, to Sweeney and Begley.

> BEGLEY
> (laughing derisively)
> Boy, oh boy. There's always one.

> WARDEN
> So what do we do now?

> FONDA
> I guess we talk.

> BEGLEY
> Boy...

FRAME GRAB #10

CUT TO:

Medium long shot from left corner and end of table past Fonda to Fielder, Cobb, Marshall, Klugman, and Binns.

FRAME GRAB #11

> BEGLEY
> (OS)
> ...oh boy.

> COBB
> Do you really think he's innocent?

CUT TO:

Close shot of Fonda.

> FONDA
> (a beat)
> I don't know.

> COBB
> (OS)
> I mean you...

FRAME GRAB #12

CUT TO:

Close shot of Cobb.

        FRAME GRAB #13

              COBB

...sat in court with the rest of us. You heard what we did. The kid's a dangerous...

CUT BACK TO:

Close shot of Fonda.

              COBB
           (OS)
...killer. You can see it.

             FONDA
He's eighteen years old.

CUT BACK TO:

Close shot of Cobb.

              COBB
Well, that's old enough. He stabbed his own father. Fourteen inches into the chest.

CUT BACK TO:

Close shot of Fonda.

              COBB
           (OS)
They proved it a dozen different ways in court. Do you want me to list them for you?

             FONDA
        (shakes his head)
No.

CUT BACK TO:

Medium long shot from right corner and end of table past Binns and Warden to Sweeney and Begley.

BEGLEY

Then what do you want?

FONDA

I just want to talk.

WARDEN

Well, what's there to talk about? Eleven men in here think he's guilty. No one had to think about it twice except you.

BEGLEY

I wanna ask you something. Do you believe his story?

FONDA

I don't know if I believe it or not. Maybe I don't.

 ***FRAME GRAB #14***

CUT TO:

Medium two shot past Fonda to Warden.

WARDEN
(cont'd)
So how come you voted not guilty?

Fonda turns away from camera to face him.

FONDA

Well, there were eleven votes for guilty. It's not easy to raise my hand and send a boy off to die without talking about it first.

WARDEN

Well now who says it's easy?

FONDA

No one.

WARDEN

What, just because I voted fast?
I honestly think the guy is guilty. You couldn't change my
 mind if you talked for a hundred years.

FRAME GRAB #15

CUT TO:

Medium two shot of Warden to Fonda.

FRAME GRAB #16

FONDA

I'm not trying to change your mind. It's just that...
we're talking about somebody's life here. We can't
decide it in five minutes. Supposing we're wrong.

DECONSTRUCTION
Scene edited by Carl Lerner

Note: There will be references below to four diagrams, which were used on pages 28–29 and 31–32 to illustrate correct camera coverage.

The first establishing shot of the jury lasts over six-and-a-half minutes, finally settling in as some of them sit around the table (the "out" frame is *frame grab #1*). The first cut is to the protagonist, Fonda (the "in" frame is *frame grab #2*). He's shown looking contemplatively out the window, his introspection and distance from the others already setting him apart.

frame grab 1

frame grab 2

frame grab 3

frame grab 4

The first two master shots in this scene (*Frame grabs #3* and *#4*) are shot from a high angle at opposite sides and ends of the table. These two completely reversed images show the most information and as many faces as possible. What cues the cut out of the shot (the "out" frame is *Frame grab #3)* is Binns, in the right near corner of screen, starting to stand up. In the beginning of the next shot (*Frame grab #4)* Binns continues to get up and then opens the bathroom door for Sweeney. Because this crucial juror's presence is needed for the deliberations to begin, the editor stays with this shot until Sweeney sits down. The editor cuts out right after Balsam asks for the jurors' attention.

The first close shot (*Frame grab #5*) sets up the importance of Balsam, the foreman. When he proposes voting right away, the editor cuts to his POV (*Frame grab #6*) down the center of the table. *Frame grab #7*, the "in" frame of the next shot, shows Balsam's reaction when one of the jurors talks about just wanting "to get outta here." It also functions as a bridge between the down-the-center-of-the-table shot in *Frame grab #6* and the next master shot (*Frame grab #8*). If the shots shown in *Frame grabs #6* and *#8* were cut together, the transition would be visually awkward, because they're only partial reversals of angles.

frame grab 5

frame grab 6

frame grab 7

frame grab 8

This next pair of completely reversed high angle master shots (*Frame grabs #8* and *#9*) now complete the camera coverage from all four corners of the table and further clarify all four juror positions, as seen in *Diagram 1*. **See Diagram 1 (on page 28).**

The "out" frame of the shot (*Frame grab #8*) sets up a cheat on the audience, because it shows only Fonda's back, and doesn't give the audience a clear view of his arm; it's not yet obvious that he's the only one who hasn't raised his hand to vote "guilty." What cues the cut out of this shot is the foreman's ending his count of only eleven votes and his turning to make eye contact with Fonda. The next shot (the "in" frame is *Frame grab #9*) lets the cat out of the bag, because Fonda is now facing the camera, and the audience sees he hasn't raised his hand.

frame grab 9

The following shot (*Frame grab #10*) has to include Fonda and Begley, since Begley is the first juror to react negatively to Fonda's vote, and the dialogue from Begley comes in tight, on the first frame, to increase the tension of the moment. The next juror to protest, Cobb, is included in the subsequent shot, *Frame grab #11*. This also foreshadows Begley and Cobb becoming the most irrationally resistant characters, with Cobb remaining the final holdout. Fonda and Binns are the only two actors who are in both shots, *Frame grabs #9* and *#10*. As a result these two actors have to be consistently on the left and right side of the screen from shot to shot. If the camera had crossed the stage line —the imaginary line that cuts through Binns and Fonda — the directions would have been flipped, and the audience would be disoriented. And because everyone sitting among them is different in both shots, there is no other stage line that has to be protected, as shown in *Diagram 2*.

See Diagram 2 (on page 29).

frame grab 10

frame grab 11

frame grab 12

frame grab 13

The editor cuts to the first close shot of Fonda (*Frame grab #12)*, when he plants reasonable doubt in the minds of the jurors and the audience. The editor also cuts to Fonda early enough so that he can take a beat before he answers, giving his dialogue further weight. The next close shot to Cobb (*Frame grab #13)* is motivated when he challenges Fonda. The editor cuts back and forth between these two jurors' close-ups for the next three shots. This confrontation foreshadows the most explosive one between any two jurors and will determine the outcome of the verdict.

The interaction shifts when Warden and Begley speak up, and the editor cuts to a group shot that includes them as well (the "out" frame is *Frame grab #14)*. This is the same angle as the one shown in *Frame grab #10,* but now the stage line runs between Warden and Fonda, who are the only actors in the following two shots, shown in *Frame grabs #15* and *#16* and *Diagram 3*. As a result, they stay consistently on the left and right sides of the screen as the focus shifts from Warden, who is facing the camera while he defends his position (the "out" frame is *Frame grabs #15*), to an angle favoring Fonda. He now takes center stage, driving home the point that someone's life is at stake (the "in" frame is *Frame grab #16*). ***See Diagram 3 (on page 31).***

frame grab 14

frame grab 15

frame grab 16

SCENE TWO: THE SECOND VOTE

The next sequence comes about half an hour later, a third of the way into the movie. Up to this point Fonda has continued to hold his ground, but despite his attempts to plant doubt in the jurors' minds, he remains the only holdout. The other jurors now pressure him to come around and vote "guilty."

INT. JURY ROOM – DAY
Medium close shot of Fonda looking out the window.

BALSAM
(OS)
Well, what about it?

Fonda turns to face them.

COBB
(OS)
You're the only one

He moves away from the window to the table and camera follows him. He turns to the camera, in a close shot.

FONDA
I have a proposition to make to all of you. I want to call
for another vote. I want you eleven men to vote by
secret written ballot.

FRAME GRAB #1

CUT TO:

Close shot of Klugman.

FRAME GRAB #2

FONDA
(cont'd, OS)
I'll abstain.

CUT BACK TO:

Close shot of Fonda.

> FONDA
> If there are eleven votes for guilty I won't stand alone. We'll...

CUT TO:

Close shot of Fiedler.

FRAME GRAB #3.

> FONDA
> (cont'd, OS)
> ....take in a guilty verdict to the judge right now.

CUT BACK TO:

Close shot of Fonda.

> FONDA
> But if anyone votes not guilty we stay here and talk it out.
> That's it. If you want to try it, I'm ready.

FRAME GRAB #4

CUT TO:

Master shot from left corner, end of table past Fonda's back to other jurors.

> WARDEN
> (claps)
> All right, let's do it the hard way.

> BALSAM
> Yeah, that sounds fair. Everyone agree? Anyone doesn't agree?
> ...Okay, fine, let's go. Pass these along there...

FRAME GRAB #5

CUT TO:

Medium shot from head of table past Balsam's back to Fonda, Sweeney, Begley, Voskovec, and Webber.

>   *FRAME GRAB #6*

Camera pans with Fonda as he walks away from table, past jurors, to water cooler at far corner of room. **The moment he stops, camera moves in slowly until he's in close-up.** He turns to look back at table, and then again looks the other way.

>   *FRAME GRAB #7*

>   CUT TO:

Medium close shot of table showing only hands holding ballots and paraphernalia on table.

>   *FRAME GRAB #8*

Camera pans from end to the head of the table as ballots are passed by jurors' hands and wind up in a pile in front of Balsam. The camera holds, shooting past Balsam to his hands as he unfolds each ballot and announces what's written on each of them.

>   BALSAM
>   (voiceover)
>   guilty... guilty... guilty... guilty... guilty... guilty...
>   guilty... guilty... guilty

Balsam opens the tenth ballot, which reads "not guilty." Camera pans up with Balsam as he stands, holding piece of paper open.

>   *FRAME GRAB #9*

>   CUT TO:

Close-up of Fonda.

>   *FRAME GRAB #10*

BALSAM
(OS)
Not guilty.

After Fonda reacts, he turns around and focus shifts to background and reveals jurors behind him.

BALSAM
(OS, reading last ballot)
...guilty.

As Fonda walks back to the table, Begley stands up angrily.

BEGLEY
Boy. How do you like that?

Warden stands up and walks away making chicken movements with his arms.

WARDEN
Another chump flaps his wings.

Fonda moves to far end of the room and in medium long shot he stands among Binns, Warden, Sweeney, Begley, and Voskovec.

BEGLEY
All right, who was it? C'mon, I wanna know.

VOSKOVEC
Excuse me. It was a secret ballot. We all agreed on that, no? If the gentleman wants it to remain secret...

COBB
(OS, shouting)
Se...

FRAME GRAB #11

CUT TO:

Medium long shot, another angle with Voskovec and Begley in left and right foreground with Cobb, Marshall, and Klugman in between.

FRAME GRAB #12

>   COBB
> ...cret! There are no secrets in a jury room!

Camera moves in as Cobb walks closer to a seated Klugman.

>   COBB
>   (cont'd)
> I know who it was. Brother you really are somethin'.
> You sit here, vote guilty like the rest of us, then some
> golden-voiced preacher starts tearing your poor heart
> out about some underprivileged kid just couldn't help
> becoming a murderer and you change your vote. If that
> isn't the most sicken... Why don't you just drop a quarter
> in his collection box?

>   KLUGMAN
> Ohhh, now just wait a mi...

Camera pans over as Klugman gets up and follows Cobb.

>   KLUGMAN
>   (cont'd)
> Listen, you can't talk to me like that!

>   COBB
> Ahh...

>   KLUGMAN
> No, who do you think you are...

>   MARSHALL
> Calm down. ...

>   **CUT TO:**

Medium close shot of Fonda, watching, seated.

MARSHALL
(cont'd OS)
...calm down.

KLUGMAN
(OS)
No, what does he think he's do...

MARSHALL
(OS)
It doesn't matter. He's...

A slight smile creeps up on Fonda's face.

FRAME GRAB #13

CUT BACK TO:

Medium shot of Cobb, Marshall, and Klugman.

MARSHALL
(cont'd)
...very excitable. Sit down.

Cobb turns back around from window and camera moves in to a close shot.

COBB
Excitable! You bet I'm excitable. We're trying to put
a guilty man in the chair where he belongs until
someone starts telling us...

FRAME GRAB #14

CUT TO:

Medium close shot of Fonda standing, looking alarmed.

FRAME GRAB #15

COBB
(cont'd, OS)
...fairy tales and we're listening!

> BALSAM
> (OS)
> Hey, uh...

CUT BACK TO:

Medium shot of Cobb. Camera pans as he moves over to Klugman and they face off in a two shot.

> BALSAM
> (cont'd, OS)
> ...come on, huh?

> COBB
> What made you change your vote?

> SWEENEY
> (OS)
> He didn't...

CUT TO:

Tight close-up of Sweeney.

> SWEENEY
> ...change his vote, I did!

FRAME GRAB #16

CUT TO:

Two shot of Cobb and Klugman.
They turn to the screen, in shock.

FRAME GRAB #17

DECONSTRUCTION

This sequence represents a turning point, which is reflected by the use of music for the first time since the opening credits. The music starts as Fonda walks back to the table and then proposes that the jurors take another vote by secret ballot (the "out" frame of that shot is *Frame grab #1).* The editor cuts very tight after that line to Klugman for a reaction (the "in" frame is *Frame grab #2),* because Klugman shares the same impoverished ethnic background with the accused boy and would seem to be the most sympathetic. After cutting back to a close shot of Fonda as he continues to discuss the vote, the next reaction shot is to Fiedler *(Frame grab #3),* who appears to be the softest character. These are red herrings, setting the audience up to think they might be the ones who will now vote "not guilty."

frame grab 1

frame grab 2

frame grab 3

The editor cuts back to Fonda, who ends his speech with, "I'm ready," which sets up the momentum for the vote (the "out" frame is *Frame grab #4).*

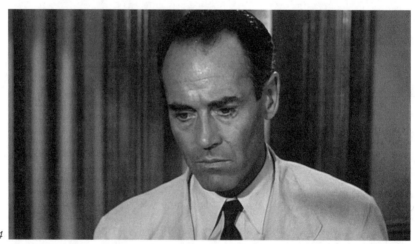

frame grab 4

The editor then cuts to show all the jurors' reactions, shooting past Fonda's back and cuts out right after Balsam leans in to distribute the ballots (the "out" frame is *Frame grab #5)*. Next is a reverse angle on many of the same jurors, as Balsam continues to lean in (that "in" frame is *Frame grab #6)*. Balsam and Fonda remain on the left and right side of the screen in both shots. The four other jurors sitting between them have their left–right positions flipped from one shot to the next. The filmmakers got away with this inconsistency, because the audience is primarily focused on Balsam and Fonda. The cut is also smoother because the editor starts the second shot (the "in" frame is *Frame grab #6)* when Fonda has already started to move away from the table.

See Diagram 4 (on page 32).

frame grab 5

frame grab 6

The camera pans with Fonda until he is at a distance from the table, then moves in to a close-up that shows him glance back at the jurors, then look away. The moment is underlined by the peaking of the musical score (that "out" frame is *Frame grab #7)*. The next shot starts with *Frame grab #8*, showing hands passing the ballots along the table until Balsam's hands receive all the ballots (the "out" frame of that same shot is *Fame grab #9)*. The tension is sustained because the editor stayed with this shot and chose to avoid cutting away to anyone's face. The audience sees all the ballots, including the "not guilty" one, before Balsam the foreman announces them. As a result, the suspenseful moment is milked because the audience can both anticipate and then experience the jurors' reactions to the "not guilty" vote.

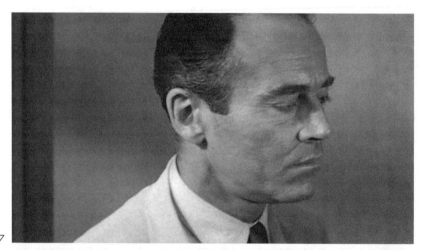

frame grab 7

frame grab 8

frame grab 9

When the foreman reads "not guilty," the editor knows the audience wants to see Fonda, so he doesn't even bother to overlap the words. He plays the whole "not guilty" line on Fonda (the "in" frame is *Frame grab #10)*.

frame grab 10

Director Sidney Lumet said that *"the cutting tempo was accelerating steadily during the movie but would break into a gallop in the last thirty five minutes or so. The increasing tempo helped enormously in making the story more exciting and in raising the audience's awareness that the picture was compressing further in space and time."* [7]

As the tension builds and the conversation among the jurors becomes more heated, the pace of the interaction shifts into a higher gear. This is evident in all the shots from *Frame grab #11* through *Frame grab #16*. In every case, the characters' lines overlap within the shots, and the dialogue is overlapped from one shot to the next. Also, a new stage line is created between Voskovec and Begley (the "out" frame is *Frame grab #11*). They make eye contact in the foreground of that shot and in the following shot (the "in" frame is *Frame grab #12*). They're also the only two jurors who are in both those shots, remaining on the left and right side of the screen, and it is the only stage line that the camera has to honor. Warden, Binns, and Fonda have "disappeared" from the first shot and are now replaced by Cobb, Marshall, and Klugman. The repositioning of the actors from one shot to another is a bit of a cheat, but it works dramatically; the audience won't notice. This is partly because the actors are anchored by Begley's and Voskovec's stage line, but also because of the volatile reaction from Cobb, whose line overlaps from one shot to the next and motivates the cut.

frame grab 11

frame grab 12

The inclusion of Cobb, Klugman, and Marshall is also justified in the shot shown in *Frame grab #12*, since the three of them now become more significant: Cobb is about to confront Klugman, with Marshall playing mediator. In the shot shown in *Frame grab #13*, Fonda is seated. Because he was standing the last time we saw him in *Frame grab #11* and will be again in *Frame grab #15*, this shot must have been "stolen" from another part of the movie. The audience will never notice, though, because the editor is giving them what they want: a smile creeping onto Fonda's face. This expression reveals that he's pleased about two things: that Klugman is standing up to the bullying Cobb and also that the jury may not be as united against him as they seemed. Then, after Fonda is attacked by Cobb (shown in *Frame grab #14*) the audience wants a different, more alarmed reaction from Fonda, which is seen in *Frame grab #15*.

frame grab 13

frame grab 14

frame grab 15

The editor now cuts to Cobb, who's still convinced Klugman voted "not guilty" and now moves over to confront him. By putting the emphasis on Klugman, the editor surprises the audience when, in the next shot, the "not guilty" voter is revealed to be Sweeney. The editor packs a punch by starting Sweeney's off-screen line on the two shot of Cobb and Klugman. The editor then cuts to Sweeney as he defiantly announces that he's the one who changed his vote (the "out" frame is *Frame grab #16*). He is also in a very tight close-up — the tightest shot in the movie so far — which is appropriate since this is one of the most surprising moments of the movie. The shock registers on Cobb's and Klugman's faces when the editor cuts back to their two shot, just as they do a double-take and then turn full-face to the screen (the "out" frame is *Frame grab #17*). Their reaction mirrors that of the audience: This is a major turning point in the movie.

frame grab 16

frame grab 17

COMEDY: *THE GRADUATE*

Comedy is not as different from drama as it may seem. The key moments are still based on emotional truth, even if they are often exaggerated. There's an especially delicate chemistry involved in creating comedy, however, because what makes something funny is not easy to analyze or predict. One thing is certain: the rhythm of delivery is all important. In theater or live performance, the actor's timing may be all that matters, but in movies the editor's timing is crucial, too. He can't wait too long for the setup of the laugh, and he also has to know how long to hold onto that moment once the laughing starts. The editor can, for instance, show an actor repeatedly trying to get up after he falls. The more he falls the funnier it gets, but there is a point when the humor peaks and exactly at that moment, the editor has to cut. The editor also has to have a sense of how long the audience will laugh and has to "open up" the cut to give the audience time so that the laughing won't interfere with the dialogue in the next shot or scene. This is especially true in physical comedy where the laughs may go on for a long time.

Verbal and Physical Comedy

Because verbal comedy is based on the meaning of words and a depth of character, many of the rules for the dialogue-driven genre apply here. The tone of verbal comedy is more realistic than that of physical comedy. The editor cuts more by the book, bound by the words and the subtlety of the actors' interactions.

Physical comedy, on the other hand, is more visceral and visual. The situations, characters, and laughs are more exaggerated. As a result the editor will be freer to break the rules and use jerky, nonsensical cuts. Basically he can do anything to get a laugh.

Character and Situation

Leading actors in comedy, especially the ones whose humor is more physical, often have a specific screen persona that doesn't vary all that much from one movie role to the next. (Examples would be the Marx Brothers and John Belushi.) The audience counts on predictable behavior from these actors, and it's up to the editor to make sure those expectations are satisfied. Whether a star is involved or not, humor is often based on exaggerating a character's physical or emotional qualities.

The situation, too, can be physical (like slipping on a banana peel) or psychological (such as mistaken identity, role reversal, or other reasons for comedic misunderstanding). The most common situation in any kind of comedy is humor at a character's expense. A classic example would be to take pleasure at someone's embarrassment or loss of dignity. Repetition that causes frustration can add to the humor and can take many forms. The editor can, for instance, keep cutting to someone trying to move an object, and failing. What adds to the humor is the character's seriousness, his not knowing how absurd and hopeless his repeated attempts are.

Foreground/background setups can also be particularly effective in heightening humor at the character's expense by exaggerating his relationship with another character, particularly his powerlessness. Contrasting their high and low positioning — say, one sitting versus one standing — can also emphasize a character's helplessness in his situation.

Subjective and Objective Views

The choice of the point of view ("POV") — whether the audience anticipates something that's about to happen or is thrown off guard — contributes significantly to physical comedy.

Let's again take as an example the classic pratfall: slipping on a banana peel. The editor could start with a long shot of the actor running down the street, then cut to a close shot of the banana skin just as his foot enters the frame, and continue that shot until halfway through the action of the foot skidding. Then the editor might cut to a medium shot of the actor completing the fall onto the pavement. Technically this would be a smooth, good cut. In this case the editor chose the "subjective" viewpoint, where the audience sees what the actor does and they react together.

The editor could also use a different approach. He could again start with a long shot of the actor running down the street, then cut to a close-up of the banana peel lying on the sidewalk. The editor might cut back to the long shot of the actor still running and stay with that shot until the actor skidded and fell on the pavement. Then he could cut to a close-up of the actor's exasperated reaction. In this case, the editor used the "objective" approach, where the audience is on the outside looking in and sees what happens before the actor does. This is a more effective cut, because you're telling the audience that the character is going to do something silly before he himself knows it, milking the pleasure of watching the character be a hapless victim. And, usually, if the joke is only on the character and not on the audience, it's funnier.

FRAME GRAB ILLUSTRATION: *THE GRADUATE*

The following two scenes from *The Graduate* straddle both verbal and physical comedy and have a dramatic — even somewhat melodramatic — undertone. In the first scene, the emphasis is more on dialogue, a cat-and-mouse scenario setting up Benjamin as the naive victim of seduction. In the second scene, the focus is on physical comedy, as Benjamin becomes trapped in the bedroom by the temptress Mrs. Robinson.

Part of the analysis of this movie — and this movie alone — will include information from the "lined script," the shooting script that the editor uses, which has lines down each page to show what part of the scene is covered by each camera angle, along with detailed notation about each of the different takes. Those shots will sometimes be identified by "slate numbers" (how each take is identified during filming).

SCENE ONE: THE DEN

The setup:
Benjamin (Dustin Hoffman), a recent college graduate, has left the party his parents threw in his honor, because Mrs. Robinson (Ann Bancroft), a friend of his parents, has pressured him into driving her home.

INT. MRS. ROBINSON'S HOUSE - NIGHT.
Master shot, dollying with Benjamin and Mrs. Robinson through hall to the bar.
Mrs. Robinson goes behind the bar.

> MRS. ROBINSON
> What do you drink, bourbon?

> BENJAMIN
> Look, Mrs. Robinson – I drove you home. I was glad to do it. But I have some things on my mind. Can you understand that?

> MRS. ROBINSON
> Yes.

BENJAMIN
All right, then.

He turns and starts to leave.

MRS. ROBINSON
What do you drink?

He stops, takes a half step back, and turns. She fixes drinks.

MRS. ROBINSON
Benjamin, I'm sorry to be this way, but I don't want
to be alone in this house.

BENJAMIN
Why not?

MRS. ROBINSON
Please wait till my husband gets home.

Camera settles in, shooting over Benjamin to Mrs. Robinson at the bar.

FRAME GRAB #1

CUT TO:

Reverse master shot to Benjamin over Mrs. Robinson.

FRAME GRAB #2

BENJAMIN
When is he coming back?

MRS. ROBINSON
I don't know....Drink?

BENJAMIN
No.

She thrusts a drink in his hand.

BENJAMIN
(con'td)
Are you always this afraid of being alone?

She lights a cigarette.

MRS. ROBINSON
Yes.

BENJAMIN
Well, why can't you just lock the doors and go to bed?

She turns to him, her back to screen.

MRS. ROBINSON
I'm very neurotic.

He makes a feeble attempt to swat at the smoke from her billowing cigarette. As she turns and exits right, he sits down, awkwardly. Dramatic, seductive piano music comes on off screen. (She's turned on the phonograph.) Benjamin reacts, sitting suddenly upright.

 **FRAME GRAB #3**

CUT TO:

Medium long shot to Mrs. Robinson over Benjamin as she returns to bar.

 **FRAME GRAB #4**

MRS. ROBINSON
May I ask you a question?
(she sits down)
What do you think of me?

CUT TO:

Medium shot of Benjamin in profile, seated.

BENJAMIN
What do you mean?

CUT TO:

Medium shot of Mrs. Robinson seated at bar.

> MRS. ROBINSON
> You've known me nearly all your life.
> You must have formed some opinion.

CUT BACK TO:

Medium shot of Benjamin.

> BENJAMIN
> Well...I always thought that you were a
> very...nice...person.

He starts to take a drink.

 *FRAME GRAB #5*

CUT BACK TO:

Medium shot of Mrs. Robinson.

> MRS. ROBINSON
> Did you know I was an alcoholic?

 *FRAME GRAB #6*

CUT TO:

Close-up of Benjamin.
He's drinking...

 *FRAME GRAB #7*

He looks up, gulping drink.

> BENJAMIN
> What?

CUT TO:

Close-up of Mrs. Robinson.

MRS. ROBINSON
Did you know that?

FRAME GRAB #8

CUT BACK TO:

Close-up of Benjamin
He starts to stand up.

BENJAMIN
Look... I think I should be going...

His torso moves across the screen.

FRAME GRAB #9

CUT BACK TO:

Medium long shot to Mrs. Robinson over Benjamin.

FRAME GRAB #10

He plunks down drink on bar.

MRS. ROBINSON
Sit down, Benjamin.

BENJAMIN
Mrs. Robinson ... if you don't mind my saying so...
this conversation is getting a little strange. Now
I'm sure that Mr. Robinson will be here any minute and...

MRS. ROBINSON
No.

BENJAMIN
What?

MRS. ROBINSON
My husband will be back very late.

He turns around and walks away, facing camera.

BENJAMIN
Oh my God.

Camera dollies with Benjamin as he moves into room for a combination long shot with Benjamin in foreground, Mrs. Robinson at bar in background.

MRS. ROBINSON
Pardon?

BENJAMIN
Oh no, Mrs. Robinson, oh no.

Benjamin is pacing back and forth in foreground, in silhouette, as Mrs. Robinson is seated seductively on bar stool, smiling.

MRS. ROBINSON
What's wrong?

BENJAMIN
Mrs. Robinson, you didn't... I mean you didn't expect...

MRS. ROBINSON
What?

BENJAMIN
I mean... you didn't really think that I would do something like that.

MRS. ROBINSON
Like what?

BENJAMIN
What do you think?

MRS. ROBINSON
Well, I don't know.

She props her foot up on the bar stool, parting her legs.

> BENJAMIN
> For God's sake Mrs. Robinson, here we are, you've got me into your house. You give me a drink. You put on music, now you start opening up your personal life to me and tell me your husband won't be home for hours.

> MRS. ROBINSON
> So?

FRAME GRAB #11

CUT TO:

Medium long shot to Benjamin through Mrs. Robinson's leg.

> BENJAMIN
> Mrs. Robinson... you're trying to seduce me.

FRAME GRAB #12

CUT TO:

Close-up (pick up shot) of Mrs. Robinson.
She's laughing.

FRAME GRAB #13

CUT TO:

Reverse master (pick up shot) shot to Benjamin over Mrs. Robinson.

FRAME GRAB #14

> BENJAMIN
> (weaker)
> Aren't you?

CUT BACK TO:

Medium long shot to Mrs. Robinson over Benjamin.

MRS. ROBINSON
Why no, I hadn't thought about it.

She turns away, closing her legs, and stubs out her cigarette.

The scene continues with a mortified Benjamin apologizing for misreading her. She forgives him, and encourages him to finish his drink.

DECONSTRUCTION
Scene edited by Sam O'Steen

The following shots were used:
> Master shot, dolly with Benjamin and Mrs. Robinson through hall to bar
> Reverse master shot to Benjamin over Mrs. Robinson
> Reverse master shot (pickup) to Benjamin over Mrs. Robinson
> Medium long shot to Mrs. Robinson over Benjamin then dolly back with Benjamin as he moves into room, for combination long shot with Benjamin in foreground and Mrs. Robinson at bar in background
> Medium shot of Benjamin, seated in profile
> Medium shot of Mrs. Robinson, seated in profile
> Close shot of Benjamin
> Close shot of Mrs. Robinson
> Close shot (pickup) of Mrs. Robinson
> Medium long shot to Benjamin through Mrs. Robinson's leg

The following shots were not used:
> Slate #15: Medium shot to Mrs. Robinson over Benjamin
> Slate #109: Insert of Mrs. Robinson's hand to turn on phonograph
> Slate #14: Medium long to Mrs. Robinson over Benjamin, camera booms down with Benjamin as he sits on ottoman
> Slate #106: Close shot of Benjamin, seated
> Slate #21: Close-up of Benjamin over bar, seen through Mrs. Robinson's leg, variable focus
> Slate #22: Medium long shot to Benjamin
> Slate #23: Big close-up Benjamin

In this key scene, Mrs. Robinson pulls Benjamin in, first with her neediness, then with her increasingly candid confessions, and ultimately with her sexuality.

As the editor, Sam O'Steen, explained, "*The theme was a jungle. You can see it in the plants, in the furniture, she was even wearing a jungle print. She was like an animal trying to devour him.*"[8]

We, the audience, know that Benjamin is way over his head, and we can pretty much see what's coming, which makes it painfully funny to watch and wait for him to "slip on the banana peel." The approach is not completely objective, however, since we identify with Benjamin and see some of what she's doing through his eyes as well. As a result, the conniving Mrs. Robinson is always one step ahead of Benjamin and even a bit ahead of the audience.

In the shooting of *The Graduate* the filmmakers paid a great deal of attention to composition within the frame, which was not only visually innovative but had dramatic and comedic resonance. In this particular scene, there's an unusual amount of foreground and background emphasis, with great discrepancy shown in the size and height of the two actors within the frame, symbolizing Benjamin's insecurity and discomfort relative to Mrs. Robinson's power over him.

There are four comic/dramatic arcs in this scene:
The first arc comes after Benjamin tells Mrs. Robinson he's leaving. In this shot (shown in *Frame grab #1*), Benjamin is in the foreground, the larger figure, when he still has some control over the situation. But then she says, "Please wait till my husband gets home," and now Benjamin is thrown, because if she's afraid to be alone, how can he say "no"? The editor makes the first cut here, because it's a turning point, the first step to Mrs. Robinson's entrapment of Benjamin. He cuts to a shot (the "in" frame is *Frame grab #2*) where her back is to the camera, in the foreground, with Benjamin in the background, looking much smaller than she. The focus is also on him, putting him on the spot visually and psychologically.

frame grab 1

frame grab 2

The second arc occurs when she says "I'm very neurotic," which throws him even more. The editor holds on this shot, where she dominates the foreground and he's in the background, while she blows smoke in his face, and he ineffectually tries to swat it away. When he sits down and she leaves him alone, the editor decides to stay on him at that distance in the long shot to underline his discomfort. The editor could have cut to a medium long shot of Mrs. Robinson over Benjamin, which booms down with him as he sits down [Slate 14] but his isolation and impotence wouldn't have been felt as much. The editor continues to hold on Benjamin, who's looking small and helpless, as Mrs. Robinson plays the dramatic, seductive music (the "out" frame of that shot is *Frame grab #3*).

An insert was shot of Mrs. Robinson putting the record on the phonograph [Slate 109], but this would not have been as effective for two reasons. First: holding onto him as the seductive music comes on — and he jumps to attention — is a very funny, awkward moment; to cut away would have weakened its impact. Second: if the editor showed her actually turning on the phonograph, he would have had to let this scene play out more in real time. The audience doesn't notice or care that in real time Mrs. Robinson could not have left Benjamin, turned on the music, and headed back to the bar (the "in" frame is *Frame grab #4*) in the three-and-a-half seconds of screen time it takes. The tension and humor is more effective because the editor made this cut in movie time.

frame grab 3

frame grab 4

The editor sets up the third arc with extra beats. Mrs. Robinson provocatively asks Benjamin what he thinks of her. When he answers that he thinks she's a nice person, the editor holds for a beat on Benjamin, letting him start to sip his drink, relax, and let his guard down (the "out" frame is *Frame grab #5*). When the editor cuts to Mrs. Robinson, he gives her a beat before she responds, showing her dissatisfaction with his polite answer, and her mind turning while she chooses what to say. This beat also sets up the impact for the third arc, when she says, "Did you know I was an alcoholic?" (the "out" frame is *Frame grab #6*). This line is shockingly intimate and throws Benjamin off guard even more.

frame grab 5

frame grab 6

After her dialogue, when the editor cuts to Benjamin (the "in" frame is *Frame grab #7*), his head is all the way down; he's in the middle of innocently swallowing his drink. That gives him a chance to look up, gulp his drink, and do a double take, thereby milking the moment. This is the first time the editor has chosen to use a close-up in this scene; he's saved it for when it really counts. The dialogue is also the tightest on this cut, from her "alcoholic" line to him, almost overlapping, because it's such a tense moment. In fact, the close-up is the only head-on angle used in the scene. When Benjamin was in the more distant medium shot previous to this (*Frame grab #5*), the editor could have used a head-on angle [Slate #106] instead of the profile, but he saved the double intensity of the straight-on close-up for Benjamin's significant reaction. For the next shot, the editor chooses the first close-up of Mrs. Robinson (the "out" frame is *Frame grab #8*) to reinforce the startling intimacy of her confession: "Did you know that?"

frame grab 7

frame grab 8

In the next shot, which again starts close on Benjamin, he's reacting strongly, but this time he's in a panic. He bolts out of his chair and says, "I think I should be going." In the "out" frame of this shot (*Frame grab #9*) the editor violates the action–cut rule that says that when an actor is standing up, cut out before the actor's face leaves the screen and definitely before we see only his midsection (which is the case here) because the shot will seem stale. In this instance, however, the editor is using the momentum of his motion to effectively cut out of that shot. Benjamin has just started standing up straight, and then in the next shot (the "in" frame is *Frame grab #10*) he's already at the bar, even though he was some distance away. (Note the distance between where Benjamin is sitting and Mrs. Robinson's bar stool in *Frame grab #3*.) Also, in *Frame grab #9* he's facing the camera, his arm by his side, and in *Frame grab #10* his back is to the camera with his arm outstretched.

frame grab 9

frame grab 10

This mismatched action and potentially awkward cut feels smooth because the editor cut out and then in to the next shot when Benjamin's energy is at its peak. And even though we don't see his glass, the sound of it being plunked on the bar at the beginning of that second shot gives the cut better flow.

Also, the audience's eyes follow Mrs. Robinson rather than Benjamin in the second shot, because we see she means business when she says, "Sit down, Benjamin." The result: the audience doesn't notice the jump cut from *Frame grab #9* to *Frame grab #10*, due to the visual momentum the editor created and our desire for him to be there at the bar right away to keep the tension going in the scene. Within the same shot, Benjamin walks away toward the camera, trying to get away from Mrs. Robinson, and he ends up in silhouette in the foreground (we can't see his face). He paces and confesses his suspicions of her (the "out" frame is *Frame grab #11*). The editor could have cut to any number of shots: a big close-up of Benjamin [Slate 21], a medium long shot to Benjamin [Slate 22] or close shots of Mrs. Robinson that were already used. But the editor chose to stay with this shot through quite a bit of dialogue, because it's working so well, the composition and staging perfectly capturing the situation. The visual emphasis is on Mrs. Robinson in the background when she is at her most seductive, poised on the bar stool with her legs parted, while Benjamin in the foreground is a shadowy figure, nervously pacing.

frame grab 11

When the editor cuts to the next shot — of Benjamin seen through Mrs. Robinson's bent leg (Frame grab #12)— the audience experiences the final and most dramatic arc of the scene. It's when Benjamin says the most memorable line of all: "Mrs. Robinson...you're trying to seduce me." The shot itself is also the most famous one in the movie, but in fact, the camera angle is not realistic at all. For one thing, it doesn't make any sense as a reverse shot. Even though she has her foot propped up on the bar stool in a previous shot (*Frame grab #11*) the position and angle of her leg doesn't match with this subsequent shot. In fact, she would have to be a contortionist to sit at the bar and have that angle through her leg really happen. But by putting him in this position inside her bent leg, the editor makes Benjamin looks smaller and more pathetic than in any of the other foreground/background shots. The contrived composition works well to exaggerate his powerlessness and the surreal situation. (There was actually another shot [Slate 21] — a close-up of Benjamin through her leg, with variable focus — which wouldn't have been as funny, because he wouldn't have been as clearly small and ridiculous.) The editor then cuts to Mrs. Robinson laughing (the "out" frame is *Frame grab #13*).

frame grab 12

frame grab 13

This is the only other instance beyond the alcoholic confession that the editor chooses to be close on Mrs. Robinson. This close-up of Mrs. Robinson does not match at all with the shot of her at the bar before this shot. It's actually a "pickup shot," meaning a portion of the angle filmed to supplement the original shooting of the same angle, usually because the original coverage was inadequate. In this shot, Mrs. Robinson's head is thrown back, her eyes are closed, and her mood is much more animated. Obviously the editor wanted this particular reaction, because it has such an unnerving effect on Benjamin and leaves him so vulnerable. Was she trying to seduce him or not? Even we, the audience, can't be sure what the laugh means. It's one of those moments where we're ahead of Benjamin but not completely ahead of Mrs. Robinson, although we suspect it's part of a ploy to make Benjamin feel guilty and embarrassed — and become putty in her hands. This close shot also doesn't match up with the subsequent pickup shot of Benjamin and Mrs. Robinson (the "in" frame is *Frame grab #14*). Her hand is not touching her ear anymore, and her head is more upright than that previous pickup shot. But the audience is focusing on the mortified reaction of Benjamin, who again looks powerless in this foreground/ background composition.

frame grab 14

SCENE TWO: THE BEDROOM

After the scene in her den, Mrs. Robinson talks Benjamin into going to her daughter Elaine's room to see her portrait. She then asks him to unzip her dress and once she gets down to her slip, he panics and says he has to go home. Before he leaves, she tells him to bring up her purse. He refuses, but she does convince him to leave her purse in her daughter's room. He nervously reenters the bedroom from the hallway.

CUT TO:

INT. ELAINE'S ROOM – NIGHT
Close shot of Elaine's portrait.
Benjamin's arm reaches out in front of the portrait to deposit Mrs. Robinson's purse on a shelf. The reflection from the glass front of the portrait shows Mrs. Robinson enter — stark naked — and just as she turns around to close the door....

 *FRAME GRAB #1*

CUT TO:

Close-up of Benjamin turned slightly away to the right. The sound of the door slams off screen. He spins his head around to the left, reacting.

 *FRAME GRAB #2*

CUT TO:

Close-up of Benjamin turned right, in profile. He spins around to the left profile, reacting.

 *FRAME GRAB #3*

CUT TO:

Close-up of Benjamin turned even more to the right, away from the camera. He spins around and faces camera, in shock.

 *FRAME GRAB #4*

BENJAMIN

Oh Go-...

CUT TO:

Close shot of woman's naked torso in profile beside doorknob. Her body starts to turn...

> *FRAME GRAB #5*

> BENJAMIN
> (OS)
> ...od.

CUT TO:

Medium close shot of Mrs. Robinson over Benjamin. She continues to turn and face him.

> *FRAME GRAB #6*

> BENJAMIN
> (OS)
> Oh...Let me out.

> MRS. ROBINSON
> Don't be nervous.

CUT TO:

Medium close shot of Benjamin over Mrs. Robinson.

> BENJAMIN
> Get away from that door.

> MRS. ROBINSON
> (OS)
> I want to say something....

CUT TO:

Close shot of breasts.

CUT BACK TO:

Medium close shot of Benjamin over Mrs. Robinson.

> MRS. ROBINSON
> (OS)
> ...first.

> BENJAMIN
> Jesus Christ!

> MRS. ROBINSON
> (OS)
> Benjamin, I want you to know that I'm available to
> you and if you won't sleep with me...

Medium close shot of Benjamin over Mrs. Robinson.

FRAME GRAB #7

CUT TO:

Close shot of mid torso.

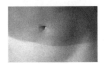

FRAME GRAB #8

CUT BACK TO:

> MRS. ROBINSON
> (OS)
> ...this time,

> BENJAMIN
> Oh my Christ.

> MRS. ROBINSON
> (OS)
> ...if you won't sleep with me this time I want you to know
> you can call me up anytime you want and we can make
> some kind...

FRAME GRAB #9

CUT BACK TO:

Close shot of breasts.

 FRAME GRAB #10

CUT BACK TO:

Medium close shot of Benjamin over Mrs. Robinson.

> MRS. ROBINSON
> (OS)
> ...of arrangement. Do you understand what I'm say...?

Screaming car sound off screen.

> BENJAMIN
> Let me out.

> MRS. ROBINSON
> (OS)
> Benjamin, do you understand what I'm say...?

> BENJAMIN
> Yes, yes let me out.

CUT BACK TO:

Close shot of mid torso.

CUT BACK TO:

Medium close shot of Benjamin over Mrs. Robinson.

> MRS. ROBINSON
> (OS)
> Because I find you very attractive. Any time you
> want you can...

Car door slams off screen. Benjamin turns, suddenly.

> BENJAMIN
> Oh, Jesus...

He moves toward her...

FRAME GRAB #11

BENJAMIN

...that's...

He ducks his head.

CUT TO:

Close shot of mid torso.

BENJAMIN
(OS)
..."him"!

His arm starts to come into frame.

FRAME GRAB #12

He pulls her away from door. His hand unlocks door and closes it shut behind him.

DECONSTRUCTION
Scene edited by Sam O'Steen

Shots that were used:
> Close shot of Elaine's portrait
> Close shot of woman's naked torso
> Close-up of Benjamin, turns
> Medium close shot of Mrs. Robinson over Benjamin
> Close shot of breasts
> Close shot of mid torso
> Medium close shot of Benjamin over Mrs. Robinson

Shots that weren't used:
> Big close-up of Mrs. Robinson, back to door
> Close-up side angle of Benjamin
> Close-up front view of Benjamin

> Midriff shot to Mrs. Robinson
> Close-up side angle on Benjamin
> Close-up front view of Benjamin
> Zoom big close-up Benjamin's eyes bulging
> Zoom big close-up of Benjamin's eyes
> Close to Mrs. Robinson over Benjamin
> Medium close-up Benjamin through Mrs. Robinson's left arm
> Medium long shot to naked body through Benjamin's arm
> Medium close-up to naked body over Benjamin's left ear
> Midriff high for left body, left hand on hip
> Camera low to midriff and breasts tilted to right side
> Breasts flat against door, camera tilted left
> Mid torso body against wall, left hand on hip
> Camera high to breasts and midriff… tilt left
> Full figure nude

The list above shows that many more shots were filmed for this scene than were actually used. There were an unusual number of angles filmed, probably because of the daring nature of the scene. But the editing choice was daring as well, and strongly illustrates another editing truism, which is not to fall into the trap of using a lot of different angles just because the director shot them.

In the first shot (*Frame grab #1*) where we, the audience, see Mrs. Robinson's naked body reflected in the glass before Benjamin does, we have the luxury of objective anticipation. We know something shocking is about to happen before the character does. The shot of the portrait starts the moment the edge of her body appears in the reflection and ends (with the "out" frame, *Frame grab #1*) just as she turns and slams the door. The first cut of his reaction (from *Frame grab #1 to #2*) is cued by the sound of the door slamming. That is, we hear the door slam at the end of that portrait shot (*Frame grab #1*), but it actually comes over the next shot, the one of Benjamin shown in *Frame grab #2*. The editor knew Benjamin's reaction was going to be powerful, so he cut to Benjamin's head spinning around, a complete half circle, and then he cut to Benjamin doing the same thing again (*Frame grab #3*), then still again (*Frame grab #4*). The three takes, all the "out" frames of the shots, are almost pure repetition, although each time his head turns a little more to the left. That means in the first two shots he ends up in profile and by the third shot (*Frame grab #4*) he's facing the camera; the editor saved the take with the most visual impact for last. The sound of Mrs. Robinson locking the door is also perfectly timed out to coincide with the last swing of Benjamin's head. The editor shouldn't have gotten away with this repetition of shots, but he knew this was a great moment and took a chance, figuring we would be willing to suspend logic and let movie time be milked as much as possible.

frame grab 1

frame grab 2

frame grab 3

frame grab 4

Benjamin's line, "Oh God," overlaps into the next shot of her naked torso (the "out" frame is *Frame grab #5*), which intensifies the moment and smooths the transition. The subsequent shot of Mrs. Robinson's face and shoulders (the "in" frame is *Frame grab #6*) could have been an awkward cut, since the angle doesn't really change from the closer body-double shot shown in *Frame grab #5*. But the cut seems smooth, because of the momentum of her starting to turn in one shot and continuing in the next, and the fact that the audience has an urgent need to see Mrs. Robinson's face.

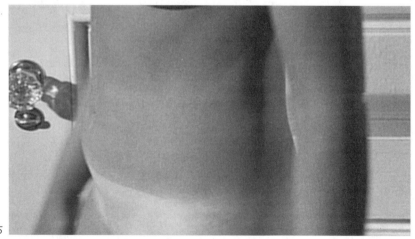

frame grab 5

frame grab 6

It should be noted that after this shot of Mrs. Robinson, we never see her face again for the rest of the scene. In fact, there are only three shots used from here on in: one shot of Benjamin past her shoulder (*Frame grab #7 and #9*) and shots of her naked breasts (*Frame grab #10*) and naked mid torso (*Frame grab #8 and #12*).

Sam O'Steen:

Originally I had close shots of her face, nude shots of her breasts and belly and close shots of Benjamin reacting to her that Mike [Nichols, the director] *had selected. But when I cut the scene together we both decided it wasn't funny. We couldn't figure out why... So I experimented. First I found an outtake* [a take not selected by the director] *of Benjamin reacting that was shot from behind Mrs. Robinson, over her shoulder.* (Frame Grabs #7 & #9) *It was the only angle where a part of Mrs. Robinson's body is on screen with him. I decided to use only that outtake whenever I cut to Benjamin so the audience would always know what he was looking at. I didn't need to cut to Mrs. Robinson's face at all.... Since I wasn't locked into using conventional cuts to establish Mrs. Robinson, and I could play her dialogue off screen, I was free to experiment.... I used subliminal cuts of her breasts and belly* (Frame Grabs #8, #10 & #12). *I tried one-, two-, and three-frame cuts and found out that three frames register, but only like a flash. I had experimented with subliminal cutting before.... You just don't know if it'll work.... But I thought it would here because Benjamin can barely look at her, yet he can't look away.*[9]

Showing only Mrs. Robinson's back and her sexual body parts made her seem disembodied and made a surreal situation seem even more surreal and absurdly funny. Also, what she specifically says — we do get the gist! — is not nearly as interesting as just staying on Benjamin's face and watching his fear and fascination with her. Also, the actor Dustin Hoffman's panicked performance completely holds up, and the editor knew that. It was certainly a nervy choice, but it worked superbly.

The mid torso shots, such as the one shown in *Frame grab #8*, were actually "stolen" from a shot intended for the end of the scene, when Benjamin pulls her away from the door, which is the last shot of the scene (*Frame grab #12*). The editor uses this throughout, probably because it was closer on the lower torso than the other angles and would add more shock value. The editor alternates using the same shots of breasts and mid torso twice. In three out of four cases, Benjamin's eyes are looking up or down in appropriate response to the breasts and mid torso, respectively. An example would be the "out" frame of Benjamin looking downward (*Frame grab #7*) to the shot of her torso (*Frame grab #8*).

frame grab 7

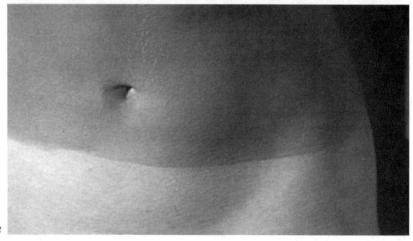

frame grab 8

One time, however (the "out" frame is *Frame grab #9*) he's staring down as if he were looking at her mid torso when what he is reacting to in the next shot are her breasts (the "in" frame is *Frame grab #10*). As O'Steen said, "*I didn't care about matching. I was cutting for performance, for the buildup of Benjamin's panic, and I knew from experience that the audience wouldn't notice, because they're having so much fun!*"[10]

frame grab 9

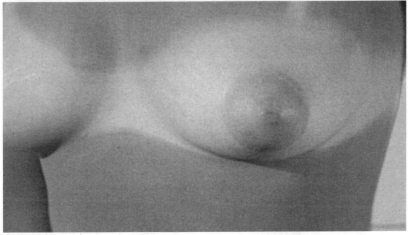

frame grab 10

When the editor cuts from the shot shown in *Frame grab #11* to the one seen in *Frame grab #12*, he underlines Benjamin's urgent need to get out of the room. The editor cuts out of the over-the-shoulder shot of Benjamin (the "out" frame is *Frame grab #11*) just as his head ducks down behind Mrs. Robinson's body. This not only shows Benjamin's eagerness to flee the room, but also creates a kind of exit cut to smooth the transition to the next shot. That following shot, a sort of entrance cut, starts just when Benjamin's arm comes into frame and shows him reaching across her torso to push it away (*Frame grab #12*).

frame grab 11

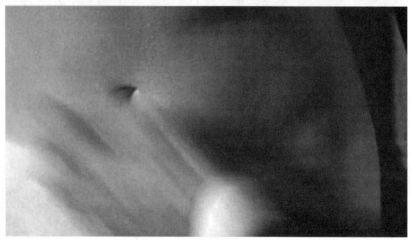

frame grab 12

The editor holds on this shot as Benjamin's arm pushes her aside, his hand unlocks the door and he slips out, slamming the door behind him. A clean exit, both visually and dramatically.

SUSPENSE: *REAR WINDOW*

The subjective and objective perspectives have particular significance in suspense as they do in comedy. Both points of view have their value, depending on the situation. Does the audience want to see the hand reach for the gun or see the gun only when it goes off? The anticipation can be more acute if the audience witnesses the gun before the character does. However, the subjective point of view can also be valuable, because the audience is afraid and surprised along with the character. The key is to milk the anticipation and take the time to build the audience's expectations. Some of the most suspenseful moments in movies are slow-moving, done with subjective camera moves. At the same time the editor has to sustain that tension. He basically has to find the balance between the slow build and the tight rope.

In a horror movie, which is an intensified variation of suspense, filmmakers prey on the fears and anxieties of the audience, fueling them with the power of the unknown. The goal for the editor is to never let go of the mood of constant menace. Cross-cutting, that is, showing first the source of terror and then the character waiting in trepidation or trying to escape, is also a classic technique. Cutaways such as a ticking clock can be very useful to maintain the tension and anxiety. Off-screen sounds, such as footsteps approaching, can add another terrifying dimension. The editor must also distinguish between creating fear and showing fear. Cutting to a frightened actor does not necessarily mean that the audience is frightened. That is why cutting to a knife coming at an actor, combined with close-up reactions of his terror, will be more effective because it internalizes the actor's fear.

HITCHCOCK: THE MASTER OF SUSPENSE AND EDITING

Alfred Hitchcock camera cut all his movies far more than most other directors — and achieved superb results. He had an unerring visual sense of where to place the camera to get the effect he wanted and then was able to masterfully cut those preconceived shots together in his head and on his drawing pad. "*I wish I didn't have to shoot the picture,*" he said. "*When I've gone through the script and created the picture on paper, for me the creative job is done and the rest is just a bore.*"[11] He also had the instinct to know what psychological buttons to push and when to push them in order to make the audience tense — and terrified.

Hitchcock brilliantly used the arsenal of techniques for creating suspense such as cross-cutting, cutaways, extreme close-ups, and, most importantly, the balance of subjective and objective camerawork. For instance, the audience might be let in on enough information to identify with the character and feel a constant sense of dread and danger, and then at a crucial moment the audience would be allowed to know more than the character did. Hitchcock might then switch back to the subjective point of view, so that at the character's most vulnerable point, the audience would also be sideswiped.

FRAME GRAB ILLUSTRATION: *REAR WINDOW*

The movie *Rear Window* allowed Hitchcock to display his techniques for building suspense in all their glory.

The setup:
Jeff (Jimmy Stewart) is a photojournalist who has broken his leg and is confined to a wheelchair in his apartment. His rear window faces many other apartments beyond a courtyard, and he's able to spy on the lives of his neighbors.

As Hitchcock said:
Of all the films I have made, this to me is the most cinematic.... It's composed largely of Mr. Stewart as a character in one position in one room looking out onto his courtyard, so what he sees is a mental process blown up in his mind from the purely visual.[12] *.... You can have a man look, you can have him see something, you can have him react to it... Without him speaking you can show his mind at work comparing things. It's limitless, I would say, the power of cutting and showing the various images, the assembly of them, the juxtaposition of imagery relating to the mind of the individual.*[13]

By shooting from the viewpoint of the immobilized man, Hitchcock makes us lean forward in our seats to glean whatever information we can hear and see from the neighbors, causing us to get frustrated, intrigued — and ultimately become full-blown voyeurs just like Jeff. In one apartment Jeff becomes aware of a bedridden woman who is constantly nagging and mocking her husband, Thornwald (Raymond Burr). As time progresses, Jeff notices that the wife has disappeared, and he begins to suspect that her husband has killed her. At first, his girlfriend Lisa (Grace Kelly), his nurse Stella (Thelma Ritter), and his police detective friend Tom Doyle (Wendell Corey) are all skeptical of his suspicion. Jeff becomes more and more obsessed with the desire to prove that the murder really happened. As the evidence piles up, Lisa becomes convinced of the murder, sneaks into Thornwald's apartment and finds the "smoking gun," Mrs. Thornwald's wedding ring. But Thornwald returns and catches her. Worse still, he sees Lisa signal across the courtyard to Jeff that she's found the ring. Jeff quickly jerks his wheelchair into the shadows. Has Thornwald seen him or not? Since Lisa is then arrested and Stella sent off to bail her out, we know that Jeff is now alone in his apartment – and in jeopardy.

INT. JEFF'S APARTMENT - NIGHT
Medium close shot of Jeff in a wheelchair.
The phone rings, Jeff answers, knowing that Doyle is returning his call. He whispers a frantic explanation of all the facts that he's uncovered that prove Thornwald murdered his wife. He ends the conversation with:

> JEFF
> Now hurry up, will ya. This fellow knows he's being watched. I'm not gonna wait around forever. Hurry up.

Jeff hangs up the phone, looks off.

                                                                    CUT TO:

Long shot, Jeff's POV across courtyard of Thornwald's darkened apartment. The phone rings again, Jeff snatches it up.

> JEFF
> Tom, I think Thornwald's left. I don't see....

He suddenly stops himself....

> JEFF
> Hello?

There's a click on the other end of the line.

                                                                    CUT TO:

Close shot of Jeff. The camera moves in for a close-up. There's a thud/door slam off screen. He reacts, startled. His eyes dart over, then his head turns as he looks over his shoulder at the source of the sound.

   *FRAME GRAB #1*

CUT TO:

Medium long shot of door, light from hallway coming through bottom.

FRAME GRAB #2

CUT TO:

Close-up of Jeff from higher angle as he slowly turns his wheelchair around, toward the door.

FRAME GRAB #3

CUT BACK TO:

Medium long shot of door. Light is still seen under the door.

CUT TO:

Medium long shot of Jeff. He moves the wheelchair back and forth in a panic, as off-screen footsteps approach.

CUT TO:

Full shot of Jeff from front angle. He starts to get out of chair.

CUT TO:

Medium close shot of Jeff. He continues to struggle to get up, then sits down in frustration.

CUT TO:

Close shot of door. Light at bottom of the door goes out.

CUT BACK TO:

Full shot of Jeff. He backs up his wheelchair in a panic, then notices his camera flash wedged next to him in wheelchair.

CUT TO:

Close shot of Jeff. He reaches into bag and pulls out bulbs, placing them on his lap.

CUT BACK TO:

Full shot of Jeff. He's backing his wheelchair up against the window as off screen footsteps get closer.

CUT TO:

Medium long shot of door. Fumbling noise off screen.

CUT BACK TO:

Full shot of Jeff. He's frozen in place, listening to one more footstep.

CUT TO:

Medium shot of door. A sliver of vertical light as door slowly opens to reveal silhouette of Thornwald, then in half light, as he moves into the room and closes door behind him.

   **FRAME GRAB #4**

CUT BACK TO:

Medium long shot of Jeff at far end of the room in half light.

   **FRAME GRAB #5**

CUT TO:

Medium long shot of Thornwald in shadows.

THORNWALD
What do you want from me?"

CUT BACK TO:

Medium long shot of Jeff.
He doesn't answer

CUT BACK TO:

Medium long shot of Thornwald.

THORNWALD
(cont'd)

Your friend, the girl, could've turned me in. Why didn't she? What is it you want? A lot of money? I don't have any money.

CUT BACK TO:

Medium long shot of Jeff.

CUT BACK TO:

Medium long shot of Thornwald.

> THORNWALD
> (cont'd)
> Say something.

CUT BACK TO:

Medium long shot of Jeff.

CUT BACK TO:

Medium long shot of Thornwald.

> THORNWALD
> Say something! Tell me what you want!
> Can you get me that ring back?

CUT BACK TO:

Medium long shot of Jeff.

> JEFF
> No.

> THORNWALD
> (OS)
> Tell her to bring it back.

> JEFF
> I can't. The police have it by now.

CUT BACK TO:

Medium long shot of Thornwald

He slowly moves forward, just starts to step down....

FRAME GRAB #6

CUT TO:

Full side shot of Jeff.

He holds up flash, covers his eyes.

FRAME GRAB #7

CUT BACK TO:

Medium long shot of Thornwald.

See impact of flash as he's awash in bright light.

FRAME GRAB #8

Then light fades back to original light as he reels backward, bringing his hands to his face.

CUT TO:

Close-up of Thornwald.

His eyes squinting in pain as he reaches for his glasses and struggles to open his eyes.

FRAME GRAB #9

CUT BACK TO:

Medium long shot, Thornwald's POV of Jeff. Distorted by the effect of the flash, becoming a superimposed faint red circle.

FRAME GRAB #10

It widens to the edge of frame to become a red mist that finally fades back to normal clarity and color. Jeff pops out used bulb, quickly looks over his shoulder to see if his rescuers, Lisa and Doyle, have returned to Thornwald's apartment.

The following sequence (already shown in **FRAME GRABS #6, #7, #8, #9 & #10**) repeats itself three more times, showing Thornwald barely moving into the room and coming out of shadows, and Jeff in progressively closer shots:

1) Medium long shot of Thornwald (barely moves out of shadows and barely closer).

2) Full side shot of Jeff as he holds up flashbulb, covering his eyes (closer and closer from full shot to medium close shot).

3) Full shot of Thornwald awash in bright light (barely closer, until last shot when knocks over chair and is in middle of room).

4) Close-up of Thornwald struggling to open eyes (same distance throughout).

5) Medium long shot, Thornwald's POV of Jeff seen with flash's red ball effect, then with normal clarity (getting closer and closer to a medium full shot).

The third time the pattern repeats itself, the editor uses four of the five sequential shots. **Then he cuts to Jeff in medium full shot, loading a bulb into the flash.** He starts to turn to look over his shoulder....

                                                            CUT TO:

Close-up of Jeff. He continues to turn, looking over his shoulder. He hears something off screen, looks back again over shoulder.

FRAME GRAB #11

                                                            CUT TO:

Long shot, Jeff's POV across courtyard of Lisa, Doyle and police in hallway outside Thornwald's apartment.

FRAME GRAB #12

                        JEFF
                   (OS)
            Li-...

                                                            CUT TO:

Medium close shot of Thornwald. He moves toward camera, arms reaching out menacingly....

JEFF

(OS)

...sa!! Doyle!!

...until his face fills screen.

FRAME GRAB #13

CUT TO:

Medium close shot of Jeff and Thornwald. Thornwald lunges toward Jeff, grabbing him by the neck as Jeff struggles to push him away.

FRAME GRAB #14

CUT BACK TO:

Long shot across courtyard. Lisa, then Doyle, see him and rush down hallway.

CUT TO:

Close shot of Thornwald. Jeff struggles to push him away.

CUT TO:

Close shot of Jeff. He struggles to pull Thornwald's hands off his neck.

CUT TO:

Medium long shot of neighbor running toward door.

CUT BACK TO:

Medium close shot of Thornwald and Jeff. Thornwald starts to tip wheelchair over.

CUT TO:

Medium long shot of Thornwald and Jeff.
Continuation of action as chair tips over and Jeff rolls over onto stomach bouncing onto bed.

FRAME GRAB #15

CUT TO:

Close shot of leg cast

FRAME GRAB #16

as Jeff continues to roll onto back.

CUT TO:

Close shot of Jeff's head and shoulders. First blurry, then in focus hanging over edge of bed, as he struggles to get up.

FRAME GRAB #17

CUT TO:

Medium close shot of Thornwald. He's moving toward camera.

CUT BACK TO:

Close shot of Jeff's head. He tries to get up, then shot becomes blurry as their bodies struggle.

CUT TO:

Medium shot of a neighbor couple coming out on terrace.

CUT TO:

Medium close shot of Thornwald and Jeff. Thornwald struggles to lift Jeff's legs up in the air and out of open window.

FRAME GRAB #18

CUT TO:

Close shot of the struggle. Starts with Jeff's back, then Thornwald's arm around Jeff, ending with Thornwald's back over Jeff.

FRAME GRAB #19

CUT TO:

Medium full shot of neighbor running out of door.

FRAME GRAB #20

CUT TO:

Medium long shot of Thornwald and Jeff. Thornwald's back to camera as he grabs under Jeff's arms to try to lift torso up and out of window.

FRAME GRAB #21

CUT TO:

Medium shot of Jeff and Thornwald shooting down over Thornwald's back at Jeff's agonized face. He hangs out of window, with arms holding on to ledge.

FRAME GRAB #22

CUT TO:

Close shot of Thornwald struggling to push Jeff away.

FRAME GRAB #23

CUT TO:

Close shot Jeff's fingers. They grip, slip, then grip ledge of window.

FRAME GRAB #24

CUT TO:

Close shot of Jeff. He struggles to hold on as Thornwald hands push on his neck and shoulders.

FRAME GRAB #25

CUT TO:

Medium shot of a neighbor couple opening window.

CUT TO:

Medium long shot of two cops and Detective Doyle running out of building and across courtyard, jumping fence.

JEFF
(OS)
Doyle!!

Camera pans up side of building to Jeff's body dangling outside window with Thornwald gripping onto his shoulders.

CUT TO:

Medium long shot of Doyle, shooting past his back to building wall, looking down at patio and cops.

DOYLE
Creel, gimme your gun!

Cop turns and tosses back gun. Doyle raises his arm to shoot.

FRAME GRAB #26

CUT TO:

Medium long shot of Doyle shooting past his back as arm continues upward to shoot, but now background includes second story window that Jeff's body is hanging from.

FRAME GRAB #27

In distance cops arrive inside Jeff's apartment and struggle to pull Thornwald off Jeff.

CUT TO:

Medium shot of cops, who struggle to release Thornwald's grip on Jeff.
One cop turns, realizing that Jeff now has nothing to hang on to.

CUT TO:

Medium shot of Jeff shooting down on his face and foreshortened body as he slowly falls.

FRAME GRAB #28

CUT TO:

Medium side shot of Jeff, shooting from ground as Jeff falls, face down, arms splayed.

FRAME GRAB #29

He falls down onto the ground.

CUT TO:

Medium close shot of Jeff, shooting from behind. He rolls onto back, to face camera, in agony and then his body is still.

FRAME GRAB #30

DECONSTRUCTION
Scene edited by George Tomasini

Hitchcock said:

I do shoot a precut picture. In other words, every piece of film is designed to perform a function. So therefore, literally, the only type of editing that I do is to tighten up. If a man's coming through the door, going into the room, then you just pull that together by just snippets. But actual creative work in the cutting, for me, is nonexistent, because it is designed ahead of time — precut, which it should be.[14] *...Where the work of the average editor comes in is when he's given a lot of film to sort out. This is when directors use many angles of the same scene. But I never do that. As a matter of fact when* Rear Window *was finished somebody went into the cutting room and said, "Where are the outtakes? Where is the unused film?" And there was a small roll of a hundred feet.* [Ninety feet of film runs a minute.] *That was all that was left over.*[15]

The typical ratio of shot film to edited film ranges from about ten to one through forty to one, depending on the director's method of working and the budget. Using those ratios, *Rear Window*, which is 112 minutes long, should have had between eleven and forty-four minutes of leftover film. Hitchcock claimed he had barely over a minute.

Another version of how Hitchcock worked comes from Sam O'Steen, who was assistant to editor George Tomasini on an earlier Hitchcock movie, *The Wrong Man*. According to O'Steen, Hitchcock never saw any film before the first cut and then when he ran it, he said:

George, what'd you do that for, you know I never do that, you just go this way and that way." But Hitchcock made only three or four changes, because the way he shot, there was only one way it would go together, and that was his way.... As a matter of fact, he had the same amount of trims [leftover film] *as he had cut* [a ratio of one to one].... *Then he ran the picture with his agent, and he loved it; at least he said he did — and that was it. Hitchcock never ran it again, never saw it. He was just gone.*[16]

Hitchcock's assistant director Herbert Colemen went on to explain:

They only shot a scene up to a certain point, then he would change the angle of the camera and start back maybe a few frames and then start the new scene, and then he would stop and go to another angle. That's the way he shot his pictures, so it was very simple for the editor. [17]

Because of the unique way in which Hitchcock worked, the primary references below will be to Hitchcock's choices rather than the editor's. However, it should be noted that Hitchcock did have a long-term relationship with his editor, George Tomasini, who had done seven movies with him before this one. So that even though he did not have the freedom to choose shots the way most editors did, he had to have the insights to be in tune with what Hitchcock wanted and the skill to finesse the cuts.

As he did in all of his movies, in *Rear Window* Hitchcock made brilliant use of both the subjective and objective viewpoints.

Hitchcock:

His [Jeff's] viewpoint becomes his mental processes by the use of the camera and the montage and this is what I actually mean by subjective treatment.... The audience are with Stewart [the actor playing Jeff]. The identification is direct and therefore they must feel superior to the other characters with him but the frustration is there all the same.... The objective treatment is also used when necessary. [18]

In fact, Hitchcock switches to an objective POV at a crucial point just before this scene. Up until then the audience has seen virtually the whole movie from Jeff's subjective POV. But then, just for a few seconds, Jeff turns away from his window and only the audience sees Thornwald leaving his apartment. By doing this, Hitchcock gives the audience the thrill of anticipation. When and how will Jeff find out what we already know? Allowing the audience to become co-conspirators with the director at that key moment is a great recipe for setting up the suspense that follows.

Previous to this scene, Jeff had the use of both sound and visuals to help him figure out what was happening beyond his apartment, even if he did strain to hear what people were saying. But now, as his attacker approaches and he remains confined to a wheelchair, sound effects play an especially powerful role in creating suspense. All Jeff has are the noises beyond his apartment — door slams and footsteps — to clue him in on his approaching attacker. Hitchcock saves the first close-up of Jeff for when he hears a door slam down the hall, and now the threat is real. His eyes dart in that direction and then his head turns. The "out" frame of the shot (*Frame grab #1*) comes after he's turned his head away from the screen toward the slammed door. The next shot is his POV of the front door and the light underneath (*Frame grab #2*). The following close-up of Jeff milks the moment, because now the camera is shooting down at him, that angle making him look more helpless. His face starts out in half shadow and now he turns until the full light falls on his face after he has slowly turned his wheelchair around in the direction of the door (the "out" frame is *Frame grab #3*).

frame grab 1

frame grab 2

frame grab 3

The editor now cuts back to the same shot of the light under the door, then back to Jeff. He moves his wheelchair back and forth in a panic and then struggles to get out of the wheelchair but realizes he can't. Then, just when he's most vulnerable, he sees the light go off under the door, meaning the killer has turned off the light in the hallway and Jeff is at the point of no return. Then the door slowly opens, first just revealing a sliver of light, then Thornwald in silhouette, then in half light with a creepy reflection of light from his eyeglasses (the "out" frame is *Frame grab #4*). This milks the arrival of the villain for all it's worth.

frame grab 4

Up until now the POV was only Jeff's, but once Thornwald enters Jeff's apartment, the POVs alternate between the two characters. In the ensuing dialogue between Jeff and Thornwald, the fact that Hitchcock cuts back and forth between Thornwald's POV of Jeff (*Frame grab #5*) and Jeff's POV of Thornwald (*Frame grab #6*) also makes Thornwald seem more human as he pleads with Jeff. (There is pathos in the way Hitchcock depicts all the villains in his movies, and in this case when Thornwald says, "Why did you do it?" Hitchcock is placing some blame on Jeff for being a Peeping Tom.) In those crucial first moments of confrontation, Jeff and Thornwald are both faceless and in shadows, particularly Thornwald, whose legs barely appear out from the shadows as he starts to come down a step further into the apartment at the end of the shot (that "out" frame is *Frame grab #6*).

frame grab 5

frame grab 6

The back and forth of POVs continue in the following four shots:

The "out" frame of the first shot (*Frame grab #7*) shows Jeff holding up a flash. The next shot reveals the impact from his POV, which is the first time Jeff and the audience sees Thornwald in full light — but just momentarily, when his image is eerily brightened from the camera's flash (*Frame grab #8*). Again sound is used significantly, since we never see the flash actually go off; we just hear and see its effect.

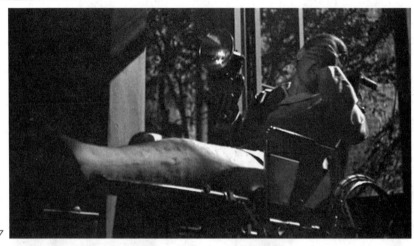

frame grab 7

frame grab 8

The next shot is a close-up of Thornwald squinting from the effect of the flash (*Frame grab #9*) and then the flash's after effects on Thornwald's eyes when he sees a red ball of light superimposed over Jeff's image (*Frame grab #10*).

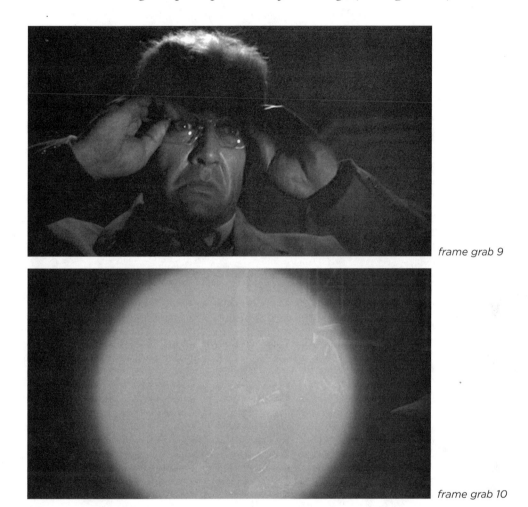

frame grab 9

frame grab 10

The previous sequence — *Frame Grabs #6, #7, #8, #9, and #10* — repeats itself three more times, with Thornwald barely getting closer to Jeff each time.

The fact that Jeff is able to hold Thornwald back by temporarily blinding him with his flashbulbs, not once but again and again *and again*, all in the space of a fairly small room, is pretty unbelievable. But the audience is willing to suspend disbelief and let Hitchcock milk movie time to the limit, because of the suspenseful intercutting of shots and because they want to buy time for Jeff. In the next shot (the "out" frame is *Frame grab #11*), he looks over his shoulder and then we see his POV across the courtyard in *Frame grab #12*.

frame grab 11

frame grab 12

Jeff's POV reaches a climax when Thornwald moves straight toward the camera and his arms reach menacingly toward Jeff (the "out" frame of that shot is *Frame grab #13*). Now the movie shifts from suspense to genuine terror, and the POV changes from subjective to objective. This starts with the shot shown in *Frame grab #14* when Thornwald's hands are wrapped around Jeff's throat.

frame grab 13

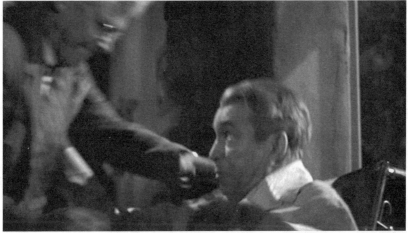

frame grab 14

Hitchcock:

Where Jimmy Stewart is thrown out of the window at the end, I just photographed that with feet, legs, arms, heads. Completely montage. I also photographed it from a distance, a complete action. There was no comparison between the two. There never is…. it's much more effective if it's done in montage because you involve the audience much more. That's the secret of that type of montage in film.[19] *…The moment the man attacks him… the moment of contact, then you are into your pieces of film. You involve the audience right in the sense of the violence.*[20]

frame grab 15

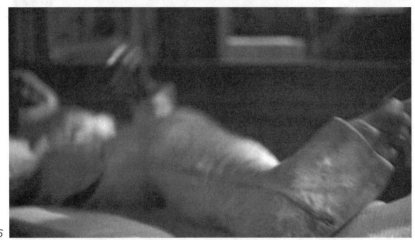

frame grab 16

frame grab 17

There are two crucial points in Jeff's and Thornwald's ensuing struggle, and in both cases Hitchcock uses the same pattern: he establishes the action with a long shot and then keeps the camera close. The first point is when Thornwald tips the wheelchair over (the "out" frame is *Frame grab #15*) and then in the shots shown in *Frame grab #16 and #17*, when he shoots close on Jeff's leg cast and head, respectively.

The second point is when Thornwald is actually lifting Jeff's legs up and over the window sill (the "out" frame is *Frame grab #18*). That is followed by a closer camera with Thornwald's back filling the frame, which captures the impotence of Jeff struggling under Thornwald's weight and power (the "out" frame of that shot is *Frame grab #19*). The visuals, in fact, consistently emphasize not only Jeff's disabled state, but also how frail his physique is, compared to Thornwald's bulky frame.

frame grab 18

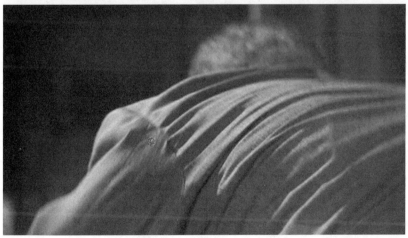

frame grab 19

When they react to the sounds of Jeff and Thornwald's struggle, the neighbors are now seen from an objective POV, an example being the shot of "Miss Lonelyheart" (*Frame grab #20*). It's a much closer angle than Jeff's actual perspective, which was all the audience had seen before this scene.

In the setup of the following two shots, Hitchcock knew it would be physically impossible to have Thornwald actually lift Jeff up in one move and hang him over the side of the building. Even if it were possible, it would slow the movie down at a crucial moment. For that reason, Hitchcock jumps the action. In the shot shown in *Frame grab #21*, Thornwald's upper torso is still above the window sill, and he's standing upright. In the subsequent shot (*Frame grab #22*), Thornwald is leaning far over the window sill and Jeff is dangling out the window. This cut works for two reasons. First, because there is that "action-cut" effect, a clear change in angle from one shot to the other. What also smooths out the transition is that in the second shot, Thornwald's body almost covers up Jeff's face, which functions as a sort of "wipe" across the screen, neutralizing the mismatch.

frame grab 20

frame grab 21

frame grab 22

Then the drama escalates with a series of even closer shots of Thornwald's face (*Frame grab #23*), Jeff's fingers (*Frame grab #24*), and Jeff's agonized face (*Frame grab #25*), which again repeat the pattern of the establishing shot followed by the "montage" effect.

frame grab 23

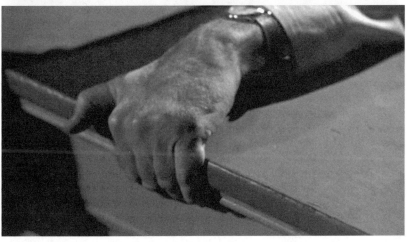

frame grab 24

frame grab 25

The second mismatched cut occurs in the next pair of shots. Hitchcock needed to show a cop throw a gun up to Doyle from the patio below and also show him aim at Thornwald, who's gripping onto Jeff's body as it hangs out the second-story window. Logistically he couldn't accomplish that in one shot, so he had to cheat the staging and cut two shots together. In the first shot Doyle's arm moves up to a shooting position (the "out" frame is *Frame grab #26*) and in the next one Doyle aims his gun toward Thornwald, who is now included in the shot (the "in" frame is *Frame grab #27*). The camera was positioned differently in each of the shots, as was Doyle, the fence behind him, and even the angle of his arm. But Hitchcock knew that the audience would focus on the movement of Doyle's gun and on Jeff hanging out of the window in the second shot.

frame grab 26

frame grab 27

The third mismatch happens when Jeff falls from the window onto the ground. In the shot shown in (the "out" frame is *Frame grab #28)*, the camera shoots straight down at him, heightening his victimization. The shot is also scarily distorted — an optical matting of his body onto the background — which shows us his face in the foreground and foreshortened body looking twisted and vertical below. The subsequent shot (the "in" frame is *Frame grab #29*) is shot from the ground level and shows Jeff in a completely different position, face down with his arms spread out. But Hitchcock counted on the momentum and emotional impact of such a dramatic fall to make the cut seem smooth.

The "out" frame of the shot shown in *Frame grab #30* reveals how the editor cut out the moment when Jeff is totally still, after falling. The timing is just right for cheating the audience into thinking that Jeff may be dead, but the editor doesn't linger long enough to keep it from being believable when Jeff turns out to be fine. (Just more broken legs, it turns out!)

frame grab 28

frame grab 29

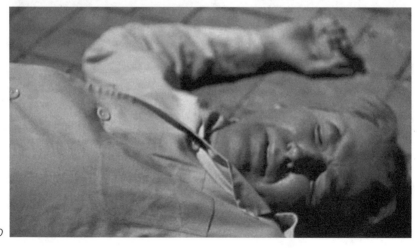

frame grab 30

MYSTERY: *CHINATOWN*

This genre is based on suspense, but it also falls into the dialogue-driven category, since mysteries rely heavily on the spoken word and what it reveals about the characters' secrets and motivations. Of course visual details provide crucial clues as well. As a result, the editor has to time exactly when he'll cut to, say, an arched eyebrow or a close-up of a weapon. The editor must also be especially aware of subtext in the dialogue, since the hidden meanings that flow beneath the surface can often motivate the cuts. For example, if an editor milks a silent pause, he can create an almost unbearable tension, because what's not being said can be more significant than what is.

Mysteries are generally more subjective than objective, because part of the fun is letting the audience solve the puzzle along with the main character, who is often a detective. In a mystery, another subjective device is to have the protagonist speak in a voiceover narrative, like many of the detectives in Dashiell Hammett and Raymond Chandler's novels, some of which were adapted into classic film noir movies.

FRAME GRAB ILLUSTRATION: *CHINATOWN*

Chinatown is true to the film noir genre in that the detective, Gittes (played by Jack Nicholson) is both honorable yet tarnished. But as Roman Polanski, the director of *Chinatown* said: "*Its private eye hero, J. J. Gittes, was no pale, down-at-the-heel imitation of Marlowe.* [Phillip Marlowe is the quintessential detective in Raymond Chandler's novels.] *Robert Towne, the scriptwriter, had conceived him as a glamorous, successful operator, a snappy dresser with a coolly insolent manner — a new archetypal detective figure.*"[21]

The female lead also deviates from the typical femme fatale. Evelyn Mulwray (played by Faye Dunaway) is sensual and mysterious but not the plotting black widow, although her incessant lying and deception make her seem so at first. She actually turns out to be the only character in the story who is operating out of purely decent motives.

Polanski said that he saw Chinatown "*not as a 'retro piece' or a conscious imitation of classic movies shot in black and white, but as a film about the thirties seen through the camera eye of the seventies…. I wanted the style of the period conveyed by a scrupulously accurate reconstruction of décor, costume, and idiom — not a deliberate imitation, in 1973, of thirties film techniques.*"[22]

Most movies that were shot in the thirties had a somewhat stagy and static look, in contrast to Polanski's movies, which have a very dynamic and innovative style. In fact, Polanski's method was so fluid that he never even shot an all-inclusive master shot. According to Sam O'Steen, who edited *Chinatown*: "*What Polanski did was maybe have people move in and out of frame, or the camera might pan back and forth or the shot may open up to include everything for part of the scene, but the camera was always active. So when I had to cut in close, it was a challenge....*" O'Steen said he loved cutting Polanski's pictures, because it was "*like a great jigsaw puzzle you put together.*"[23]

The first scene of *Chinatown* takes place in an office where the actors are seated most of the time, so there was little opportunity to use a dynamic shooting style, but even here Polanski's subtly probing camera adds brilliant tension to the scene.

The setup:
Gittes is hired by Evelyn Mulwray to spy on her husband. He discovers Mr. Mulwray with another girl, and the story ends up in all the newspapers, because he's the city's chief engineer. Gittes continues to follow Mulwray, who discovers that someone is suspiciously diverting water in the middle of a drought. Gittes also finds out that the woman who hired him is not Evelyn Mulwray, and the real Mrs. Mulwray slaps him with a lawsuit. When Evelyn Mulwray mysteriously drops the lawsuit, Gittes tells her that someone is out to get her husband. Soon after that Mulwray is murdered, and when Gittes decides to investigate the water diversion himself, he practically gets his nose sliced off by a couple of hoods.

SCENE ONE: THE OFFICE

The first scene takes place about an hour into the movie, a little less than halfway through. Gittes knows that Evelyn Mulwray is hiding something from him, but he doesn't know exactly what, and he's not too thrilled with this wealthy, evasive woman who has gotten him into professional and physical jeopardy.

INT. GITTES' OFFICE – DAY
Medium shot of Gittes standing at open door of inner office.
He looks back at his secretary.

                                                                    CUT TO:

Close shot of secretary. She mouths "Mrs. Mulwray," pointing inside.

CUT BACK TO:

Medium shot of Gittes at door. He opens the door wider to a medium long shot that reveals Evelyn Mulwray looking out the window, her back to the camera. Gittes takes a beat, then he starts to swing the door shut behind him.

CUT TO:

Medium close shot of Evelyn. Door slams off screen, startling her. She turns to look at him.

 *FRAME GRAB #1*

CUT TO:

Medium long shot of Gittes.
He makes eye contact with her.

 *FRAME GRAB #2*

He turns away and walks to cabinet behind desk. He looks back at her.

GITTES

Drink?

CUT BACK TO:

Medium close shot of Evelyn.

EVELYN

No....thank you

She moves away from the window toward the camera until she's in close-up. She looks back at him, sits down, and takes a puff of her cigarette.

EVELYN

What is your usual salary?

CUT BACK TO:

Medium long shot of Gittes.

                           GITTES

Thirty-five dollars daily for me, plus twenty for my
associates, plus expenses.

He turns around, looking over some papers on his desk, drink in hand.

                           GITTES
                          (con't)
Plus a bonus if I show results.

He sits down, continuing to look at papers.

                                           CUT TO:

Close-up of Evelyn, in three-quarter profile. She takes a puff of her
cigarette.

                          EVELYN
Whoever's behind my husband's death, why have
they gone to all this trouble?

                                         CUT TO:

Medium long shot of Gittes.
He's still looking down at papers.

                           GITTES
Money. How they plan to make it out of emptying the
reservoirs...that I don't know.

                                   CUT BACK TO:

Close-up of Evelyn.

                          EVELYN
I'll pay your salary plus five thousand dollars if you find
out what happened to Hollis and who is involved.

   *FRAME GRAB #3*

CUT BACK TO:

Medium long shot of Gittes.
He finally looks up at her, takes a beat, leans in to push intercom.

> GITTES
> Sophie, draw up one of our standard contracts for
> Mrs. Mulwray.

> SOPHIE
> (OS, through intercom)
> Yes, Mr. Gittes.

He continues to eye Evelyn warily and sits back, drink in hand.

> GITTES
> Tell me something....did you get married before or after
> Mulwray and your father sold the water department?

FRAME GRAB #4

CUT TO:

Close-up of Evelyn, head on. She reacts, startled.

FRAME GRAB #5

> GITTES
> (OS)
> Noah Cross is your father, isn't he?

She looks away, looks back at him.

> EVELYN
> Uh...yes, of course.

She looks down.

CUT TO:

Insert shot of Evelyn's hands. She flips her purse open, pulling cigarette out of case.

FRAME GRAB #6

                    EVELYN
              (OS)
        It was sometime after. I was just out of grade school
        when they did that.

CUT TO:

Close shot of Gittes. He watches her.

FRAME GRAB #7

                    GITTES
        Then you married your father's business partner?

CUT BACK TO:

Close-up of Evelyn, head on.
She makes eye contact for a moment, then looks down, brings cigarette to mouth and just as she starts to light it...

                    GITTES
              (OS)
        You've already got one going, Mrs. Mulwray.

She puffs on her cigarette, laughs nervously.

                    EVELYN
        ...oh.

She takes cigarette out of her mouth, looks down.

                    GITTES
              (OS)
        Does, uh...

FRAME GRAB #8

CUT TO:

Insert shot of ashtray. She stubs out cigarette.

FRAME GRAB #9

> GITTES
> (OS)
> ...my talking about your father upset you?

> EVELYN
> (OS)
> Why no...

CUT BACK TO:

Close-up of Evelyn, head on. She's looking down.

FRAME GRAB #10

She looks up.

> EVELYN
> ...yes, a little. You see Hollis and my f... my father had a falling out finally.

> GITTES
> (OS)
> Over you or over the water department?

> EVELYN
> Not over me. Why should... it be over me?

> GITTES
> (OS)
> Then it was over the water department.

> EVELYN
> Yes. Hollis felt that the water should belong to the public and I don't think... my father felt that way.

CUT TO:

Medium long shot of door opening. Sophie enters carrying file.

>   EVELYN
>   (OS)
>   Actually it...

FRAME GRAB #11

CUT BACK TO:

Medium long shot of Gittes at his desk.

>   EVELYN
>   (OS, cont'd)
>   ...was over the Van der Lip Dam. You know
>   the dam that broke.

Gittes looks over as file is handed to him.

>   GITTES
>   ...Oh yeah?

>   EVELYN
>   (OS)
>   Yes. Hollis never forgave him for it.

>   GITTES
>   Never forgave him for what?

He looks up at her.

FRAME GRAB #12

>   EVELYN
>   (OS)
>   For talking him into building it. They never spoke
>   from that time on.

He looks up at her, then down, signing contract.

GITTES
You sure about that?

EVELYN
(OS)
Of course I'm sure.

Gittes holds contract out, sets it down at far edge of table. .

GITTES
Sign here.

He holds out a pen as camera pans over to include Evelyn. She leans over desk and signs. .

GITTES
(con't)
The copy's for you.

FRAME GRAB #13

DECONSTRUCTION
Scene edited by Sam O'Steen

Since this scene is mostly about Evelyn hiding the truth, more is revealed in the dialogue's subtext and by what's not being said. As Gittes probes Evelyn with questions and the pressure builds, the editor uses progressively closer shots and creates tighter responses with overlapping dialogue. The editing is also motivated by eye contact, because when Evelyn looks at Gittes and when she looks away reveal a great deal about her truthfulness and evasiveness. Evelyn's cigarettes are also a significant detail in this scene, and the editor cuts to her grabbing for them when Gittes' questions makes her squirm.

The scene starts with Gittes entering his office — and virtually ignoring Evelyn. In fact, he slams the door and startles her without announcing himself, showing his hostility. The editor chooses to hold on Evelyn as her eyes follow him (the "out" frame is *Frame grab #1*). The editor cuts to Gittes when he makes eye contact with her (the "in" frame is *Frame grab #2*). But Gittes holds the contact only for a moment, then turns away, only half glancing back when he offers her a drink, then continues to avoid looking at her as he rifles through the papers on his desk.

frame grab 1

frame grab 2

The editor cuts back to Evelyn when she offers him a large sum of money to find out who killed her husband (the "out" frame is *Frame grab #3*).

frame grab 3

There is a cut for Gittes' reaction and he doesn't take his eyes off Evelyn for the duration of this shot until he asks her a significant question: "Did you get married before or after Mulwray and your husband sold the water department?" At that point the editor cuts (the "out" frame is *Frame grab #4*).

frame grab 4

frame grab 5

The editor then cuts to Evelyn's surprisingly startled reaction to his question (the "in" frame is *Frame grab #5*), which foreshadows the powerful and evil role that Evelyn's father, Noah Cross, plays in the story. In fact, the editor makes the most of Evelyn's reaction by using her head-on close-up for the first time. She was in three-quarter profile before this, as shown in *Frame grab #3*. The editor also overlaps Gittes' question over her close-up, adding tension to the moment. Gittes knows that when he's questioning Evelyn here about her father and husband being partners, he's also including the fact that Noah Cross is her father. Gittes doesn't know the significance of Noah Cross yet, but he knows that Evelyn had the opportunity to tell him about her connection to Cross in a previous scene but she didn't, so he follows that line of questioning now. The editor stays on Evelyn's close-up as Gittes presses her to admit Cross is her father. She looks away before she answers and looks back at Gittes before she finally makes the admission. She then averts her eyes again by looking down, which cues the cut to an insert shot of her grabbing for a cigarette. The "in" frame and "out" frames (the latter is *Frame grab #6*) show Evelyn's hands at peak movement, which makes this insert shot blend in smoothly and also serves to underline her nervous energy. Up to this point, Gittes has been shown only in medium long shot. His close-up (the "in" frame is *Frame grab #7*) is saved for his reaction to Evelyn's fumbling for a cigarette. Her nervousness makes him realize the father-daughter connection may be a key to unlocking her secrets. As a result, Gittes puts pressure on her by making her acknowledge what had already been mentioned before, that she married her father's business partner.

frame grab 6

frame grab 7

Again the editor cuts to her head-on close-up and slightly overlaps the dialogue, showing her avoidance once more. The "in" frame of the shot starts with her briefly making eye contact, not saying a word, then shows her looking down to light up and smoke. When Gittes tells her, off screen, that she's already got one cigarette going, the editor stays with her close-up, to show her discomfort until she looks down again (the "out" frame is *Frame grab # 8*). That downward look cues the cut to another insert of her nervous hands stubbing out the cigarette she'd previously lit (*Frame grab #9*).

frame grab 8

frame grab 9

Over that shot, Gittes asks her if the mention of her father upsets her, and her off-screen response is "Why no…" When the editor cuts to Evelyn's close-up (the "in" frame is *Frame grab #10*), her eyes are looking down in avoidance again, and then she looks up and admits that she is, "…yes, a little," upset.

frame grab 10

Part of the editor's job is to cover up problems and make the most of what he has. The actress Faye Dunaway's line readings are somewhat uneven in this movie. An example is her dialogue over the shot of the ashtray (*Frame grab #9*) and her subsequent line in her close-up (*Frame grab #10*). Breaking up the two lines visually — cutting from an off-screen to an on-screen line — makes that inconsistency less obvious. Throughout the movie, editor O'Steen struggled with the unreliable quality of Dunaway's performance: "*I had to change her performance in so many ways.... she used to give the weirdest line readings.*" However, O'Steen was able to use Dunaway's hesitations and voice fluctuations, which, he said, "*worked for the part, because she was the one with something to hide.*"[24]

As Gittes continues to ask Evelyn questions about her father, the editor stays on the close shot of her to show her revealing hesitations. When Gittes asks Evelyn if her father and husband had a falling out over her or the water department, the question clearly throws her. But after that the pressure is somewhat off Evelyn, as she sidesteps the loaded question by presenting a hard fact — the dam breaking — as the reason why the two men no longer speak. At this point the editor can afford to cut away and take a breather, allowing the secretary to enter with the contract (the "out" frame is *Frame grab #11*). The editor cuts out here on a "awkward" shot of the secretary's midsection, but clearly the timing of her handing Gittes the contract mattered more than following any rule.

frame grab 11

When the editor cuts to Gittes, he seems somewhat disinterested as Evelyn continues to talk about the dam. His interest perks up when he asks Evelyn what her husband never forgave her father for, after which he makes eye contact with her in *Frame grab #12*. This is also a loaded question but Evelyn has a straightforward answer for it, so there is no need to cut to her. When Evelyn says her father and husband haven't spoken to each other for some time, we see Gittes look up again, because Gittes know that's not true: his assistant had previously photographed the two of them arguing. But Evelyn obviously doesn't know that, so again there is no need to cut to her. Also, by staying on Gittes, the audience gets to watch him become the one who is now withholding information. The scene ends with a commentary on the tenuous nature of their professional relationship: a long shot of Evelyn signing a contract, and Gittes watching her warily (the "out" frame is *Frame grab #13*).

frame grab 12

frame grab 13

SCENE TWO: THE CONFESSION

In the fifty minutes that have passed between the two scenes, the audience has gone through the frustrating journey, with Gittes, of peeling back the layers of Evelyn's lies and secrets. Evelyn and Gittes have also become romantically involved, which raises the emotional stakes even higher. And now Gittes feels betrayed, since he's become convinced that the woman he thinks is Mulwray's girlfriend is being held against her will by Evelyn and that, worse still, Evelyn has killed her husband in a jealous rage. The scene starts with Gittes rushing to the house where Evelyn has kept the girl in hiding.

EXT. STREET - DAY
Long shot of car speeding down a residential street. It passes a bungalow and turns into the driveway. Gittes get out of the car and heads to the front door.

                                                            CUT TO:

Medium shot of Gittes at the front door. He knocks on the door and a Chinese servant (KAHN) opens it. Gittes starts to push his way in, but Kahn holds him back.

                          KAHN
              You wait.

                          GITTES
              You wait.

They argue in Chinese as Gittes pushes past him and camera follows him inside. A breathless Evelyn rushes down the stairs, coming between them.

                                                            CUT TO:

Medium shot of Kahn, Evelyn, and Gittes.

                          EVELYN
              How are you? I've been calling you.
                   (to Kahn, waving him off)
              It's all right.

CUT TO:

Medium shot over Gittes to Evelyn and Kahn.

> EVELYN
> Have you...have you slept?

> GITTES
> Sure.

Kahn closes door and starts to head up stairs.

> EVELYN
> Have you had lunch? Kahn can fix you something.

> GITTES
> Where's the girl?

> EVELYN
> Upstairs. Why?

> GITTES
> I want to see her.

> EVELYN
> She's... she's having a bath right now, why do you want
> to see her?

> GITTES
> Going some place?

Gittes moves past her into living room and crosses in front of half-packed suitcases. Camera lingers on luggage for a beat.

> EVELYN
> (OS)
> Yes, we have a... 5:30 train to catch.

CUT TO:

Medium close shot of Gittes. Camera pans with him as he moves across room then pans down to telephone. He picks up receiver and dials.

                    EVELYN
              (OS)
          Jake?

                                        CUT TO:

Medium close shot of Evelyn. Camera pans with her as she moves across room toward Gittes until they're both in a two shot.

                    GITTES
          ... J. J. Gittes for Lieutenant Escobar.

                    EVELYN
          Look, what's the matter?? What's wrong? I told you
          we've got a 5:30....

                    GITTES
              (cutting her off)
          You're going to miss your train!
              (into phone)
          Lou, meet me at 1972 Canyon Drive...
          Yeah, soon as you can.

                    EVELYN
          Why did you do that?

Camera pans with him as he moves past her, away from camera.

                    GITTES
          Do you know any good criminal lawyers?

                    EVELYN
              (OS)
          No.

Camera settles into medium long shot as he sits down on couch, opens cigarette case.

> GITTES
> Don't worry.... I can recommend a couple. They're
> expensive but you can afford it.

Shot now includes Evelyn's back in the foreground.

> EVELYN
> Will you please tell me what this is all about?

He lights cigarette, pulls folded handkerchief out of his pocket, lays it on table and opens it to reveal a pair of eyeglasses inside.

> GITTES
> I found these in your backyard in your pond. They
> belonged to your husband, didn't they?

FRAME GRAB #1

CUT TO:

Close-up of Evelyn reacting, surprised.

FRAME GRAB #2

> GITTES
> (cont'd, OS)
> Didn't they?

> EVELYN
> I don't know...yes...probably.

CUT TO:

Close shot of Gittes as he stands up into camera.

FRAME GRAB #3

> GITTES
> Yes positively!

Camera follows him as he walks away from her.

                              GITTES
                            (cont'd)
                    That's where he was drowned.

He turns to look at her.

                                                    CUT BACK TO:

Close-up of Evelyn.

                              EVELYN
                            (disbelief)
                    What?

                              GITTES
                            (OS)
                    There's no time to be shocked by the truth
                    The coroner's...

                                                    CUT TO:

Close-up of Gittes.
                              GITTES
                    ...report proves that he had salt water in his lungs when he
                    was killed, just take my word for it, all right? Now I want to
                    know how it happened and I want to know why and I want
                    to know before Escobar gets here because I don't want to
                    lose my license.

                                                    CUT BACK TO:

Close-up of Evelyn.

                              EVELYN
                    I don't know what you are talking about. This is the craziest,
                    most insane...

He grabs her.

GITTES
(yells, OS)
STOP IT!!... I'm gonna make it easy for ya.

CUT BACK TO:

Close-up of Gittes.

GITTES
You were jealous. You had a fight. He fell. He hit his head.
It was an accident. But his girl is a witness.

CUT BACK TO:

Close-up of Evelyn, looking at him in disbelief.

FRAME GRAB #4

GITTES
(OS)
You had to shut her up. You don't have the guts to
harm her but you got the money to keep her mouth shut.
Yes or no.

EVELYN
NO!!!!

CUT BACK TO:

Close-up of Gittes. He takes a beat.

GITTES
Who is she? And don't give me that crap about
your sister because you don't have a sister.

CUT BACK TO:

Close-up of Evelyn.

EVELYN

I'll tell you.... I'll tell you the truth.

CUT BACK TO:

Close-up of Gittes, blowing smoke out of his nose.

FRAME GRAB #5

He calms down, for just a beat.

GITTES

Good. What's her name?

A beat.

EVELYN

(OS)

Katherine...

A beat.

GITTES

Katherine who?

CUT BACK TO:

Close-up of Evelyn. A beat.

EVELYN

She's my daughter.

FRAME GRAB #6

CUT BACK TO:

Close-up of Gittes.

In a fury, he swings his arm at her.

FRAME GRAB #7

CUT TO:

Medium close shot over Gittes to Evelyn, being slapped.

FRAME GRAB #8

GITTES
I said I want the truth!

EVELYN
She's my sister.

He slaps her again.

EVELYN
(cont'd)
She's my daughter.

He slaps her again.

EVELYN
(cont'd)
My sister, my daughter!

He slaps her again – and again. She's crying.

GITTES
I said I want the truth!

He grabs her and throws her across the room, making her fall onto the couch. She struggles to sit up.

EVELYN
She's my sister and my daughter!!

She's sobbing, then looks off suddenly.

FRAME GRAB #9

CUT TO:

Medium long shot of stairway as Kahn rushes down stairs.

FRAME GRAB #10

> EVELYN
> (cont'd, OS)
> Kahn, go back! For God's sake, keep her upstairs, go back!

CUT TO:

Close-up of Evelyn in profile. She turns to camera, tears streaming down her face. She look up at Gittes, then away from him.

> EVELYN
> My father and I...
> (closes her eyes, then looks up at him)
> Understand? Or is it too tough for you?

FRAME GRAB #11

CUT TO:

Close-up of Gittes looking down at her.

FRAME GRAB #12

CUT BACK TO:

Close-up of Evelyn. She makes eye contact, then looks away for a long beat. She cries, laying her head down.

> GITTES
> (OS)
> He raped you.

She looks up at him, then looks away again, devastated.

FRAME GRAB #13

CUT BACK TO:

Close-up at Gittes, reacting.

 FRAME GRAB #14

He takes a beat

                    GITTES
              Then what happened?

CUT BACK TO:

Close-up of Evelyn.

                    EVELYN
              I ran away.

                    GITTES
                   (OS)
              To Mexico.

                    EVELYN
                  (nods)
         Hollis came and took care of me.

 *FRAME GRAB #15*

CUT BACK TO:

Close-up of Gittes.

                    EVELYN
                   (OS)
              I couldn't see her.

 *FRAME GRAB #16*

CUT BACK TO:

Close-up of Evelyn, looking down, tears streaming down her face.

 *FRAME GRAB #17*

She looks up at him.

> EVELYN
> I was fifteen... I wanted to but I... I couldn't...
> Now I want to be with her. I want to take care of her.

CUT BACK TO:

Close-up of Gittes.

> GITTES
> Where are you going to take her now?

> EVELYN
> (OS)
> Back...

CUT BACK TO:

Close-up of Evelyn.

> EVELYN
> ...to Mexico.

> GITTES
> (OS)
> Well, you can't take the train. Escobar will be looking
> for you everywhere.

> EVELYN
> (standing up)
> H.. h.. how bout a plane?

> GITTES
> (OS)
> No, that's worse.

CUT BACK TO:

Close-up of Gittes.

> GITTES
> You better just get out of here. Leave all this stuff here.

CUT BACK TO:

Close-up of Evelyn.

> GITTES
> (OS)
> Where does Kahn live? Get the exact address.

> EVELYN
> All right.

Camera follows her as she backs away toward stairs — and looks down.

> EVELYN
> (cont'd)
> Uh...those didn't belong to Hollis.

She turns away toward stairs.

> GITTES
> (OS)
> How do you know?

She turns back, looks at him.

> EVELYN
> He didn't wear bifocals.

She looks down at glasses again, back at him, then spins around to head up stairs.

FRAME GRAB #18

CUT BACK TO:

Close-up of Gittes, his eyes following her up the stairs.

FRAME GRAB #19

He looks down, thinking. He walks for a beat, looks down again.

CUT TO:

Insert of eyeglasses on handkerchief.
He picks them up and turns them over in his hand. Hand starts to leave frame...

FRAME GRAB #20

CUT TO:

Medium full shot of Gittes, as he puts glasses inside jacket pocket.

FRAME GRAB #21

He's thinking, then looks up.

CUT TO:

Medium long shot of staircase.
Evelyn and teenaged girl appear in stairway

      EVELYN
   Katherine, say hello to Mr. Gittes.

Camera moves in slightly on two women.

> KATHERINE
> (shyly)
>
> Hello.

CUT BACK TO:

Medium full shot of Gittes.

> GITTES
> (smiles gently)
>
> Hello.

CUT BACK TO:

Medium long shot of stairs.
Evelyn nods to daughter, who heads back upstairs.

> EVELYN
> He lives at 1712 Alameda. Do you know where that is?

CUT TO:

Close shot of Gittes.
Camera moves in closer, he reacts strongly.

> GITTES
> Sure.

He looks down, deep in thought.

 FRAME GRAB #22

CUT TO:

Medium long shot of Gittes looking through window at street.
In the foreground Gittes closes blinds and in the background, through the
window, Evelyn, Katherine, and Kahn get into car and drive off.

DECONSTRUCTION

While the first scene was about hiding the truth, this one is about revealing the truth. Previously, Evelyn's evasive looks and actions spoke louder than what was said, but in this scene Gittes and the audience are demanding more, and the change in tone is clearly reflected the way the scene is shot and edited.

The moment Gittes enters the house, he and Evelyn are crowded within the frame. The intimacy of how these actors are positioned reflects their previous sexual intimacy — and Gittes' anger — and as that fury escalates, so does the momentum of the editing.

The scene really picks up pace when Gittes shows Evelyn the "smoking gun," the eyeglasses that he insists are her husband's (the "out" frame is *Frame grab #1*). The editor has saved Evelyn's first close-up for her important reaction to this evidence (the "in" frame is *Frame grab #2*). The editor also overlapped the dialogue slightly when he cut to the shot of Evelyn, satisfying the audience's urgent need to see her reaction.

frame grab 1

frame grab 2

When Gittes demands her to answer whether the glasses are, in fact, her husband's, the editor makes a high-energy visual choice. The point where he cuts to Gittes (the "in" frame is *Frame grab #3*) comes in the middle of his jumping up to challenge her. The editor stays with Gittes' energy as he paces.

frame grab 3

frame grab 4

Now there is a batting back and forth of close-ups between Gittes and Evelyn, and the dialogue overlaps, as Gittes accuses Evelyn of killing her husband. When Gittes implies that Evelyn might harm the girl, by saying "the girl is a witness," it's an especially painful accusation for Evelyn, so he cuts to her agonized, wordless reaction (the "in" frame is *Frame grab #4*). Then Gittes asks Evelyn if his allegations are true, and she vehemently yells out "no!" The intensity of her denial puts a bit of doubt in Gittes' mind, and his rat-a-tat questioning loses some of its momentum. There's a shift now in the pacing because of the ebb and flow of Gittes' anger. Instead of overlapping dialogue, the editor gives the actors beats before they speak their lines.

When Evelyn promises to tell the truth, the editor cuts to Gittes (the "in" frame is *Frame grab #5*) and gives him a beat by letting him blow smoke out of his nose before he continues to question her.

frame grab 5

frame grab 6

But it's the calm before the storm, because now another, more powerful, wave of anger appears after the editor cuts to Evelyn and she confesses that the girl is her daughter (the "out" frame is *Frame grab #6*).

With this answer, which Gittes assumes is a lie, he completely loses his temper and slaps her hard. The editor stays with this shot until Gittes has already swung his arm around (the "out" frame is *Frame grab #7*). When the editor cuts to the shot that now includes Evelyn (the "in" frame is *Frame grab #8*), her face has already jerked away from the impact of the slap. This classic technique works here, because the audience experiences the sound of the slap on the cut, which makes them blink and think they've seen the slap, even though they haven't. The sound of the slap really plays a few frames later over that second shot of Evelyn, but because we hear instantaneously and our vision is slightly delayed, that sound seems to come on the actual cut.

frame grab 7

frame grab 8

The editor then stays on the second shot, which shoots past Gittes to Evelyn, and now Gittes slaps Evelyn four more times as she continues to infuriate him by saying over and over what he believes are lies: that the girl is her sister, then her daughter. The editor maintains the tension by staying with this shot through the point when Gittes throws Evelyn onto the couch. The dramatic arc peaks after her violent fall against the couch, when she turns to him and blurts out, "She's my sister *and* my daughter!" Then there's a break from this intense moment when she reacts to something off screen (the "out" frame is *Frame grab #9*). The editor then cuts to what she sees: the servant Kahn coming down the stairs (the "in" frame is *Frame grab #10*). This lull gives the audience and Gittes time to let Evelyn's bizarre and shocking confession sink in.

frame grab 9

frame grab 10

Now there's a shift in mood from anger to pathos, and again the pace slows. And although the previous cuts were propelled by direct eye contact, now the motivation for cutting to Evelyn is based both on looking and looking away, which reflects the pain and shame of her confession. After the shot of Kahn, the editor cuts to a close-up of Evelyn showing her eyes dart to Gittes; then she looks away for her devastating confession: "My father and I…" The editor continues to hold on her as she closes her eyes for a moment, then gives Gittes a defiant look and says: "Understand? Or is it too tough for you?" (the "out" frame of that shot is *Frame grab #11*). The cut to Gittes' close-up (the "in" frame is *Frame grab #12*) comes on the first frame after her line, because the editor knows the audience is dying to see Gittes' reaction. The editor holds on him as he sustains eye contact with Evelyn and subtly clenches his jaw.

frame grab 11

frame grab 12

In the next cut to Evelyn, she's making eye contact with him; then she looks away and sobs, letting her forehead fall down on the table. It is at this devastating moment that the editor plays Gittes' off-screen line "he raped you." The editor holds on Evelyn's close-up as she looks up at him pleadingly and shakes her head as if trying to erase the memories and then continues to stay on her, only cutting out of this shot after about nine seconds, when she finally looks away in shame (the "out" frame is *Frame grab #13*). The editor is now compelled to cut back for Gittes' reaction (the "in" frame is *Frame grab #14*) which is the same as his previous close-up, and this time the editor gives him a very long beat — around six seconds — to show the reality sinking in on Gittes. He looks at her, looks down, his eye darting around in anger until, finally, he looks back at her and softly asks what happened after the rape.

frame grab 13

frame grab 14

The editor now cuts to Evelyn as she reveals her tragic story in painstaking detail. Her eyes briefly dart over to Gittes twice, but the editor cuts when she looks away again (that "out" frame is *Frame grab #15*). Then an interesting thing happens. The next cut to Gittes, a brief shot of his looking at her (the "out" frame is *Frame grab #16*) is not really motivated by any particular reason, since the off-screen line that plays over this shot — "I couldn't see her" — does not beg for a particular reaction from Gittes. There are several possible explanations for cutting to Gittes here: The editor may have been motivated to cut away to Gittes so that when he cut back to Evelyn (the "in" frame is *Frame grab # 17*) her poignant line ("I was fifteen") would have more impact. It's also possible that the editor may have made the cutaway to Gittes so that he could change to another take when Dunaway spoke that crucial line. As was mentioned in the previous scene, the actress' performance was somewhat erratic and often had to be protected. In fact, in this shot of Evelyn (*Frame grab #17*) it is obvious from her hair being more matted down that this is a different take from the previous ones, shown in *Frame grabs #11, #13*, and *#15*. Nicholson's performance is so consistent, however, that cutaways to his close-ups (shown in *Frame grabs #12, #14*, and *#16*) could be fall-backs for whatever adjustments the editor had to make with Dunaway's line readings.

Another possible reason why the editor cut to Gittes (shown in *Frame grab #16*) is that the director may have used it as an opportunity to take out some unnecessary dialogue. In the original screenplay, after Evelyn talks about her husband taking care of her and that she couldn't see her daughter, Evelyn says: "but I don't want her to know. I don't want her to know." Gittes then says, "So that's why you hate him," and Evelyn says, "…no… for turning his back on me after it happened! He couldn't face it…. I hate him." It's possible that this dialogue was eliminated in shooting rather than in the cutting room, but regardless of when those dialogue cuts were made, the choice is a very smart one. There's no need for Evelyn to elaborate here or to justify her hatred for her father. Less is definitely more in this case.

frame grab 15

frame grab 16

frame grab 17

frame grab 18

frame grab 19

An entirely new dramatic twist occurs after Evelyn's confession, when she tells Gittes that her husband didn't wear bifocals. She delivers the line off-handedly as she heads toward the stairs but does make eye contact with Gittes as she tells him. Then the editor cuts at the moment she starts to spin around and head up the stairs (the "out" frame is *Frame grab #18*). When the editor cuts away from her, she's at the bottom of the stairs, but on the other side of the cut (the "in" frame is *Frame grab #19*) Gittes is already looking up at the top of the stairs. The editor needed to cut for the intensity of his reaction, for performance, rather than for matching, because this is such a key moment.

The editor then holds on this shot of Gittes to show his mind turning, which allows the audience's minds to turn as well: to the realization that the owner of the glasses will lead to the identity of the murderer. Whose glasses could they be, if not Mulwray's? Who is old enough to wear bifocals and would have wanted Mulwray dead?... Noah Cross, of course! This moment is the first time since Gittes arrived at the bungalow that triggers music, to underline the powerful truth that's being revealed. The editor continues to hold on this shot as Gittes takes a beat, looks down, deep in thought, then continues to stay with him for a total of about fourteen seconds as he walks over to the table and looks down again. This cues the cut to the insert shot of Gittes picking up the eyeglasses from the table (the "out" frame is *Frame grab # 20*). In this insert shot Gittes would have had to lean over the coffee table to pick up the glasses, but in the next shot (the "in" frame is *Frame grab #21*), Gittes is standing up straight and is just about to slide the glasses into his breast pocket. This jump cut is a classic editing technique that works partly because in *Frame grab #20* Gittes' hand is seen almost leaving the frame and it's at peak motion, and that movement continues into the next shot. It also works because we want the editor to get on with it and maintain the dramatic momentum in the scene.

frame grab 20

frame grab 21

In the insert shot, the hand that's supposed to be Gittes' is not that of Nicholson, the actor portraying him. O'Steen explained that "*If he* [Polanski] *needed an insert shot of an actor's hands he'd just do it himself, because it was easier — and he knew what he wanted in terms of timing.*"[25] This is part of the reason why the inserts, which normally can feel static and disruptive, are unusually fluid in Polanski's movies. But even when the inserts are of a woman's hands, like the shot of Dunaway's in the previous scene, O'Steen and Polanksi were able to make them seem visually dynamic by always cutting in motion.

The musical score continues to play over this period of revelation for Gittes and during his subsequent heartfelt meeting with Evelyn's daughter. When Evelyn then tells Gittes Kahn's address, which is where they're going to hide from the police, the editor cuts out tight, the moment she says her line, to Gittes' strong reaction. And now the music swells. The editor also underlines the drama visually, by cutting to Gittes in the middle of a camera move-in, and then stays on Gittes for a beat as he looks down contemplatively (the "out" frame is *Frame grab #22*).

frame grab 22

We later find out Kahn's address is in Chinatown, where Gittes had experienced romantic loss once before. He had said earlier, after he made love to Evelyn, "I tried to keep someone from getting hurt and I ended up making sure she was hurt." The editor's holding on the shot of Gittes foreshadows the death — in Chinatown — of Evelyn, another woman he cannot protect from tragedy.

ACTION

When an audience views a performance, their muscle movements mirror what they're watching, a phenomenon called "kinesthesis." This can happen in such situations as sporting events, magic acts, or movies. In an action movie, for example, when there's a lot of energy and excitement on screen, the audience will respond not only to the motion of the actors and objects but also to the movement from cut to cut. Some cuts are meant to feel smooth and seamless, but other edits, especially in this genre, are supposed to jolt the audience and give them a strong gut reaction to what they're seeing. In a fight scene, for instance, the editor wants the audience to flinch when the actor takes a punch. An editor is also subject to kinesthesis. His own body will instinctively react to rhythm and motion on the screen, which will "tell" him where to cut.

Story points always have to be made, but in an action scene the editor isn't as tied down to the structure of the screenplay as he would be in a dialogue-driven scene. He doesn't have to search for subtle moments. Even the conflicts between the characters are more exaggerated. The editing goal — to always cut in motion, to never complete an action — gives scenes in this type of movie their crucial momentum. Fortunately, because of that and the fact that the picture is not as married to the dialogue, the editor can take footage out more easily, too. The editing style — the visual rhythm from cut to cut — becomes faster, more visible, and usually more stylistic. Because the goal is to keep the audience on edge and emotionally unsettled, the editor has more freedom to break the rules. He can go a little wild on pans, tilts, and zooms. The audience is on such an adrenaline ride, most likely they won't see a jump cut as jarring. In fact, they probably would be bored by a matched cut and prefer the bounced-around effect. Because there are fewer constraints and the action mostly dictates what has to be done, the editor will probably spend less time cutting this kind of scene than any other.

Action scenes are sometimes storyboarded, because the logistics and cost of them may require specific planning. If the director is technically overwhelmed by how to cover a particular scene, the storyboard can be very helpful. However, sometimes the carefully illustrated frames of the storyboard can't be exactly duplicated in the actual shooting, because of limitations on the set or location, and because the movie takes on its own life. Some scenes — especially those that are a one-time event such as a building being blown up — will be shot with multiple cameras covering different angles simultaneously. The editor will have many choices and the luxury of making matched cuts when he wants to.

THE CHASE, THE RACE: *BUTCH CASSIDY AND THE SUNDANCE KID, THE FRENCH CONNECTION*

Cross-cutting — whether it's between pursuer and pursued or between competitors in a race — forms the core of this type of scene. The stakes are high, and the editor has to be very clear in showing which characters the audience is supposed to identify with, and where the characters are in relation to each other. This consistency is crucial, because if the audience is confused, both their involvement and the momentum of the scene itself are seriously weakened. Since pursuer and pursued are not always seen within the same shot, the editor has to find other ways to establish a common geography between the parallel streams of action. One way is to use a marker, a memorable spot in the scene that the pursuer, too, will later pass (a bridge, for example). Another way for the editor to keep the action continuous is by weaving a fabric of cutaways between the two or more active threads of the story. The cutaway shots can be static ones, like inserts or close-ups — say, a shot of hands on a steering wheel during a car chase — which heighten the audience involvement and punctuate the drama with emotion. Such shots are also useful in bridging time lapses, so that the editor can eliminate footage. This is a good example of where real time — showing the entire chase or race — is not nearly as interesting as movie time.

The nature of the cutaway shots will determine their length. A still image, closer shot, or even a tracking shot of an actor in motion can be shorter because the audience can get the information quickly. With a long shot or just a more complicated shot that shows a lot of information, the audience needs more time to get their bearings. Shots of pursuer and pursued don't necessarily need to be the same length. For the most part the cuts come faster as the action escalates and heads toward a resolution. However, alternating between a fast pace and slow pace can also heighten the impression of speed and create unique emotional impact — for instance, a chase scene on horseback could have short, high-energy fast cuts interwoven with shots in slow motion of the riders falling to their death. There are no hard-and-fast rules for editing as long as the cuts keep the audience in an increasingly heightened state of involvement from buildup to climax.

THE FIRST CHASE SCENE — ARRIVAL OF THE POSSE

FRAME GRAB ILLUSTRATION: *BUTCH CASSIDY AND THE SUNDANCE KID*

The following pivotal scene is a variation of the chase scene, involving the pursuer and pursued. Only in this case, the pursued — Butch's gang — is not running away, because neither they nor the audience learn until the end of the scene that there's a posse on the train. This sequence is modeled after a classic and climactic scene from *High Noon*, the fifties Western, where the heroic former sheriff waits for the train to bring a murderous posse. The scenes from both these Westerns effectively use cross-cutting to show the arrival of the train and the people waiting for it, but the seventies version is less static and more stylized. In *Butch Cassidy* the good guy/bad guy distinction is also ambiguous, and the tone has a unique way of shifting back and forth between being ominous and humorous.

In the previous scene, Butch Cassidy (Paul Newman), the Sundance Kid (Robert Redford), and the gang blow up a bank safe inside the train. The explosives they use are more powerful than they anticipated, and dollar bills come flying out of the vault and the train. The gang scrambles alongside the train, laughing and grabbing at the floating money, putting everyone on a high… just before the arrival of another train, which, unknown to the gang, carries a group of legendary lawmen that will end up relentlessly pursuing Butch and Sundance.

EXT. TRAIN — DAY
Medium long shot of billowing black smoke, moving horizontally.

FRAME GRAB #1

CUT TO:

Close shot of Butch reacting.

FRAME GRAB #2

Camera moves in on him.

CUT TO:

Close shot of Sundance reacting.

FRAME GRAB #3

He leans in.

CUT TO:

High long shot of robbers and train in foreground and approaching train and smoke in background.

FRAME GRAB #4

CUT TO:

Medium long shot of train in full view.

FRAME GRAB #5

CUT TO:

Close shot of Butch and Sundance.

FRAME GRAB #6

BUTCH
What the hell is that?

CUT TO:

Medium close shot of train moving straight toward camera.

FRAME GRAB #7

Train continues to move toward camera until the front (cowcatcher) is in close shot.

FRAME GRAB #8

CUT TO:

Close shot of engine.

FRAME GRAB #9

CUT TO:

Close shot of smokestack.

FRAME GRAB #10

CUT TO:

Close shot of top of train and steam vents.

FRAME GRAB #11

CUT TO:

Close shot of empty cabin.

FRAME GRAB #12

CUT TO:

Medium shot of train car.

FRAME GRAB #13

CUT TO:

Close-up of Butch and Sundance.

FRAME GRAB #14

CUT TO:

Close shot of train whistle.
Camera moves in on whistle as it blows.

FRAME GRAB #15

CUT TO:

Medium close shot of train car as door slides open.

FRAME GRAB #16

CUT TO:

Medium close shot of car with horses galloping out.

FRAME GRAB #17

CUT TO:

Medium shot of car with horses galloping out.

FRAME GRAB #18

CUT TO:

Medium shot, from behind, of horses galloping away.

CUT TO:

Medium close shot of horses, another angle from behind, of horses galloping away.

CUT BACK TO:

Close shot of Butch and Sundance.

BUTCH
Whatever they're selling, I don't want it.

DECONSTRUCTION
Scene edited by Richard C. Meyer

The buildup to the arrival of the train and the posse starts with the audience seeing only black smoke moving across the distant horizon and hearing the chugging sound. The editor, Richard C. Meyer, cuts to shots of Butch and Sundance hearing the sound and looking off to see what's making it.[26] The editor then cuts to still another shot of the smoke and to shots of the other two robbers reacting. When the editor cuts to yet another shot of the smoke, this time the smoke is billowing more and appears slightly closer, with parts of the bank's train in the foreground to show that the train is getting nearer (the "out" frame is *Frame grab #1*). The tease of not actually seeing the train, only its smoke and its sound, makes the robbers — and the audience — strain to see (as Butch and Sundance do in *Frame grabs #2* and *#3*, the "in" frames of each shot). The editor also cuts out of both shots using motion to underline the impact: a camera move onto Butch and a body move from Sundance.

frame grab 1

frame grab 2

frame grab 3

Then the editor cuts to a master shot of the two trains and robbers shown in clear relation to each other: the bank's train is in the foreground and the arriving train appears in the distance, in full view for the first time (the "out" frame is *Frame grab #4*). Although Butch and Sundance did not seem to be anywhere near each other in their previous close-ups (*Frame grabs #2* and *#3*), in this master shot they are standing right next to each other, but the audience won't notice this mismatch, because their focus is on the arriving train.

frame grab 4

The next shot, a closer view of the train, still moving horizontally, is the first clear shot of it (*Frame grab #5*). In the next shot Butch and Sundance are standing together in a medium shot, showing increasing concern (the "out" frame is *Frame grab #6*).

frame grab 5

frame grab 6

The editor creates a building sense of impending danger both with his choice of shots and by their length. The first shot of the train (*Frame grab #1*) is more than two seconds long. The subsequent shots (*Frame grabs #4, #5* and *#6*) are about four seconds long. These shots are longer because the editor is milking the mystery and can take his time. The train, which had been moving in a relatively non-threatening horizontal direction, is next shown moving straight at the camera: The editor has saved the most dramatic shot of the train for last. This shot, over six seconds long and the longest in the scene, starts with *Frame grab #7*, showing the train in a cloud of smoke, and ends with *Frame grab #8*, where the front end of the train completely fills the screen. The editor cuts out the moment the train stops. The constant, chugging sound — which has been used up until now as a slowly building threat — is topped by the screech of the train coming to a halt.

frame grab 7

frame grab 8

Now the threat is more real and the pacing changes markedly. The scene also becomes more stylized as the editor cuts to close shots, showing different parts of the train. The tension builds with a shot of the black, dripping pistons and engine (*Frame grab #9*), a shot of the black smoke and smokestack (*Frame grab #10*), as well as steam and its vents (*Frame grab #11*). The buildup continues with the eerie shot of an empty cabin (*Frame grab #12*) and the mysteriously closed door of the train's car (*Frame grab #13*). These shots of the train are only about a second long, but they feel shorter because of how close the angles are. The sounds that play over these shots are also a reflection of the danger ahead. First we hear the train's eerie hissing and its idling noise, which sounds almost like a heartbeat — putting pressure on both the robbers and the audience as they watch and wait. That sound is accompanied by the subtle sounds of the pistons turning and the steam coming out of the vents. Our fearful reactions are then mirrored in the faces — in close-up now — of Butch and Sundance (*Frame grab #14*).

frame grab 9

frame grab 10

frame grab 11

frame grab 12

frame grab 13

frame grab 14

The dramatic turning point comes with the shot of a train whistle: The editor cuts in the middle of a camera move that ends up in a tight shot, and cuts out just after the whistle blows its full steam (the "out" frame is *Frame grab #15*).

The shot of the whistle blowing is barely over a half second long, but feels even shorter because of how fast the camera is moving and how close the shot is. The surprising, high-pitched whistle sound, coming after the lull of the train's subtler sounds, helps to set up this turning point. The editor then cuts to a straight-on shot into the train car, revealing a empty black space (the "out" frame is *Frame grab #16*). The audience should actually be able to see the horses of the posse inside the car from this angle, since the subsequent shot shows them bursting out (the "in" frame is *Frame grab #17*). In reality, the actors had to ride their horses on a ramp from the other side of the car in order to get them up to speed, so that previous shot would have been impossible to capture. But as it turns out, the dark empty shot (*Frame grab #16*) is not just a necessary cheat; it made the next cut work very effectively. After the mysterious black void inside the train, the bursting out of all those galloping horses is both shocking and thrilling. The grind of the sliding door that announces their appearance only adds to the excitement.

frame grab 15

frame grab 16

The difficult stunt of the horses jumping out was shot with multiple cameras, and the editor used the first two camera angles in order of their impact. The editor chose the most exciting angle for the initial burst, where the camera is shooting more from below and at a closer angle, which makes the horses' appearance scarier. The editor cuts into this shot the moment we see the first horse's head at the edge of the door, and cuts out when the second and third horses show themselves (that "out" frame is *Frame grab #17*). The next shot (the "in" frame is *Frame grab #18*) is not a match to the previous shot. In *Frame grab #17*, the first horse is well away from the car and the second horse is almost halfway out, while in *Frame grab #18* only the front legs of the second horse have emerged. But a matched cut would probably have been boring, and even a jump cut wasn't necessary. The editor's goal was to capture energy from one shot to the next and create the most momentum possible. These shots are also short, like the previous shots of the train and, again, they seem even shorter because of the intensity of the moment and the speed of the horses.

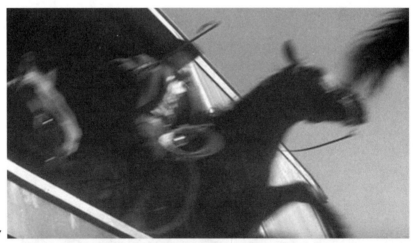

frame grab 17

frame grab 18

The next two shots are not as dramatic visually, since the horses are galloping away from the camera, but they let the audience clearly see the number of the threat: six men on horseback, to be exact. And, as is characteristic of the movie's dark humor, this ominous scene is capped off by Butch's wry line: "Whatever they're selling, I don't want it."

THE SECOND CHASE SCENE — THE CAR & THE TRAIN

FRAME GRAB ILLUSTRATION: *THE FRENCH CONNECTION*

The selection from *Butch Cassidy and the Sundance Kid* showed the pursued waiting for the pursuers. In contrast, this scene from *The French Connection* shows the pursuer, a cop driving a car, very actively chasing the pursued, a villain inside a train. Because the sequence from *The French Connection* was shot in a more improvised, less choreographed style than the scenes from *Butch Cassidy*, it offered different challenges for the editor, Jerry Greenberg.

The setup:
Popeye Doyle (Gene Hackman) is a hard-nosed New York City cop who stumbles onto a very big, impending heroin deal. The French drug dealer's associate, Nicoli (Marcel Bozzuffi), knowing that Doyle may be onto them, has just gunned down innocent bystanders on Doyle's home turf in his failed attempt to kill Doyle. In response, an enraged Doyle pursues Nicoli on foot, but Nicoli manages to elude Doyle by jumping onto an elevated subway train. A desperate Doyle runs into the street, flags down a car, and forcibly takes it. Now the chase between the elevated train and the car begins. The editor intercuts from exterior shots of the train and Doyle driving, to interior shots of Nicoli walking through the train and ultimately shooting a cop. After that, the editor cuts to the train's POV as it speeds along the tracks, then back to Doyle driving.

(*Note:* I have chosen two sections from the sequence that follows — with a gap in between — to show an escalation of the chase and, as a result, a contrast in both the shooting and editing styles. They will be referred to as Part I and Part II.)

PART I

Long shot of street shooting past Doyle and dashboard.

 FRAME GRAB #1

CUT TO:

Close shot of Doyle in car with street in background.

 *FRAME GRAB #2*

CUT TO:

Long shot of elevated train, seen past playground in foreground.

 *FRAME GRAB #3*

CUT TO:

Long shot of car under elevated train, seen past playground in foreground.

 *FRAME GRAB #4*

CUT TO:

Close shot of Doyle looking up, then camera pans over and up to medium long shot under elevated train track.

 *FRAME GRAB #5*

CUT TO:

Medium long shot of Nicoli walking away from camera through train car.

 *FRAME GRAB #6*

Nicoli walks to the front of the train and the front cabin, pointing his gun at the motorman's head to make sure he doesn't stop at the next station.

Meanwhile Doyle has arrived at that station and runs up to the platform, expecting that he has beaten Nicoli there. Instead, he finds the train racing past him and the other startled people waiting on the platform. He runs back to the car and resumes his chase, driving more aggressively than ever.

PART II

Medium shot of Nicoli and motorman, gun pointed at motorman's head.

FRAME GRAB #7

CUT TO:

Long shot of train on tracks.

FRAME GRAB #8

Train moves toward the camera.

CUT TO:

Long shot, POV from car racing through streets.

FRAME GRAB #9

CUT TO:

Medium shot through windshield of Doyle.

FRAME GRAB #10

CUT BACK TO:

Long shot, POV of car, racing through streets.

FRAME GRAB #11

CUT BACK TO:

Close shot of Doyle through windshield, looking straight ahead, then up.

FRAME GRAB #12

CUT TO:

Medium long shot, Doyle's POV of elevated tracks.

FRAME GRAB #13

CUT BACK TO:

Long shot of elevated tracks showing car below and train above, with playground in foreground.

FRAME GRAB #14

CUT TO:

Long shot, Doyle's POV of street. Car approaches back of truck, then truck starts to turn left, cutting off car.

FRAME GRAB #15

CUT BACK TO:

Close shot of Doyle through windshield, frantically steering away.

FRAME GRAB #16

CUT BACK TO:

Long shot of car and truck side by side.

FRAME GRAB #17

Car gets sideswiped by the truck.

CUT TO:

Close shot of Doyle in car, even more frantically steering.

FRAME GRAB #18

CUT TO:

Medium long shot, Doyle's POV of street corner.

FRAME GRAB #19

CUT TO:

Camera pans unsteadily from sidewalk to street.

CUT TO:

Medium side shot of car as it drives past camera and turns back onto street.

CUT BACK TO:

Long shot, Doyle's POV of street.

CUT BACK TO:

Close shot of Doyle through windshield.

CUT BACK TO:

Long shot, Doyle's POV of street.

CUT BACK TO:

Close shot of Doyle through windshield.

CUT BACK TO:

Long shot, Doyle's POV of street.

CUT TO:

Medium close shot of Doyle's legs and feet on car pedals.

CUT BACK TO:

Close shot of Doyle through windshield.

CUT BACK TO:

Long shot, Doyle's POV of street.

CUT TO:

Close-up of Doyle through windshield.

FRAME GRAB #20

CUT TO:

Long shot, Doyle's POV of street and a woman wheeling baby carriage.

FRAME GRAB #21

CUT TO:

Tight close-up of Doyle.

FRAME GRAB #22

CUT TO:

Close shot of woman, then zoom in to tight close-up of woman.

FRAME GRAB #23

CUT BACK TO:

Close-up of Doyle through windshield.

FRAME GRAB #24

CUT TO:

Medium long shot of buildings and street.

FRAME GRAB #25

CUT TO:

Camera pans unsteadily pans from street to sidewalk.

CUT TO:

Long shot of woman and carriage alongside car and it drives past them and smashes through piles of garbage cans and boxes.

FRAME GRAB #26

DECONSTRUCTION
Scene edited by Jerry Greenberg

This sequence was groundbreaking, not only because it wasn't the usual two cars chasing each other, but also because of the cinema verité style of shooting. The director, William Friedkin, said, "*Most of the camerawork was done on actual locations, not sets… with handheld cameras; you can see the shakiness sometimes, but it has a verisimilitude, a sense of reality, as if the camera just happened upon the scene. I had worked in documentary film for years, and I had learned how to achieve an induced documentary style and* The French Connection *was the first fiction film where I had a chance to try that out….*" The cutting process was improvised accordingly: "*A lot of the editing was developed in the cutting room. There is sort of an elliptical style of the editing in that you're not really sure where the next cut is coming from, and certainly neither the shots nor the editing of the shots fall into any conventional pattern.*"[27]

The style of shooting and editing shifts to reflect the escalation of danger and drama. The change occurs between the last shot of Part I, as Nicoli is moving through the train car (*Frame grab #6*), and the first shot of Part II (*Frame grab #7*), when he points a gun at the motorman's head. Between those two shots, Doyle has been thwarted from intercepting the train as he expected, because Nicoli has hijacked it at gunpoint —and now is forced to resume the chase.

frame grab 6

frame grab 7

As a result, Doyle experiences an escalation of frustration and aggravation. Friedkin said, "*This chase embodies the character of Popeye Doyle. He is totally obsessive. He will go through any obstacle to get his man and to break a case. He doesn't care if he endangers innocent lives.*"[28]

As Doyle's pursuit increases in intensity, the footage also becomes more raw and high energy. Doyle's POVs also reflect this escalation. *Frame grab #1*, Part I, the first shot from inside the car, is fairly stable, but in Part II the POVs become speedier and more erratic, as the example in *Frame grab #11*. In that shot, according to Friedkin, the camera was "*mounted on the bumper of Hackman's car. And this is actually traffic; these are cars that have no idea a guy's coming at them at 90 miles per hour.*"[29]

frame grab 1

And although the length of the cuts does not really change from one part to the next, they seem to be shorter, because the car is moving faster in the latter shot, and the action is more exciting.

frame grab 11

When an editor is intercutting between pursuer and pursued, he has to make sure the audience always knows where the two elements are in relation to each other. In Part I the train is always in close proximity to the car, which is established when Doyle looks up — a continuation of the same angle seen in *Frame grab #2*. Then the camera pans over and up to his POV under the tracks (that 'out' frame is *Frame grab #5*). In Part II, the relationship of train to car is reinforced when the editor cuts from Doyle again looking up (the "out" frame is *Frame grab #12*) to another shot of his POV under the tracks (the "in" frame is *Frame grab #13*).

What's also interesting to note is that in Part I, the shot of Doyle is a side angle, as seen in *Frame grab #2*. In Part II, as the scene escalates, Doyle is shot straight on through the windshield, which creates an eerie intensity (a prime example is *Frame grab #12*).

frame grab 2

frame grab 5

frame grab 12

frame grab 13

Even more effective are the two sequential shots which show the train and car in relation to each other: in Part I, there is a long shot of the train on the elevated track (*Frame grab #3*) and then, from the same distance, a shot of the elevated track and the car below it (*Frame grab #4*). Better still, in Part II, the editor uses a shot where the car is right under the train (*Frame grab #14*). That shot has the car and train moving in the opposite direction from those previous two shots, which might have been done so it would seem like a different shot or just because it's visually dynamic. Whatever the reason, the filmmakers pulled it off. It would have been more problematic to reverse the shots in *Frame grabs #3* and *#4*, because the previous shot (*Frame grab #2*) shows Doyle moving in the same left-to-right direction. But the shots before and after *Frame grab #14* are straight on (*Frame grabs #13* and *#15*), giving the editor more flexibility to flip the direction of the shot.

frame grab 2

frame grab 3

frame grab 4

frame grab 13

frame grab 14

frame grab 15

Another way reversed movement is used to create visual excitement is with the juxtaposition of opposing POVs. *Frame grab #8* (the "in" frame) shows the train moving toward the screen, but in *Frame grab #9* (the "out" frame), the car is driving away from the screen and in the opposite direction.

frame grab 8

frame grab 9

The dynamic pairing of contrasted POVs continues through throughout the scene. As Doyle drives wildly, the perspective shifts from outside the car (*Frame grab #10*) to inside the car going the other direction (*Frame grab #11*).

frame grab 10

frame grab 11

The editor captures the excitement of Doyle's hitting the truck by cutting first to Doyle's blurry POV of the truck veering into the frame (the "out" frame is *Frame grab #15*), then to a close angle on Doyle as he frantically tries to steer away (the "out" frame is *Frame grab #16*). The editor then cuts to a more distant shot clearly showing the car next to the truck (the "in" frame is *Frame grab #17*) and stays with this shot until the car gets sideswiped by the truck.

frame grab 15

frame grab 16

frame grab 17

He cuts back to Doyle, still steering (the "out" frame is *Frame grab #18*). The editor shows the result of his out-of-control driving by cutting in on an out-of-focus handheld shot of Doyle's POV of the street (the "in" frame is *Frame grab #19*).

frame grab 18

frame grab 19

After the editor cuts to Doyle's battered car "recovering" from this mishap, there are a series of POVs of the street showing Doyle driving more wildly, intercut with shots of Doyle getting more and more aggravated by the obstacles in his race to catch up to the train. When the traffic clears a bit, the editor cuts to another shot of Doyle, but now he has a relatively relaxed expression (*Frame grab #20*), which creates a lull and set up for an even more dramatic arc.

frame grab 20

What happens next, the near-miss of a woman and a baby carriage, is the most memorable editing moment in the sequence and, arguably, the entire movie. The effect was achieved without stunt work, just editing finesse. As Friedkin explained, "*It was very easy to do and it was made with movie magic and a knowledge of cutting. We weren't really driving at her that fast, we were zooming at her that fast with a stationary camera.*"[30]

The editor first establishes the woman and baby carriage from a distance (the "out" frame is *Frame grab #21*). He then cuts to the tightest close up of Doyle yet, showing him in shock (the "out" frame is *Frame grab #22*), which creates the anticipation of danger. Then the editor maximizes the near-miss effect by cutting in to the terrified woman on an erratic zoom-in motion and staying on her until he's at a very tight close-up (the "out" frame is *Frame grab #23*). The editor cuts to Doyle's reaction, a close shot of his most agonized expression yet, as he continues to steer away (the "out" frame is *Frame grab #24*).

frame grab 21

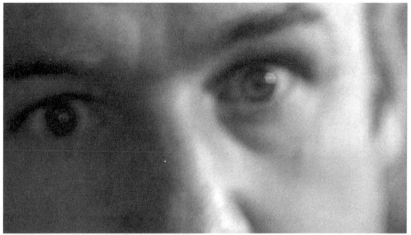

frame grab 22

frame grab 23

frame grab 24

After Doyle almost misses hitting the woman and carriage, the editor uses the same kind of dizzying, handheld POV shot of the street (the "in" frame is *Frame grab #25*) that he used after Doyle collided with the truck (*Frame grab #19*). In both cases the editor cut on camera movement to sustain the out-of-control energy of those moments.

frame grab 25

Once the car is a safe distance away, the editor can afford to show an actual angle of the car in relation to the woman and carriage. And even though the height of the drama has passed, the editor still gets to cap off the sequence by showing the car plowing through a pile of boxes (*Frame grab #26*).

frame grab 26

This chase scene was, Friedkin explained, "*a set piece, you know, a real blast-out chase at the center of the picture, to relieve all this* [police surveillance of drug dealers prior to this scene] *that was leading nowhere.*"[31]

THE BATTLE SCENE

In editing a battle scene, the approach is similar to that of the chase scene: The editor must constantly be aware of the goals of each of the two opposing forces and which camp the audience is supposed to identify with. He must also maintain constant tension and momentum that ultimately builds to a climax. But instead of a single direction of movement by a pursuer and his pursued, the battling enemies are usually moving toward each other. As a result, one side must mostly move right to left, the other side left to right, to preserve the audience's sense of direction and avoid confusion.

The greater challenge with a battle scene is to keep the audience clear on geography, because battles involve more actors than in a chase, and the actors' movements are generally less linear. If the armies are regimented, well matched, and in open terrain, the editor will have an easier time keeping the audience from getting confused. If the battle is more disorganized and chaotic, it may be more difficult for the editor to keep the audience oriented, but he has more freedom to make unconventional cuts.

THE FIGHT

As with a chase or battle scene, in a fight scene the editor has to stick with a chronology and some sort of resolution, but he has even more license to use unconventional cutting techniques that create disorientation and bring on the unexpected, because fights are almost always unruly. The editor can, for example, abuse his audience by sending their eyes off in one direction and then in the opposite direction. Rules about camera angles and moves can be seriously broken, and usually should be. The pace does not necessarily get faster and faster; it can vary from slow to fast and back to slow, but the tension must always be there.

A common belief is that you have to show the crowd's reaction to a fight, but it's only really necessary when you're using such a cutaway to make a story point, as a way to eliminate footage, or as a bridge to cover up problems. It's generally easier to cover up mistakes in a fight, because of its tumultuous nature. If, for instance, a punch is not framed correctly and the exact impact is not seen on screen, a sharp sound and then cutting to the visual impact of the punch (the head snapping back) will still work. In fact, it may be more effective than a literal depiction of the punch, because hearing something violent happen off screen or just seeing the reaction to that violence is often more powerful.

THE SEX SCENE: *BODY HEAT*

Overall, sex scenes are a challenge to pull off, because the filmmakers are depicting the most intimate human experience in a medium that is anything but intimate. Also, what makes something erotic is very subjective, so the editor has to be especially sensitive to what the director intended and what the audience desires. And often, the less you show and the more you imply, the more powerful the erotic effect.

A sex scene is similar to a fight scene — without the crowd watching, of course, and without a clear winner or loser! All sex scenes have an inherent excitement, but some may be particularly wild and edgy, and would be shot and edited similarly to a fight scene, in which the editor could break the rules to create a kind of disorientation or even turmoil.

If the characters are falling in love, the filmmakers may want to create a gentler mood, and the scene may often take the form of a montage accompanied by music and could be cut with dissolves. But even in a romantic montage, the editor can break rules, because the desired effect may be ethereal or surreal. There may not be musical accompaniment, since silence provides its own form of intensity.

FRAME GRAB ILLUSTRATION: *BODY HEAT*

Body Heat, with its sultry tone and fatalistic plotline, pays homage to the film noir movies of the forties. The movie also subtly parodies itself, which gives it a self-conscious style all its own. The protagonist, Ned Racine (William Hurt), fits the film noir bill as a cynical loner living on the edge of the law. Matty (Kathleen Turner) is the classic femme fatale, someone who has the beauty and powerful allure to make a man do anything to have her. In this eighties incarnation, however, Matty is more sexually aggressive and cagier than her forties predecessors in the way she manipulates Ned into murdering her husband. The first pivotal sex scene from the movie involves a choreographed seduction. The visual and narrative structure had to be pre-planned, because the audience has to believe that Matty and Ned are lusting after each other. But they must also later realize, that every move Matty made was calculated to draw the luckless Ned into her intricate web. It's a balancing act of passion and plotting, which the filmmakers pulled off completely.

The setup:

It's a steamy midsummer night and Ned has followed Matty to a bar, where she tells him about the wind chimes in her house and how their ringing always made her feel cool. Ned asks to see the chimes and Matty agrees, although she warns him he's going to be disappointed. When they're together on Matty's veranda, he admires and touches the chimes and then barely strokes the side of her face, at which point she asks him to leave. She then exits and he follows her, reluctantly.

                                                                    CUT TO:

EXT. MATTY'S HOUSE — NIGHT

Medium shot of Matty. She's waiting for him outside her front door. He comes out and stands close to her.

> MATTY
> Thank you. I'm sorry. I shouldn't have let you come.

> NED
> You're not so tough after all, are you?

> MATTY
> No, I'm weak.

She kisses him on the mouth, then quickly turns around and heads inside, closing the door behind her. Once inside, she briefly makes eye contact with Ned through the glass pane of the door, then turns around and disappears inside. The camera holds on Ned for a moment.

                                                                    CUT TO:

Long high shot of cars. Ned walks into frame and heads over to his car and bangs on it in frustration.

                                                                    CUT TO:

Medium long shot of porch and chimes.

CUT BACK TO:

Long high shot of Ned and cars.

FRAME GRAB #1

Camera booms down on him until he's in medium close shot. He looks up at chimes.

FRAME GRAB #2

CUT TO:

Medium shot of chimes.

FRAME GRAB #3

CUT TO:

Medium close shot of chimes.

FRAME GRAB #4

CUT TO:

Close shot of chimes.

FRAME GRAB #5

CUT TO:

Close-up of Ned, camera shooting down on him. He's full of frustration.

FRAME GRAB #6

He exits the screen.

CUT TO:

Medium long shot of Matty through glass panes in front door. Ned appears in foreground, on the outside looking in at her.

FRAME GRAB #7

Ned tries the door. It's locked. **Camera stays with him in close shot in as he moves along house, trying to get in.**

CUT TO:

Close-up of Ned's face through slats of Venetian blinds.

FRAME GRAB #8

CUT TO:

Medium full shot of Matty inside house, watching him.

FRAME GRAB #9

CUT BACK TO:

Medium long shot of Matty through slats of blinds with Ned in foreground, watching her.

FRAME GRAB #10

Ned turns away and walks back to the right toward door, camera shooting close behind him.

CUT TO:

Close shot of Ned through glass panes of door, looking inside at her.

FRAME GRAB #11

He moves to the left past door.

CUT BACK TO:

Close shot of Ned, shot from behind. He's still moving to the right.

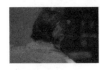

FRAME GRAB #12

CUT TO:

Close-up of Ned looking past curtain of glass door.

FRAME GRAB #13

He moves to the left, to the center of glass.

CUT TO:

Close shot of Matty inside house.

FRAME GRAB #14

CUT TO:

Close shot of Ned through glass door.

FRAME GRAB #15

Camera moves in for a close-up.

CUT TO:

Medium long shot of Ned in foreground, Matty in background.
Camera moves with him as he grabs stool and smashes glass in door.

FRAME GRAB #16

CUT BACK TO:

Close shot of Matty, inside house, mouth parted.

FRAME GRAB #17

CUT BACK TO:

Medium long shot of Ned as he continues to move through doorway toward Matty.

FRAME GRAB #18

Camera follows him inside and moves in for a close shot as he grabs her and kisses her.

FRAME GRAB #19

CUT TO:

Close shot of his back as her hands grasp him.

FRAME GRAB #20

Her hands continue to run down his back.

CUT TO:

Close shot of Ned and Matty kissing. She pulls away and flings her body around so her back is up against him.

FRAME GRAB #21

CUT TO:

Medium full shot of Ned and Matty with her back still up against him, shooting from below.

FRAME GRAB #22

His hand grabs her breast, the other hand slides down her skirt between her legs.

FRAME GRAB #23

She whispers, "yes, yes," and turns around to face him. He starts to pull up bottom of skirt.

CUT TO:

Close shot of Ned and Matty kissing. She starts to unbutton his shirt.

CUT TO:

Close shot of Ned and Matty, lower angle to include her face and only his torso as she opens his shirt and kisses his chest.

CUT TO:

Close shot of back of Matty's skirt. He pulls skirt up.

CUT BACK TO:

Close shot of Ned and Matty as she continues to kiss his chest.

CUT BACK TO:

Close shot of the back of Matty's skirt. Ned's hand hikes the skirt up and he slides his hand under her panties.

CUT BACK TO:

Close shot of Ned and Matty, her face inside his shirt. She pulls away and the moment her face leaves the frame....

CUT TO:

Medium shot of floor. Matty falls into shot onto her back, in profile from the waist up. She hikes up her skirt.

CUT TO:

Close-up of Matty's face, her eyes closed.

CUT TO:

Medium long shot of Matty through reflection of glass door. She's facing away from camera, lying down, and Ned is kneeling behind her as he slides her panties off her knees.

FRAME GRAB #24

CUT TO:

Medium shot of Ned and Matty, reverse angle from inside house. Camera shoots past his back to show her knees up in the air as Ned continues to pull panties off her legs.

FRAME GRAB #25

CUT TO:

Close shot of Ned's hand dropping panties on the floor.

FRAME GRAB #26

CUT BACK TO:

Close-up of Matty's face, eyes still closed.

FRAME GRAB #27

CUT TO:

Close shot of Ned looking down at her, smiling.

FRAME GRAB #28

NED
(whispers)
Yes... right.

CUT TO:

Medium shot of Matty from waist up, camera shooting down at her.

FRAME GRAB #29

MATTY

Please do it.

Ned's head and his body come into frame and he moves on top of her.

DISSOLVE TO:

Shot of headboard. Pan down to medium close shot of Ned with Matty in his arms. The camera moves in on Ned for a close-up, looking satiated.

CUT TO:

High shot of Matty and Ned in bed in same position. He still looks spent — until Matty slides her hand between his legs and starts rubbing him and turning him on.

FRAME GRAB #30

He grabs her and kisses her.

CUT TO:

EXT. MIAMI STREET — DAY
Ned is walking down the street, a smile of satisfaction on his face.

FRAME GRAB #31

DECONSTRUCTION
Scene edited by Carol Littleton

Lawrence Kasdan, who directed this scene from *Body Heat*, and Carol Littleton, who edited it, will be quoted throughout the following deconstruction. (The symbol † indicates quotes from both that were taken from supplemental interviews for the movie's DVD; all of Kasdan's quotes come from this source. The rest of Littleton's comments are from my interview with her for this book.)

BO: *You and the director are of the same generation and share the same appreciation of film noir.*

CL: *Both Larry and I were aware of the homage to film noir and we really wanted it to speak to our generation at that time, and I think the very fact that we were so aware of certain noir moments and that we let them play all the way, we were taking a chance, because they could be just ridiculous, but we loved it. And we really had faith that the audience would enjoy this too.... And the dialogue in* Body Heat *is highly stylized. It's the dialogue of tough dames and tough guys and it is not language as we speak it. It's writerly... it's Raymond Chandler....*[32]

†CL [Speaking with Lawrence Kasdan about the script when they first met]: *I told Larry that what I loved above everything else was the fact that it had an extraordinary sense of humor, and he said, "Oh really?"* [I asked myself] *"Did I say the wrong thing?" He said, "You're the only person that I've talked to who understood that there was a sense of humor."*[33]

†LK: *When I was looking for an editor, I was absolutely set on getting a woman, because I wanted this very sexual movie to not just be some male fantasy. I wanted a woman's voice in there in the moment when we were making all the judgments about the sexual aspects of the movie and luckily I met Carol Littleton, who then wound up cutting most of my movies and who I've known now for twenty-five years.*[34]

CL: *I guess what I was looking for more than anything else, and I know this is a thing that Larry was concerned about as well, is that we did not want the film in any way to seem pornographic or in any way to seem sexually explicit; we wanted it to be suggestive, because we really felt that what is suggested on the screen, [in] one's imagination is far more powerful.... Once the act of making love actually starts, what's there to show? Not much. It's everything that precedes that is really evocative.*

BO: *You also had to set up, from the start, that Matty's seduction was all manipulation, without giving it away. Was that tricky?*

CL: *It was very tricky. The audience had to be with him [Ned] or just before him but not miles ahead of him, so we had to very careful how much we showed when certain things happened, because we really didn't want it to seem as though he was manipulated at all until it falls apart. That was a big challenge.*

Matty asks Ned to leave — because she's supposedly afraid she'll be too "weak" to resist him — and after she leaves him to go inside, the editor holds on Ned to show his frustration. She cuts to a distant high angle showing him walk toward his car and just stand there helplessly, finally banging on the hood of the car with his fist. The editor cuts to his POV of the chimes, then back to the same high shot of Ned as the camera starts to boom down (the "in" frame is *Frame grab # 1*). The editor cuts out of this shot just when the camera stops moving and when he looks up at the chimes (the "out" frame of that same shot is *Frame grab #2*).

frame grab 1

frame grab 2

BO: *That high angle with the camera booming down and in on him, certainly underlines his character's powerlessness, his lack of control over the effect Matty has on him.*

CL: *…Oh, absolutely. It's like, "It's over, buddy. You don't know it yet, but…." There are several moments that are real noir moments, and that was one of them. This extraordinary crane shot: it's up on the height of the crane, then the crane comes all the way down.*

The editor cuts to Ned's POV of the chimes (*Frame grab #3*), then another that is closer than Ned's actual perspective (*Frame grab #4*), and then cuts to a third angle on the chimes that is even closer, to emphasize his mounting frustration (*Frame grab #5*).

frame grab 3

frame grab 4

frame grab 5

The sound of the chimes is presented literally in the beginning of the scene, when Matty shows them to Ned and he brushes them with his hand. But once she's left him alone, and he continues to look at them, they also represent an interior, emotional state: his pent-up sexual frustration and longing. It's characteristic of film noir to use sound to show introspective emotion, and because this movie is both homage and parody, it's intentionally obvious here.

CL: *In the script it was described that Ned Racine is obviously being seduced by Matty, but he looks up and he sees these wind chimes. The sound of the wind chimes seduces him, and he makes up his mind once he has been more or less seduced by their sound. Larry shot different sizes* [of the chimes], *not knowing exactly how we were going to do this. We discussed that a lot. From the beginning we've heard them faintly and as we go up the stairs* [to Matty's veranda] *they kind of build, a little tingle, tingle. We were specific about not really hearing them until they were out there on the veranda, on the upstairs veranda. Then once he brushes them, it just builds. Outside* [the house], *of course, the breeze does kick up, so it's like the heat of the night, the same way the fever overcomes him. And of course it climaxes here with the cuts to the different sizes of the chimes (Frame grabs #3, #4, and #5).*

The sound gets louder as the editor chooses closer and closer cuts of the chimes. However, that noise continues to peak over Ned's first close-up (the "in" frame is *Frame grab #6*), which doesn't make sense geographically, but it certainly works dramatically. This is where Ned is driven the craziest by the sounds inside his head, which cause him to make his move back to the house. Music, too, underlines the importance of this moment, for when he starts to move out of that shot and take action, the first notes of the score creep in. In this first close-up of Ned the camera again shoots down at him, underlining both his powerlessness and his fever, as his face glistens with sweat.

frame grab 6

The moment Ned exits the frame, which he does in the "out" frame of this shot, the audience knows he's going back to the house. This is the first arc of the scene and the editor holds on this close-up for over six seconds before he starts to move, trusting the importance of this decision-making moment.

BO: *When he makes a decision to go back to the house, you hold on that shot of him for a long time.*

CL: *A long time.*

BO: *You also give the moment energy by cutting out on his move off screen.*

CL: *It's liberating. Seductive, too.*[35]

After Ned's close-up, the editor cuts to an exterior shot of Matty posing in the center of the room — dramatically, almost magically, framed by the doors' beveled glass. The editor holds on this shot until Ned moves into the foreground and stares in at this vision of her (*Frame grab #7*). Then, within that same shot, the camera follows closely behind Ned as he moves in darkness along the house until he ends up standing just beyond the blinds. The next shot is to Matty's POV: a close-up of Ned looking in at her from behind the blinds (the "out" frame is *Frame grab #8*).

frame grab 7

frame grab 8

The editor then cuts to a shot of Matty inside the house (*Frame grab #9*). In the next shot she is still posing provocatively (the "in" frame is *Frame grab #10*), but she's again seen from Ned's POV. He's in the foreground looking in on her, and the editor continues to stay close to him as he moves in darkness along the house.

frame grab 9

frame grab 10

The next angle switches back again to Matty's POV of Ned's face; now he's positioned within the glass pane (the "in" frame is *Frame grab #11*). The editor cuts back to Ned's POV as he moves once again in darkness along the outside of the house (*Frame grab #12*). In the next shot (*Frame grab #13*), the editor cuts back to Matty's POV, and this time Ned is once again peeking at her, this time from behind the curtain.

frame grab 11

frame grab 12

frame grab 13

The following shot, the closest yet of Matty, is again an interior shot as she stares at Ned and straight into the camera (*Frame grab #14*). The editor then cuts back to Matty's POV, and Ned holds the same intense eye contact through the glass door (*Frame grab #15*). This shot of Ned is especially powerful, because he's in the center of the screen. Up until now, in all the shots that have shown Matty's POV, Ned has been obscured or framed by something that makes him look caged and a bit scary: for example, by the Venetian blinds (*Frame grab #8*), the glass panes (*Frame grab #11*), and the edge of a curtain (*Frame grab #13*).

frame grab 14

frame grab 15

Also, *Frame grab #15* is arresting, because now Ned is perfectly still. Previously, he was always in motion, even if minimally, within the shots and in the transitions. The shots of Matty inside the house, on the other hand, show her as always still. By interweaving their contrasting motion, the editor created the effect of Ned as a pacing animal and Matty as a poised bird. What's also interesting is that the audience never questions whether Matty would, in real life, stand there motionless while Ned keeps moving back and forth, looking at her from all the doors and windows. The audience buys into this contrived situation and milked movie time, because the editor continuously sustains the tension.

The editor chose to never let Ned leave the frame completely in any of the shots of him (the sole exception is the "out" frame after *Frame grab #11*), which also helps maintain the edge and the visual momentum. The psychological pressure is also sustained by eye contact. There's always dead-on eye contact in the interior shots of Matty (*Frame grabs #9, #14,* and *#17*), which has a sexual power all its own, and with the POV shots there's always either eye contact and/or camera or character motion in the "in" or "out" frames.

The editor also creates a visually dynamic effect when switching between Ned's and Matty's POVs, because the left-right direction is repeatedly reversed. Examples are when Ned moves first to the right, then to the left, then to the right again in *Frame grabs #10, #11,* and *#12,* respectively. This effect also makes directional sense by following the exit/entrance rules of editing.

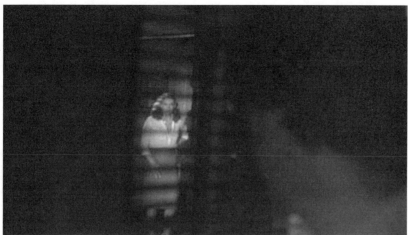

frame grab 10

frame grab 11

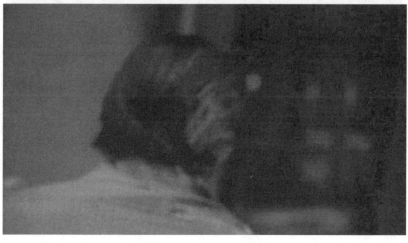

frame grab 12

The close shot of Ned, which starts with *Frame grab #15* and cuts out during a camera move in on him, visually sets up the momentum for him to take action. Just before the editor cuts out of this shot and again in the next shot, Ned's looking down at the doorknob, which shows his intent to get inside the house. Then he grabs the stool and smashes the glass door (the "out" frame of that shot is *Frame grab #16*).

frame grab 15

frame grab 16

In the sequence just described (*Frame grabs #7* to *#16*), the editor creates a brilliantly constructed series of shots that show both Matty's sexual manipulation and Ned's mounting frustration. She does this by developing a pattern of intercutting among three perspectives: Ned's POV of Matty from the outside looking in, Matty's POV of Ned from the inside looking out, and interior shots of Matty. What's amazing, though, is that this sequence was not the result of pre-planning, but instead of plans gone awry:

CL: *There was definitely a plan to boom down on him* [Frame grabs #1 and #2] *and have him come forward* [Frame grab #6], *but the rest of the scene with Matty when he returns to the house* [starting at the end of the shot with Frame grab #6] *was largely constructed, reconstructed, and rethought out because of the camera problem.... This particular sequence was not intended to be cut this way at all.*

frame grab 1   frame grab 2   frame grab 6

BO: *Can you explain?*

CL: *When this was done back in 1980-81, the Steadicam was a new piece of equipment that wasn't yet very reliable... sometimes it would work, and sometimes it wouldn't. We got the dailies of Bill Hurt* [Ned] *from the outside, the angle going into the house, where he's pacing back and forth* [Frame grabs #10 and #12] *and sees Matty Walker on the other side of this front door with the little panes of glass.* [Frame grab #7] *And he walked back and forth several times and he stopped, picked up the chair and smashed through.* [Frame grab #16].

frame grab 7   frame grab 10   frame grab 12   frame grab 16

[But] *when we got the dailies the lab called (Technicolor here in New York), they said, "Half of it's streaking, there's no image." I said, "Well, ship what you've got, we'll look at it in the dailies and we'll figure out what we're going to do..." I knew that once we wrapped that location — and we were within a day or so of wrapping it — we were never going to be able to go back, because the wrecking ball was coming right away to destroy part or all of the house. The ground under the house where we were shooting had turned into a sinkhole. So I looked at everything and told Larry, "I'm going to take the parts of the takes that we've got that work and just string them together, and we'll look at that in dailies." So I just cut them together, all of that angle, and we had enough to get him to A to B to C, but there was not one complete take that we could use. [The director's] idea of being behind Bill* [Ned] *over his shoulder and literally going with him... having it be a moment that was seen largely from his POV, wasn't going to happen, so we had to figure out a way that we could cut the pieces together. That meant we were going to have to do the reverses* [reverse angles], *but we were scheduled to get out of this house. We talked it over with* [producer] *Fred Gallo and the first AD* [assistant director] *Michael*

Grillo and we said, "Let's just take the windows and doors and set decorating back to L.A., we'll figure out which shots we need; we'll shoot them in L.A. and then put this sequence together there." This is one of the last sequences that went together because we had that problem. We got these extra shots of Matty, different sizes of Matty, because we were just going to be shooting across Ned, through the window seeing her.

BO: *You're talking about Frame grabs #9, #14, and #17.*

CL: *We had a medium shot* [Frame grab #9] *and close-ups* [Frame grabs #14 and #17] *of her standing inside, yeah. Those were shot after we knew we had a camera problem.*

frame grab 9   frame grab 14   frame grab 17

BO: *As well as the shots of Ned from her POV* [Frame grabs #8, #11, #13, and #15]

frame grab 8   frame grab 11   frame grab 13   frame grab 15

BO: *So if you hadn't had a camera problem, the entire sequence where he's pacing outside the house would have basically been one shot.*

CL: *Essentially a Steadicam shot from Ned's point of view… we didn't have anything to cut away to.*

BO: *You were just going to have that moving camera stay on him until he moves through the doorway towards Matty* [Frame grab #18].

frame grab 18

CL: *Then he grabs her* [at the end of the same shot: Frame grab #19].

frame grab 19

The Steadicam stopped there... The rest of these [Frame grabs #20 through #29] *were shot in the house, the scene that came right after he breaks through.*

frame grab 20   frame grab 21   frame grab 22   frame grab 23   frame grab 24

frame grab 25   frame grab 26   frame grab 27   frame grab 28   frame grab 29

BO: *A movie critic could look at that sequence and say, the filmmakers' conception was brilliant, the way they intercut those shots of him pacing outside, her looking at him, then his looking at her as if he's a caged animal. Don't you feel that it is a better scene because of the camera problem?*

CL: *I think so, I really do. And who knows, if we ever had a complete Steadicam shot to look at, whether we would've seen that it didn't work.... I do think it wouldn't have been as much fun.*

BO: *It's also more stylized and in keeping with the film noir genre. It's movie time: that she's just standing there like a gilded bird, waiting....*

CL: *Waiting for him to do something. He's not going to open the door.*

BO: *I can see a little mismatch from the reshoots: In the medium shot of her inside (Frame grab #9), she's standing away from the stairs at the bottom of the railing, which doesn't match with where she stands in the Steadicam shots shown in Frame grabs #16 and #18. Also, there is no curtain on the door in the Steadicam shot shown in Frame grab #16, but there is in the re-shoot shown in Frame grab #15.*

CL: *There are a lot of mismatches in* Body Heat.

BO: *But, of course, this is all working beautifully, so the audience never notices.*

The dramatic peak of the scene, when Ned smashes the glass, is augmented by the editor's use of sound. Up until now, the editor allowed the sound of the chimes to play under the action, but once Ned crashes through the door, the pressure inside his head is released and the chimes stop. That's when the real passion — and the swelling music — takes over and the score continues to play for the rest of the scene. When Ned does finally break that glass (*Frame grab #16*), the obvious editing choice would have been to stay on Ned as he moves into the house. Instead, the editor cuts back to the same close shot of Matty she used in *Frame grab #14*. Only this time, in *Frame grab #17*, Matty's mouth is parted and she looks aroused. This shot reveals that Ned's forcing his way in and aggressively "taking her" is a complete turn-on to Matty — and to the women in the audience!

frame grab 16

frame grab 17

BO: *You could have stayed on that Steadicam shot that followed him inside, but right in the middle of it, you cut again to that close shot of her, this time showing her more excited, looking almost orgasmic. I home in on* Frame grab #17, *because I think it's such an editing moment that clearly reveals a female sensibility.*

CL: *It's the take when she gasps; yes, I do remember putting that together there. That was her biggest reaction of the shots we had of her.*

BO: *I think it's very much a female fantasy, the excitement of being taken, somewhat violently, when Ned smashes through — and guys would not necessarily pick up that.*

CL: *That's true.*

Then the editor cuts back to the shot of Ned continuing to enter the house (the "in" frame is *Frame grab #18*). She stays with this dizzying, handheld camera move until Ned grabs her, kisses her and she kisses him back, to show that she is least as much the aggressor as he is (the "out" frame of this shot is *Frame grab #19*).

frame grab 18

frame grab 19

The first shot the editor uses after the kiss is of Matty taking the initiative again by running her hands down his back and grasping it (the "in" frame is *Frame grab #20*).

frame grab 20

The next two shots are examples of the film's playful, contrived choreography — and how it underlines Matty's "look at me" posing and manipulation. *Frame grab #21* is the "out" frame of a shot where Matty pulls away from kissing Ned and flings her body around so her back is up against him, wanting him to look at her.

frame grab 21

The editor milks that moment by cutting to the more distant angle of the same "look at me" pose (the "in" frame is *Frame grab #22*).

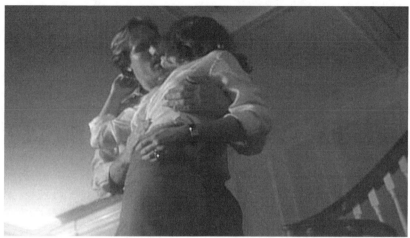

frame grab 22

The editor holds on this shot to show him rub her breasts and then run his hands down between her legs (*Frame grab#23*).

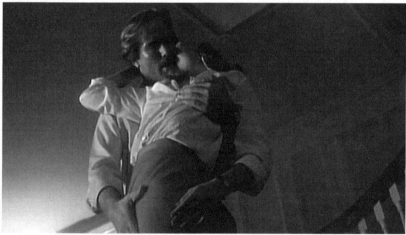

frame grab 23

CL: *What's really suggestive and unbelievably seductive in my mind is the angle shown in* [Frame grab] *#22 and #23..*

BO: *Why?*

CL: *I guess because first of all, that angle is amazing, you get her long legs, her long torso — there's something that's very dangerous, like sex is dangerous.... You don't know that it's a setup but you know that this guy is in her house —not that the husband can come home anytime, I don't mean that — but they both step way over the line, and you know that the rest of the movie is going to be downhill from here. But the danger... and sex are kind of marvelous together.*

BO: *It is also intriguing because of the way she presents herself to him.*

CL: *Yeah, I think so. I think because it's just a very staged moment, but it also says so much about both of them.*

BO: *His voyeurism and her narcissism.*

CL: *Yes, and* [Frame grab] *#22 and #23 is a total noir shot shooting up at the ceiling; it has a big Dutched angle* [in which the camera is tilted] *that's an incredibly beautiful Germanic noir, really expressionistic shot. We were seduced by the movie, too, and* [the actors] *were so beautiful.*

BO: *You definitely held our attention in that shot.*

CL: *We held on that shot a long time because he fondles her.*

BO: *I thought that could have been a difficult cut to make, from Frame grab #21 to #22, to a more distant shot of the same angle.*

CL: *Oh yes, absolutely. I just knew that their action had to match. You really had to use movement to pull that off.*

BO: *Did the director intend those two* [Frame grabs #21 and #22] *to be cut together?*

CL: [It was] *my choice. Obviously when they come in, he grabs her, they kiss, this follows a progression and then the hands down the back* [Frame grab #20] *and* [Frame grabs #] *21 and 22, these were takes that were taken all the way through, and the action's the same. If we were talking about whatever scene number this is, this* [the above-mentioned frame grabs] *would probably be an A, B, and C angle.*

The editor cuts back and forth to more shots of them kissing, her kissing his chest, his hiking up her skirt and sliding his hand under her panties. She then pulls away and initiates another "look at me" move by lying down and hiking up her skirt; but we only see her from the waist up. Then the editor cuts to a distant shot, a reflection from the glass door of Ned sliding Matty's panties off her knees (the "out" frame is *Frame grab #24*). The next reverse shot (the "in" frame is *Frame grab #25*) implies Ned's continuing to remove the panties by the movement of his arms and her legs.

frame grab 24

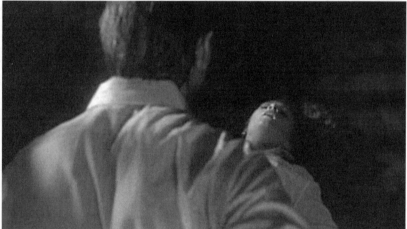

frame grab 25

CL: *The reflection of the action in the windows* [Frame grab #] *24, showing both of them on the floor, is the most voyeuristic of all of them. It's the most graphic, in the sense of graphic design of a shot. The framing of the door, the framing of their action, the frame within a frame…. The most we ever see, really is in* [Frame grab #] *24 and whose point of view is it? It's ours. It's a real Peeping Tom shot. We're showing her actually disrobing in the beginning of actual lovemaking in that shot rather than showing it literally, which might have been in* [Frame grab #] *25. They shot all the way through in* [Frame grab #] *24 and* [Frame grab #] *25, but there was definitive selection not to show too much in* [Frame grab #] *25. You're not going to show literally what's happening.*

BO: *So there was more graphic footage at the end of that shot* [Frame grab #] *25?*

CL: *It was simulated, but yeah….*

BO: *So by cutting away to the panties....*

CL: *You're staying away from the action.*

The next cut (*Frame grab #26*) is to a shot of Ned's hand dropping her panties onto the floor.

frame grab 26

CL: *There's one shot I would have to say, number [Frame grab #] 26, that I did not want in the movie. I did not like the panties going down, [but] Larry loved it; he said it's a guy thing, gotta leave it in. I just really didn't like that.*

BO: *Because everything else was more implied.*

CL: *And this was very, very specific. Yeah, he found that to be irresistible.*

BO: *I guess the panty shot represents more of a guy's fantasy. What would you have cut to instead of the panties?*

CL: *I would have just cut to her face.*

After the shot of the panties, the editor cuts to a close-up of Matty looking very turned on (*Frame grab #27*). She then cuts to a close-up of Ned lustfully looking at what he's just undressed, shown in *Frame grab #28*). The fact that the audience, once again, doesn't see her from the waist down but only imagines what Ned is seeing, is another example of the editor's feminine touch — and the power of suggestion.

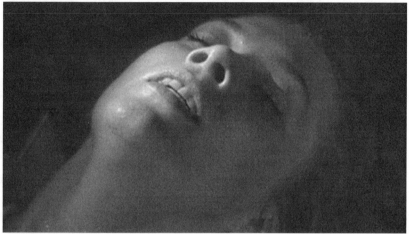

frame grab 27

frame grab 28

The editor then cuts to the climactic shot: a theatrically-posed high angle shooting down on Matty, her arms and hair dramatically splayed out on the floor (the "in" frame is *Frame grab #29*). In this shot, Matty is again only seen only from the waist up.

frame grab 29

BO: *Did you worry about Frame grab 29?*

CL: Y*eah, it's a little posey. I worried about her hair being laid out that much. I tried taking that out. He* [the director] *didn't like it, but we would've had to go from* [Frame grab #] *28* [Ned's close-up] *to the headboard and that's not right.*

After Ned moves on top of her, the shot dissolves to the headboard of her bed.

BO: *Did you shorten the beginning of that high shot so you wouldn't have too much of that theatrical pose?*

CL: *Yeah….*

BO: *Was there any discussion with the director about this foreplay sequence?*

CL: *I think it was one of those cases where we really needed to see how the film played from the beginning down to this point and this is one of the last things that I cut, so when Larry and I were looking at it one of the first things we saw was, oh whoa, this is way too long. I think that the part where the scene got too long was starting with* [Frame grab #] *19 through to the end. I used all the angles, but basically* [less] *of each shot… and the action was just shortened quite a lot.*

BO: *When the director hired you, it must have been a plus that you're not only a woman but also a musician, that you're more sophisticated about music than most editors.*

CL: *It was just a lucky coincidence…. When it came time for us to talk about a composer, I strongly recommended John Barry. Larry wanted the film to be as close to the film noir genre as possible, and we knew we needed to have some kind of a jazz score for that, not only because of the steamy and sexual suggestion, but it needed to be evocative of a time when jazz was used a lot in Hollywood scores…. I think one of the biggest contributions to the film was John Barry's score.*

BO: *You also have a unique perspective on the connection between music and dialogue.*

CL: *When I'm editing I would have to say that I'm very aware of the musicality of the language, and I don't disrupt it, if it's working well, especially with writer-directors [who] have a strong identification with the language. For instance, in* Body Heat, *the language itself is seductive because it's hyper-stylized, and he [the director] used it and didn't shy away from it. It was absolutely laid out there. He didn't know if an audience was going to laugh when they heard that arch dialogue or not. But I felt that if we're going all the way, I have to embrace that language.*

BO: *How did the audience react to this scene when you previewed it? Could you hear a pin drop?*

CL: *Absolutely. They just gasped.*

BO: *This is a classic example of less is more in a sex scene and how powerful that can be.*

CL: *Oh, yeah.*

BO: *Did you have some concerns about this scene?*

CL: *I think we were really concerned when we previewed the film, we thought well, if we can get by this scene, if the audience can buy this scene, we'll be okay, but if there's a laugh when he forces his way in by crashing through this French door, grabbing her and throwing her on the ground, and going through the love making scene and seduction the way he does…. Little did we know the scene after this was the one the audience laughed at.*

BO: *The post-coital scene of them in bed?*

CL: *Yes, the scene is in the movie but the dialogue is out; they laughed at the dialogue. Matty said something to the effect, if I can remember, "I didn't want this to happen," and the audience just — she did want it to happen of course, she wanted to be seduced. So we had to lose the dialogue, and they're just in bed and she reaches for him and that's it* [shown in Frame grab #30].

And the shot of Ned Racine the next morning when he was walking across the little street, he's sort of self-satisfied [the "in" frame of the shot is Frame grab #31]. *We never saw that as being very funny, but it was a huge laugh. I think the audience was unbelievably uncomfortable with the last moment of the scene, where she's groping him before, you don't know how long it's going to go on. Then we just cut to daylight and he's walking across the street, and* [the audience was] *terribly relieved, I think.*[36]

frame grab 30

frame grab 31

This is a classic example of the fact that an editor always has to be aware of the domino effect. What follows and precedes a scene definitely has an impact of the scene he is working on, and those results can be surprising. It should also be noted that, even though there is no nudity or graphic sex in this scene from *Body Heat*, this is arguably the most memorable. There are other sex scenes later in the movie that are much more explicit and show quite a bit of nudity, but this scene is the most erotic. There's a powerful buildup of tension and then exhilaration, when Matty finally lets herself be taken by Ned. And then, once they finally connect, the audience is shown just enough to completely stimulate their sexual imagination.

THE MUSICAL

The musical genre, in its traditional form, is constraining for an editor, because he is basically locked in by the score. As music editor Suzana Peric says, "*You have music that's married to picture, and you have to cut with those two elements always tied together. Say you're in a musical sequence, somebody's singing on the stage, and now you'd like very much an angle of this performer at a certain point — you cannot cut in the middle of a song to another verse. The lips have to be in sync with the song.*"[37]

In a conventional musical not only are the pictures and music joined, but also the story itself is told mostly through singing. And because the purely narrative scenes are shot in a different style from the musical ones, the director and editor can find it challenging to combine the two. This is much less of a problem if the leading character is a musical performer, because then the transitions are often not as abrupt. In fact, there's a history of musicals that have starred famous singers rather than professional actors — movies usually written with minimal narrative and often created primarily as a vehicle to showcase the star. An example would be the Elvis Presley rock 'n' roll movies from the fifties; their negligible plots were just a way to show off Presley's talents and charisma. Within a decade of those movies, however, the musical took on a whole new form.

FRAME GRAB ILLUSTRATION: *A HARD DAY'S NIGHT*

Like earlier musicals, *A Hard Day's Night*, made in the sixties, displayed the Beatles as performers and personalities. It, too, had a thin story: the filmmakers tracked the daily life of the Beatles, culminating in a television broadcast of them in concert before their adoring audience. In several musical numbers the Beatles sang on camera to songs pre-recorded either in rehearsal or in concert, and the editor was locked into showing them mouthing the words to their songs. However, they were usually shot from the unique movie-within-a-movie perspective, which gave the editor a chance to play with the multiple points of view of TV cameras, crew, and monitors. But it was when the Beatles' music played over various sequences that *A Hard Day's Night* dramatically broke away from the traditional musical.

The director of *A Hard Day's Night*, Richard Lester, had done some avant-garde work in television commercials and short films. Strongly influenced by the cinema verité and New Wave movements, he used handheld shots, jump cuts, and the juxtaposition of extremes: slow motion and fast motion, close shots and long shots, realism and surrealism. The movie's innovative shooting and editing style broke many rules, which reflected the liberating spirit of the Beatles themselves. The first third of the movie, as director Lester said, *"was shot in real places with* [the Beatles]*… being hounded and told what to do and where to go, so there's a certain moment when they break out and refuse and run down the fire escape and go into a field and just be idiots. That sense of relief was what we were trying to do. And that was cut with the music 'Can't Buy Me Love' and it's when the film begins to take off."*[38]

To reflect this energy and spirit, the director used more revolutionary film techniques here than in any other musical sequence in the movie. Although its style may seem commonplace now, at the time this sequence was groundbreaking. (The film was a precursor of the music videos that took off in the eighties, when the audience would come to expect a kind of anarchy and pace in both the shooting and editing.) But no matter how dizzying and absurd the visuals were, the editor was still tied to the emotions, continuity, and rhythm of the song.

The setup:
The Beatles (John Lennon, Paul McCartney, George Harrison, Ringo Starr) were being pestered by their manager and especially by the TV director they were working with, who didn't like them improvising and generally clowning around during rehearsal. The following sequence starts with them running away from the tedious work in the studio. The building's door bursts open, and the Beatles appear outside, at the top of the fire escape, with Ringo yelling "We're out!"

The song "Can't Buy Me Love" kicks off with a series of shots showing the Beatles flying down the stairs. The next shot shows them running away from the camera, like children, into an open field.

EXT. FIELD — DAY
Long shot from helicopter of the Beatles running around.

"I may not have a lot to give,
but what I've got I'll give to you.
I don't care too much for money,
Money can't buy me love.
Can't buy me lo-ove
Everybody tells me so.
Can't buy me lo-ove, No, no, no, no!
Say you don't need no diamond rings, and I'll be sa-...

 *FRAME GRAB #1*

                                              CUT TO:

Medium long shot of Beatles kneeling on field, in starting position.

 *FRAME GRAB #2*

"...tisfied. Tell me that you want the kind of things that money...

They set off running — and then fall down.

                                         CUT BACK TO:

Helicopter shot of Beatles running around.

" ...just can't buy. I don't care too..."

 *FRAME GRAB #3*

                                              CUT TO:

Medium long shot of Beatles, continuation of them goofing around.

 FRAME GRAB #4

"...much for money, money can't buy me love."

CUT TO:

Close shot of Paul, making faces.

FRAME GRAB #5

(A scream, then instrumentals)

Handheld camera pans over to Ringo and George.

FRAME GRAB #6

CUT TO:

Close shot of ground.

FRAME GRAB #7

Camera pans over to a shadow and boots and legs, then up to Ringo, who runs toward camera, which pans down again to show his legs and boots, ending with an empty shot of cement ground.

CUT TO:

Medium handheld shot of the Beatles; they bump together and then run apart.

FRAME GRAB #8

CUT TO:

Long shot from helicopter with continued action of the Beatles running apart.

FRAME GRAB #9

CUT TO:

Medium long shot of the Beatles still clowning around.

"Can't buy me lo-ove, everybody tells me so.
Can't buy me lo-ove, no no…"
They run out of the frame, the last one being John.

 *FRAME GRAB #10*

CUT TO:

Medium long shot from helicopter of the Beatles running.
Camera pulls up higher as the Beatles continue to run.

"…no, no!
Say you don't need no diamond ring
And I'll be satis-…"

 *FRAME GRAB #11*

CUT TO:

Medium shot of John, jumping down from sky.

 *FRAME GRAB #12*

"…fied."

CUT TO:

Medium shot of George, jumping down from sky.

 *FRAME GRAB #13*

"Tell me that you…"

CUT TO:

Medium shot of Paul, jumping down from sky.

" ... want the..."

FRAME GRAB #14

CUT TO:

Medium long shot of Ringo, standing with bent knees.

FRAME GRAB #15

He barely jumps up and down.

"... kind of things that money just can't..."

CUT TO:

Long shot from helicopter of the Beatles, with George running around, tangled in jacket.

"...buy. I don't care too much for money, money..."

FRAME GRAB #16

CUT TO:

Close shot, shooting down at Paul, Ringo, and George's faces as they chatter away.

FRAME GRAB #17

"...can't buy me love. Can't buy me lo-..."

CUT TO:

Medium long shot from helicopter of the Beatles running around.

"...o-ove, Lo-"

FRAME GRAB #18

CUT TO:

"...o-ove, Lo-"

Long shot from helicopter, another angle of the Beatles.

FRAME GRAB #19

"...o-ove. Buy me lo-ove. Ohh."

CUT TO:

Close shot of a farmer's rubber boots.

FRAME GRAB #20

(Last musical beat.)

Camera pans up to a medium long shot of the farmer with the Beatles in background.

FARMER
I suppose you realize this is private property!

The Beatles walk off the field, moving past him.

GEORGE
Sorry we hurt your field, mister.

Ringo taps his hat in mock salute and as the Beatles exit frame, the farmer turns to look after them in disgust.

DECONSTRUCTION

Scene edited by John Jympson

This freewheeling sequence is technically a montage, since the Beatles don't sing on camera and the song plays over a series of shots, but it plays like a musical number. The editor, John Jympson, times out the Beatles' movements within the shots and from cut to cut, so they seem to be dancing to the rhythm and tempo of the song, even when they're doing pratfalls or just running around like goofy children. The editor sometimes starts a shot on a downbeat or on an emphatic word, but the cuts don't present themselves the way they might in a more traditional montage. The style of shooting and editing appear spontaneous, reflecting the Beatles playful, manic energy. As music editor Peric says, "*The sequence is very percussive, and it kind of goes with their running and their freedom. There's something that feels random, not structured, but it's random on purpose; everything's on purpose.*"[39]

The cuts are motivated not only by the movement of the Beatles and their music, but by the dynamic camera as well. The entire sequence is shot in sped-up motion with no dialogue, even when the Beatles are talking, which creates a feeling reminiscent of silent movies and slapstick. The editor uses dizzying, handheld shots and swooping helicopter shots for momentum, and contrasting camera distances and angles to surprise and shake up the audience. He stays on the first helicopter shot for over twenty-six seconds, so the audience could get into the spirit of fun by watching the Beatles scamper around crazily (the "out" frame is *Frame grab #1*). The editor sets up a contrast of movement in the transition from the unsteady helicopter camera and Beatles running to the next shot where the four of them are motionless at first, shot from the ground in a kneeling position, as if getting ready for a race (the "in" frame is *Frame grab #2*).

frame grab 1

frame grab 2

Also, there is no attempt to match coverage by the two cameras in the next two shots: from the helicopter shot, where each of the four Beatles stands at a distant corner of the cement square (the "out" frame is *Frame grab #3*) to the medium long shot covering the same action, showing them closer together (that "in" frame is *Frame grab #4*).

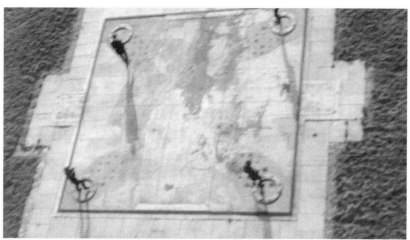

frame grab 3

frame grab 4

frame grab 5

frame grab 6

The next transition is unpredictable, starting with a distorted close angle of Paul (the "in" frame is *Frame grab #5*). The camera ends up moving unsteadily closer, then away from him over to a blurry shot of Ringo and George (the "out" frame is *Frame grab #6*).

frame grab 7

The editor again confounded the audience's expectations by cutting to a shot of the cement pavement (the "in" frame is *Frame grab #7*). Next the camera pans down to Ringo's boots and legs, then up Ringo, and down to more boots and legs, ending with another empty frame of concrete pavement.

frame grab 8

The next dizzying, handheld shot has the four Beatles running into each other and bumping apart, almost leaving the shot in *Frame grab #8*.

In the subsequent shot the action is continuous as three of the band members push away from each other, shown now from the perspective of the helicopter shot (the "in" frame is *Frame grab #9*).

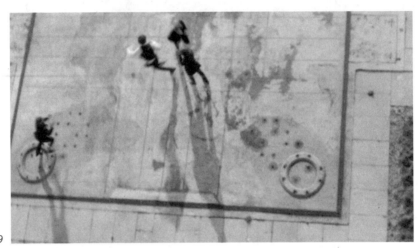

frame grab 9

The action continues in the next shot (*Frame grab #10*, which is the same angle as seen in *Frame grab #4*) until all four Beatles have run out of it, clearing the frame.

frame grab 10

The editor then used another helicopter shot, but this one starts closer on the four, who are running full bore, the camera moving with them and then pulling back and swooping around (the "out" frame is *Frame grab #11*). This is one of the most euphoric moments of the sequence because of the way the editor cut in and out on the dramatic camera moves, and timed the joyful racing of the Beatles to coincide with the second half of the spirited lyrics "no, no... no ... no!!"

frame grab 11

The next cut takes the audience by surprise as John absurdly jumps down from the sky (the "in" frame is *Frame grab #12*)

frame grab 12

followed by similar zany leaps by Paul and George (*Frame grabs #13* and *#14*). The shot after that creates a contrast in movement again, by cutting to Ringo standing with bent knees (the "in" is *Frame grab #15*), who holds the pose so that he barely moves within the shot.

frame grab 13

frame grab 14

frame grab 15

There's even greater change from fast motion to no motion, and from distance to closeness, in the next two shots: from a helicopter shot (the "out" frame is *Frame grab #16*) to the very close shot of all four Beatles lying still on their backs, heads together (the "in" frame is *Frame grab # 17*).

frame grab 16

frame grab 17

The latter half of the word "lo-ove" motivates the cut to another helicopter shot, which starts close on one Beatle; then the camera pulls up and swoops around, showing all of them clustered together (the 'out' frame is *Frame grab #18*). The next helicopter shot (the "in" frame is *Frame grab #19*) shows them from a higher angle in a totally different position, all lined up. Though this action is mismatched, it transitions smoothly because, again, the second half of the spirited "lo-ove" is the impetus to cut, and the clockwise swoop that started in that first shot continues around in the same circular direction when the editor cuts to this second helicopter angle. And, once again, the editor created a feeling of elation by combining that camera motion with the gleeful running of the Beatles.

frame grab 18

frame grab 19

This climactic, giddy shot sets the audience up for a surprise, when the editor cuts to a farmer's boots (the "in" frame is *Frame grab #20*). It is here that the last musical note plays out, effectively bringing them, and the audience, down to earth. This shot also plays out in real time, not sped-up motion, as the camera pans up to the farmer, showing the Beatles in the background. There is dialogue for the first time as well, when the farmer scolds the band members for trespassing. The shot ends as the Beatles walk off, not at all contrite about breaking the rules.

frame grab 20

THE MONTAGE

A montage is an impressionistic sequence of silent, disconnected images that are linked to tell a condensed part of the story. A montage can show the passage of time, a change of place or event, a change in a relationship, or even the internal transformation of a character — his unspoken thoughts or subconscious feelings. Because music almost always binds the images together, the visuals are, in essence, dictated by the music and cut to its rhythm. Usually the screenplay is not specific about what pieces of film should be used, and often it's not clear until the end of the editing process how much of the story needs to be told and how much screen time can be afforded to show a montage.

The editor has a lot of control in choosing pieces of film that are most effective, especially since he is not restricted by the screenplay's plot and dialogue. But because a montage takes the audience out of straight storytelling, it can also be disruptive. If it only gives the audience pleasing music and visuals, it can lull the filmmakers into thinking they're adding something meaningful to the movie even when they're not. Influenced by the rule-bending movies of the sixties and MTV videos of the eighties, the style of cutting a montage has changed, but it still has to be consistent with the style of the rest of the movie. For instance, a conventional movie shot in a static way cannot suddenly have a hyperactive, erratic montage.

THE FIRST MONTAGE

FRAME GRAB ILLUSTRATION: *BUTCH CASSIDY AND THE SUNDANCE KID*

In *Butch Cassidy* there are three montages, which were mostly created to show more of the character of Etta (Katharine Ross), who was considered to be underwritten as the female lead. Of the three montages, the one described below probably reveals more about Etta's character than any of the others. The montage also expresses a lot about who Butch is: a fun-loving trickster with a melancholy edge and an unrequited love for Etta. However, the value of this scene could be questioned, since it's sandwiched between two exciting bank robberies. In fact, according to music editor Peric, "*In the middle of the film you have this 'Raindrops Keep Falling On My Head'* [the song that accompanies the montage].... *It's important to know how she* [Etta] *relates to them, but it was kind of strange. The song has absolutely nothing to do with the movie, anything before or after, but it is something that is remembered so vividly from the film.*"[40]

Why did this somewhat incongruous montage become one of the most memorable scenes in the movie? Because the cinematographer created a glowing, magical look, the actors were gorgeous and charming, the song was completely infectious — and the editor was able to somehow put all these elements together to make magic. To this day, you cannot hear "Raindrops Keep Falling on My Head" without picturing the playful, touching visuals. That's the best proof that a montage really works.

The setup:

Etta is asleep in bed with Sundance, and is awakened by Butch's voice calling her name, as he circles around her house on a bicycle. He invites her to join him, and she runs out of the house and jumps on the bicycle's handlebars. The montage and song starts with Etta and Butch riding away from her house.

EXT. TOWN — DAY
Long shot of Etta and Butch on the bicycle heading away from the town and down the hill.

"Raindrops keep falling on my head,"

CUT TO:

Long shot of Butch and Etta through fence as camera pans with them and they ride in closer to a medium long shot.

"And just like the guy whose feet are too big for his bed,
Nothing seems to fit."

CUT TO:

Medium shot of Butch and Etta, shooting past fence as they continue riding.

"Those raindrops are fallin' on my head,
They keep fallin.'"

   ***FRAME GRAB #1***

CUT TO:

Close shot of branch out of focus. Apple starts to go into focus.

FRAME GRAB #2

It is snatched from the branch by Butch's hand.

"So I just did me some talkin' to the sun."

Camera pans down to Butch, who's holding the apple, until Butch and Etta are medium shot. He hands her the apple and rides with her behind a tree.

FRAME GRAB #3

CUT TO:

Medium shot of Butch and Etta riding toward the camera.

FRAME GRAB #4

Etta takes a bite of the apple, feeds Butch a bite.

"And I said I didn't like the way he got things done, sleepin' on the job,
Those raindrops are falling on my head, they keep falling.
But there's one thing..."

CUT TO:

Close shot of a tree branch. Camera pans down and over to bicycle for medium long shot of Butch and Etta heading toward camera through grazing cows.

"...I know. The blues they sent to meet me won't defeat me. It won't be long..."

CUT TO:

Medium long shot through fence, as they ride down hill past camera.

"...till happiness steps up to greet me."

CUT TO:

Medium long shot of Etta and Butch, shot through slats of wood structure.

"Raindrops keep falling on my head,"

CUT TO:

Medium long shot of Etta and Butch, repeated action (another take). until slats become denser and until the screen is virtually black.

*"But that doesn't mean my eyes will soon be turning red,
Cry-..."*

CUT TO:

Long high shot inside barn. Open doorway shows Etta jumping off bicycle and entering barn. She climbs up ladder toward camera as it pans over and past her to show Butch down below, riding on his bicycle around in circles.

*"...in's not for me,
'Cause I'm never gonna stop the rain by complaining.
Because I'm free. Nothing's worrying me."*

(The lyrics stop and a circus/vaudeville score accompanies the following.)

CUT TO:

Medium shot of Butch riding on bicycle.

CUT TO:

Medium shot up at Etta watching from the barn.

CUT TO:

Medium shot of Butch clowning some more on bicycle.

CUT TO:

Long shot of Butch riding in foreground, Etta up above in background watching from the barn.

CUT TO:

Medium close shot of Butch clowning on bicycle.

CUT BACK TO:

Full shot of Etta watching from barn.

CUT TO:

Medium shot of Butch riding in circle past camera.

CUT BACK TO:

Full shot of Etta throwing hay at him.

CUT TO:

Medium long shot of Butch as hay falls on him and he rides away.

CUT TO:

Close-up of Etta, smiling.

CUT TO:

Medium long shot of Butch riding toward camera, clowning.

FRAME GRAB #5

CUT BACK TO:

Close-up of Etta, pinning up her hair, pensive.

FRAME GRAB #6

CUT TO:

Medium close of Butch on bicycle, grinning.

FRAME GRAB #7

CUT BACK TO:

Close-up of Etta, laughing.

FRAME GRAB #8

More shots of Butch clowning around on the bike, with Etta laughing and applauding. Butch backs his bike into a fence and falls off, annoying a cow that then chases him. Butch jumps back on the bike, races to Etta, who jumps out of the barn and onto bike's handlebars.

"Raindrops keep falling on my head,"

Cow chases them, and camera pans over to long shot of Butch and Etta riding off away from camera.

*"But that doesn't mean my eyes will soon be turning red,
Cryin's not for me,
'Cause I'm..."*

DISSOLVE TO:

Medium long shot of Etta and Butch walking, their arms around each other.

"...never gonna stop the rain by complaining, because I'm free,"

FRAME GRAB #9

CUT TO:

High long shot of Butch and Etta walking.

"Nothing's worrying me."

DECONSTRUCTION

Scene edited by Richard C. Meyer

The visual transitions could have been a problem, because the shots of Etta and Butch on the bicycle are either too similar in angle, coming from the same right to left direction, or don't match in action and physical context. What helped a great deal was that the cinematographer liked to obscure photographic images, so there were many times in this sequence where Butch and Etta were shot through fences, branches, and leaves. The editor took advantage of this by frequently starting and ending shots when the actors are partly or completely hidden, which mostly wipes the shot clean and functions as an entrance or exit cut — and creates visual intrigue. An example of this would be *Frame grab #1*, where Etta's face is completely obscured, but Butch's face is only partly obscured. A few frames later, the "out" frame of the shot shows just a blur of two faces. The following shot functions as an entrance cut, because that shot starts with a blur and soon focuses in on branches and an apple (that frame is *Frame grab #2*).

frame grab 1

frame grab 2

In the shot of Etta and Butch riding behind a tree (the "out" frame is *Frame grab #3*), the branches in the foreground help distract the audience from the mismatches that occur from this shot to the next one, where Butch passes the apple to Etta (the "in" frame is *Frame grab #4*). First of all, there is no side of a tree or shade in the second shot, even though they pass right by a tree in the previous shot. Etta is also holding the apple in a different arm, but the editor made the cut at a point where Etta's arm bent the same way in both shots. Also, the dramatic angle change from side shot (*Frame grab #3*) to the frontal shot (*Frame grab #4*) forces he audience to adjust their eyes and not notice the mismatches.

frame grab 3

frame grab 4

In the sequence where Butch is fooling around on the bicycle, the editor uses the same close-up of Etta three times in order to capture many aspects of her personality. Right after one of the shots, where Butch is clowning around on the bicycle (the "out" frame is *Frame grab #5*), the editor makes an unexpected transition to a shot of Etta with a more serious expression (the "in" frame is *Frame grab #6*). The juxtaposition makes her seem especially introspective and more beautiful in repose than in any other shot.

frame grab 5

frame grab 6

In contrast, the other shots show her being charmed by Butch's boyish antics; she is either smiling, making faces, or applauding. The cut from "out" frame of Butch in *Frame grab #7* to the "in" frame of Etta laughing in *Frame grab #8* is a clear example of that.

frame grab 7

frame grab 8

After Etta and Butch ride away from the angry cow, the editor dissolves to a shot of Butch and Etta that reveals the most about their loving relationship. The shot starts just as Butch starts to put his arm around Etta, and the editor stays on this shot to give her time to lean in on him as pulls her close (the "out" frame is *Frame grab #9*).

frame grab 9

Overall, the style of editing reflects the type of the montage — in this case, romantic and impressionistic. According to music editor Peric, *"the least editing you do the better, to not to break up that feeling. It's a very lyrical, pastoral montage. The song goes with the flow; there's nothing that points to a certain cut.... The tempo doesn't change, it's gentle and very melodic, and so the sequence of the ride on the bicycle is as melodic as that song."*[41]

To achieve this, most of the time entire phrases of the song (and sometimes more than one phrase) remain intact within each shot that the editor used. Actually, the montage was originally cut to a different song, so inevitably the editor had to adjust the length of the shots and the timing of the cuts accordingly. Because even though the composer is influenced and inspired by the mood and rhythm of the song that originally accompanied the montage, he is, according to Peric, *"always going to change something, because the songs in their nature are not* [as] *even as a metronome.... It's just the human factor that goes into a performance and makes that performance special."*[42]

THE SECOND MONTAGE

FRAME GRAB ILLUSTRATION: *THE BIG CHILL*

The editor of *The Big Chill* was faced with a different challenge: she cut all the montages to existing songs. *The Graduate* had started the trend in the sixties by using pre-recorded music to accompany the movie. *The Big Chill* broke new ground in the eighties, because of the extent to which the filmmakers used pre-recorded songs — nineteen Billboard hits in all. Another innovation in *The Graduate* had been the use of two consecutive songs to accompany a single montage. Again, *The Big Chill* went further, an example being the movie's climactic sequence, where the editor used three songs and montages virtually back to back. The songs from both movies were recorded in the sixties, but in *The Graduate* the music was from the time being depicted.

In *The Big Chill*, however, the songs played a significantly nostalgic role. The movie is about a group of college friends who met in the sixties and are now reunited fifteen years later over the suicide of a college friend. They miss that simpler, more idealistic time, and the music is used throughout to reinforce that state of mind. Most of the action takes place in a single location, a house, and one song often played multiple roles. Sometimes it is used to link events and various characters in different parts of the house, and then continues as background music when those characters gather in a group.

Lawrence Kasdan and Carol Littleton, the director and editor of *Body Heat*, also worked together on *The Big Chill*. (The symbol † refers to quotes from both that were taken from supplemental interviews for the movie's DVD; all of Kasdan's quotes come from this source. The rest of Littleton's comments are from my interview with her for this book.)

BO: *The varied use of a song is not that unusual, but what's unique is the degree and frequency with which you used the songs in* The Big Chill *and how successful you were at integrating that music into the movie.*

CL: *Some of it was source, some of it score, some of it would comment on the scene, some of it was contrapuntal to the scene but it would all be one song. Sometimes maybe we just got lucky. We just tried a lot of things.*

BO: *At the end of the movie you used three songs back to back, which is very unusual.*

CL: *At the time I didn't think about it at all, we just knew we wanted the film scored with pop songs that were popular when they were in college, when they were young. It was a challenge, of course. It became part of the fabric of the film.*

BO: *As music editor Peric says of the movie, "Music plays a character in the movie itself. It has a role and it depicts who these people were, who they are now, how they related. It definitely has a function and, I thought, very well chosen...."*

CL: *She's absolutely right. Larry wanted the pop music to be a voice for the film, another character, something as big as the image on the screen. And if you analyze each of the songs, they meant something....*[43]

†CL: *We just started with a library of music, matching it against the scenes to find out which ones actually worked best rhythmically and thematically.... Larry and Meg [the director's wife] actually researched songs, tunes that were popular before and including 1969 and of course they were the tunes I loved, hits you know that I loved when I was in college as well.*[44]

†LK: *There were some songs that had to be in, they were favorites of mine. There were others where we'd try one or two or three different songs and try not to comment on the action directly, but in some oblique way to support the feeling of the movie in that moment.*[45]

This opening montage introduces all the characters in their various lives: Harold (Kevin Kline), Sarah (Glenn Close), Karen (JoBeth Williams), Michael (Jeff Goldblum), Meg (Mary Kay Place), Sam (Tom Berenger), Chloe (Meg Tilly), Nick (William Hurt).

The montage begins with:

A black screen with sounds of splashing water and a man and a little boy talking.

CUT TO:

INT. BATHROOM
Close shot of a boy in the bathtub playing with a toy. He starts to sing and the phone rings off screen.

CUT TO:

Close shot of Harold, who turns to the camera reacting, as the phone as continues to ring.

CUT TO:

Medium long shot of Harold in foreground, Sarah in background. She picks up phone on bedroom nightstand, her back to the camera.

SARAH
Hello?...Yes, this is Dr. Cooper.

CUT BACK TO:

Close shot of the boy playing.

CUT BACK TO:

Medium long shot. Sarah turns to a profile, hangs up phone.

CUT TO:

Medium two shot of the boy and Harold still playing, they look up, reacting.

FRAME GRAB #1

CUT TO:

Medium close shot of Sarah standing there, devastated.

FRAME GRAB #2

(Prelude to song: "I Heard it through the Grapevine" begins.)

CUT TO:

Close shot of a man's bare calf.

FRAME GRAB #3

A man's hands come into frame and pull sock up on calf. Pinstriped pant leg falls down just as the title *The Big Chill* appears over the pinstriped fabric.

FRAME GRAB #4

(Titles continue throughout this sequence.)

"Ooh, ooh, I..."

CUT TO:

Close shot of a coffee cup next to phone and woman's hand playing with cup.

"...bet you're wonderin' how I..."

CUT TO:

Close shot of Karen sitting in her kitchen, upset. Camera pulls back to medium close shot.

FRAME GRAB #5

"...knew, 'bout your plans to make me blue with some other guys you knew before. Between the two of us...."

CUT TO:

Close shot of a man's hands buttoning up dress shirt.

FRAME GRAB #6

"...guys you know I loved you more. It took me by surprise..."

CUT TO:

Close shot of Michael looking down, also upset.

"...I must say when I..."

CUT TO:

Medium shot of Michael's hands rummaging through a pile of papers.

"...found out yesterday. Don't you know that I..."

CUT TO:

Medium long shot of Michael in foreground and his wife in background watching him get more agitated. She goes over and hands him what he was looking for, and hugs him.

 *FRAME GRAB #7*

"...heard it through the grapevine, not much longer would you be mine. I heard it through the grapevine. Oh, I'm just about to lose my mind. Honey, honey..."

CUT TO:

Close shot of a woman's red-nailed hands buckling man's belt.

 FRAME GRAB #8

"...well, through the grapevine [backing vocals: not much longer, would you be my..."

CUT TO:

Close shot of Meg looking upset.

"...baby. Ooh, ooh..."]

CUT TO:

Medium close shot of Meg's hands throwing files into briefcase.

"I know a man ain't supposed to cry..."

CUT BACK TO:

Close shot of Meg. Camera pulls back to show Meg walking away from desk to window. She smokes, staring out at cityscape.

FRAME GRAB #9

"...but these tears I can't hold inside. Losin' you would end my life, you see, 'cause you mean that much to me."

CUT TO:

Close shot of man's hands tying shoelaces...

FRAME GRAB #10

Hand then rubs smudge off toe of shoe.

"You could have told me yourself that you loved someone else."

CUT TO:

Close shot of Sam taking a drink, looking pensive.

"Instead I heard it through the grapevine,"

CUT TO:

Close shot of a tray as he sets down glass next to four little empty bottles of vodka.

"not much longer would you..."

CUT BACK TO:

Close shot of Sam. He looks up as camera pull backs to show him in medium long shot and that he's in first class — and that he's reacting to stewardess standing over him.

FRAME GRAB #11

"...be mine. Oh, I heard it through the grapevine and I'm just about to lose my mind. Honey, honey, well... [backing vocals: "through the grapevine,"

CUT TO:

Close-up of stewardess smiling.

"not much longer would you be..."

CUT TO:

Insert of magazine cover in stewardess' hands, which open it up to reveal *Us Magazine* with Sam on the cover.

"...my baby. Oooh, ooh ...]"

CUT TO:

Close shot of Sam smiling, holding up empty vodka bottle and wanting more.

(Music continues)

CUT TO:

Close shot of woman's hands on knot of man's tie.

FRAME GRAB #12

Her hands slide tie knot up to neck.

"People say be-..."

CUT TO:

Close shot of Chloe's face and bent knee. Leg comes straight up in air.

FRAME GRAB #13

"..lieve half of what you see"

CUT TO:

Close shot of pointed foot up in air.

FRAME GRAB #14

Foot comes down to join other pointed leg on floor.

FRAME GRAB #15

"Oh, and none of what you hear. But I can't... "

CUT BACK TO:

Medium close shot of Chloe in leotard. She turns and lies back, stretching her legs, then props herself up on her side and lifts leg up and down.

FRAME GRAB #16

"...help but be confused. If it's true please tell me, dear. Do you plan to let me go for the other guy you loved before? Don't you know that I heard it through the grape-..."

CUT BACK TO:

Tight close-up of man's upper forehead and back of brush.

FRAME GRAB #17

Brush smooths hair across forehead.

"...vine, not much longer..."

CUT TO:

Close shot of hands on car steering wheel, one hand holding lit cigarette. Pan over as the hand stubs out cigarette in car ashtray, then reaches into glove compartment to get one of two bottles of pills.

"...would you be mine. Oh, I heard it through the grapevine. Oh I'm just about to lose my mind. Honey, honey, well... [backing vocals: through the grapevine, not much..."

CUT TO:

Close shot of car seat. His hand comes into frame, pops top and empties several kinds of pills onto seat and picks up two of them. Hand leaves frame.

FRAME GRAB #18

"...longer would you be my baby. Oooh, ooh] I know a man ain't supposed to cry but these tears I can't hold in-..."

CUT TO:

Close-up of Nick's sunglass-covered eyes in rear view mirror.

FRAME GRAB #19

"...side. Losing you...

CUT TO:

Medium shot of back of black Porsche.

FRAME GRAB #20

Car drives away from screen until it's in long shot.

"...would end my life, you see, because you mean that much to me. You could have told me..."

CUT TO:

Close shot of flat surface. Wrist and shirt cuff come down into shot. Then woman's red-nailed thumbs enter shot and snap cufflink shut.

"....yourself that you loved some-..."

CUT TO:

Close shot of woman's hand holding man's wrist. As she sets the wrist down, the cuff slides up to reveals three stitched-up slashes.

   *FRAME GRAB #21*

Woman's hand slides up cuff to cover the scars.

"...one else. Instead I heard it through the grapevine, not much longer would you be mine."

The last credits roll and the shot dissolves into a long shot of a field, pulling back to show Harold staring out at it.

DECONSTRUCTION

Scene edited by Carol Littleton

Some montages, especially romantic ones, are primarily intended to depict mood and feeling. Because of this, the editing is often minimal, with the musical phrases remaining intact from cut to cut. (This was the case with the "Raindrops Keep Fallin' on My Head" montage in *Butch Cassidy and the Sundance Kid*.) However, when a sequence conveys more information and story, the music and editing is usually less static, and more energized. The opening montage of *The Big Chill* is a case in point: it has an unusually dense narrative which, according to film editor Littleton, was "*very carefully scripted almost shot for shot.*"[46]

In an opening sequence, such as the one in *The Big Chill*, the way the main titles appear and are timed out also contributes a great deal to the overall effect — unless all the credits are saved for the end of the movie, which is the exception rather than the rule. As a result, the editor will carefully plan how both visuals and the superimposed credits work in tandem with the music.

THE CHARACTERS

CL: *What Larry really wanted, one of the main themes in the film, is that the seeds of who we were when we were young are still with us when we're older, and he wanted to show that from the very beginning. I wouldn't call the credit sequence necessarily foreshadowing the whole film, but certainly each one of these vignettes gave you a very, very good indication of who the person was.*

The editor had to establish a great deal about each character without the advantage of dialogue. The details about them also have to resonate, since they leave their lives behind once the montage ends and the movie starts. These introductory shots of each character are emotionally linked by some mysterious news that upsets them all, and they're visually linked by shots of a mysterious male figure, who's being dressed by a man's hands and then by a woman's. The opening montage stands apart from the rest of the movie as a unique kind of narrative that almost functions as a film unto itself. It even has a climax with a surprise twist, when the audience finds out that the body being dressed is a corpse, a man who has just committed suicide. The establishing shots of the other characters — which range from two to seven for each person — not only establish profession and lifestyle, but end up revealing some insight into each personality as the characters respond to the upsetting news.

Frame grab #1 sets up an affectionate father and son in very comfortable surroundings. Their reaction to wife/mother Sarah's tear-streaked face (shown in *Frame grab #2*) sets up the momentum for the song and the spreading of bad news to begin. Sarah's devastated reaction also sets up what we later find out to be the romantic involvement she had with the suicidal character.

frame grab 1

frame grab 2

When Karen is introduced, all we see is her manicured nails and wedding ring. In the next shot (*Frame grab #5*), she is sitting in her designer kitchen, looking upset and somewhat isolated.

frame grab 5

CL: *With the coffee cup and the whole thing, I mean everything about that, you can read suburban housewife instantly.*

The first cut of Michael shows him upset as well, the next shot establishes his messy writer's desk, and the third shot (*Frame grab #7*) reveals his cluttered urban apartment and wife.

frame grab 7

CL: *With Jeff Goldblum [Michael] I think you understand right away that his relationship with his wife is not particularly warm and she doesn't accompany him [to the funeral]. And you get a lot of... who he is and the world he lives in.... He has big ideas about his life, but he's never thoroughly engaged emotionally.*

The first shot of Meg reveals a sadness more repressed than Michael's. The next cut shows that she has files and a briefcase, and the subsequent shot (the "out" frame is *Frame grab #9*) shows the impressive city view from her office.

frame grab 9

CL: *I remember this particular image [Frame grab #9]. We had it pushing in and pushing out. We had also panning over and panning off, so it was a question of which image size and what movement worked with that place in the song.*

BO: *Why does the pull back, or, as you say, the "pushing out," which ends with Frame grab #9, work best?*

CL: *I think because she's the one person who really wants to have what Sarah has, which is a career and a family. She's a career corporate attorney, and it seemed wonderful to have the cityscape below her as kind of an anonymous thing.*

BO: *It feels very lonely.*

CL: *Yes, it's very isolating and her back is to camera and obviously she's mourning.*

The first shot of Sam shows him being somewhat stoic, sitting in an airplane's first class section (the "out" frame is *Frame grab #11*). Subsequent shots show that he's on the cover of a celebrity magazine and that he's boozing it up and flirting with a stewardess.

frame grab 11

CL: *The Sam character is wonderful, because he's a celebrity and he wants to make sure everybody knows…. The narcissism, it's extreme.*

Chloe and Nick, the next two characters who get the news, end up linked together at the end of the movie. The first shot of Chloe shows her tears flowing (seen in *Frame grab #13*); then we see that she's doing stretching exercises in her leotard and tights (*Frame grabs #14, #15* and *#16*).

frame grab 13

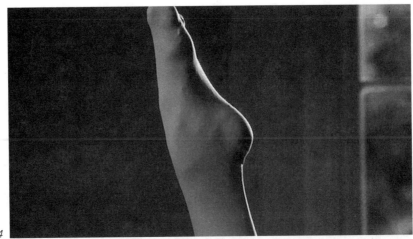

frame grab 14

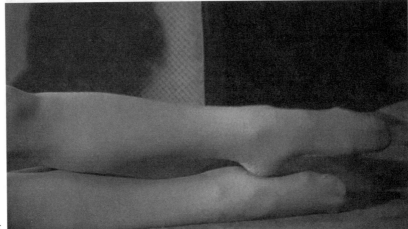

frame grab 15

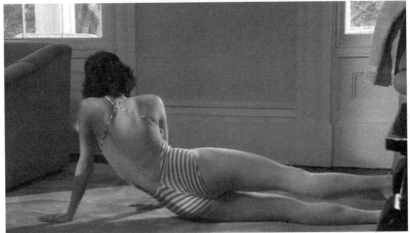

frame grab 16

BO: *She not only has a gorgeous body, but we sense that her youth makes her more openly vulnerable and sets her apart from the others.*

CL: *Absolutely. I think it was the contrast between the younger generation and the older one, and she's not a part of this brotherhood and friendship this particular clique had from college.*

BO: *You introduce her in close shot looking the most upset of any of them* [Frame grab #13].

CL: *She is the most upset…. They always discount her as arm candy, but then they find out she really loved Alex* [her boyfriend and the one who committed suicide].

In contrast, Nick, the next character, is presented as a cipher. The first two cuts of Nick don't show his face, just his hands on the steering wheel driving, smoking, and popping pills. The editor adds visual intrigue here: she starts the shot with an empty car seat before Nick's pill bottle is popped open and pills are dropped onto it. After Nick's hand picks up a couple of pills, it leaves the screen with only the pills left (*Frame grab #18*). The only shot of Nick's face shows him out of focus, behind his dark glasses, in *Frame grab #19*. What contributes to the mystique is his black beaten-up Porsche speeding off (*Frame grab #20*).

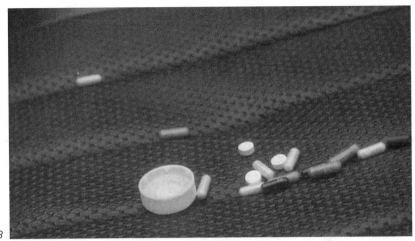

frame grab 18

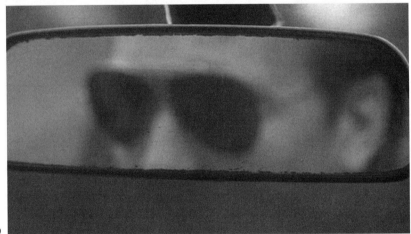

frame grab 19

frame grab 20

BO: *Nick is a mystery; you never see his eyes.*

CL: *But then you see his car* [Frame grab #20] *and you realize all the information you get from his car. He does drive a Porsche but it's barely running and he reaches for the glove compartment and he gets the pills* [Frame grab #18].... *He's the bad boy they love because he's such a slouch, and then you realize he was in Vietnam and he was a casualty of the war, too* [like Alex]. *Interesting that Nick would have taken Alex's place, in a sense, at the end.* [Nick ends up living where Alex did and being paired up with Chloe.]

BO: *Did you always intend for Chloe to come just before Nick, and to somehow foreshadow their connection?*

CL: *I know that Harold and Sarah came first and I know Nick came last, and I think there was a certain amount of shuffling as we went through, as I went through it.... I largely remember trying to make this whole sequence into a tapestry that had a lot of yin and yang. That you would understand by the grief of the women and going through the different vignettes, that you would put the pieces together a little bit like a detective at work so each image would be evocative in its own way.*[47]

THE BODY PARTS

The shots of the Alex's dead body are placed between each character's introductory shots. The shots of the male hands dressing the body are cleverly shot in a way that the audience never gets ahead of the fact that the man isn't dressing himself.

†LK: *One of the first ideas that I had for the movie was for the title sequence in which we would see this figure being dressed* [Frame grabs #3, #6, and #10] *and we might think he was dressing himself.*[48]

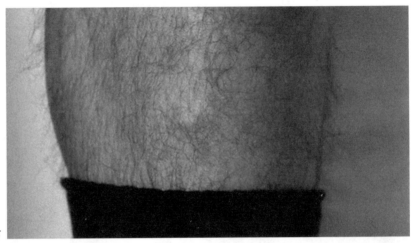

frame grab 3

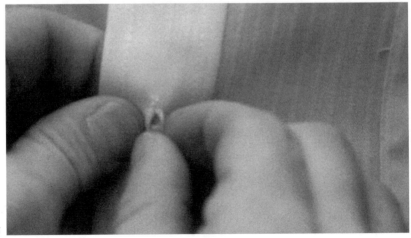

frame grab 6

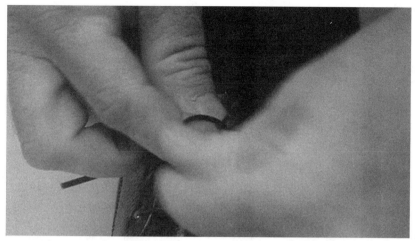

frame grab 10

BO: *Was the order that the body parts specifically described in the script?*

CL: *The part that was specifically described was the actual motion with the hands, of course, because Larry wanted it to be somewhat ambiguous whether this guy was alive or dead. So that part was pretty well choreographed, the idea of the corpse and the red fingernails [Frame grab #8] and how highly art directed it was, was very much a reflection of what was written in the script.*

BO: *First you're supposed to think it's a man dressing himself, and then maybe his lover when you see the beautiful female hands buckling his belt. [Frame grab #8]*

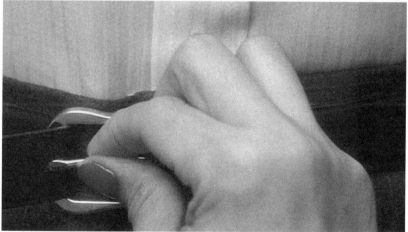

frame grab 8

CL: *Well, I do think we needed to make certain that it seemed ambiguous. We needed the audience to be let on to think that this might be very sexual.... In fact the title sequence is very evocative and then you realize bit by bit that she's dressing a corpse.*

BO: *You're not predictable in the sequencing of male and female hands or in your choice of body parts, but then you show the tie and sliding up to the neck* [Frame grab #12], *so you're moving closer to the head.*

frame grab 12

CL: *You're getting close.*

BO: *And you do save the intimacy of the man's forehead and hair* [Frame grab #17] *to be the next to last shot.*

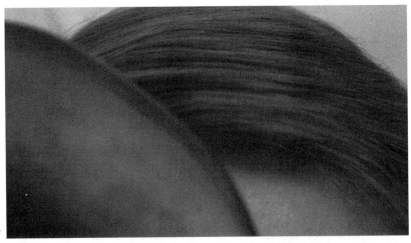

frame grab 17

CL: *Why the hair there? I guess it's the most intimate of all the frames of Alex.*

BO: *And then comes the last body part of Alex.*

CL: *Of course it was revealed at the end the slices of the wrist* [Frame grab #21].

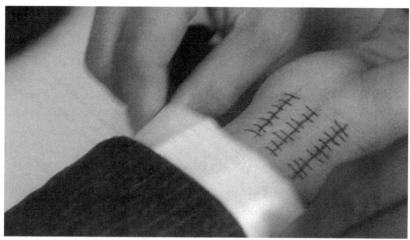

frame grab 21

THE MUSIC AND MOVEMENT

BO: *Was the song "I Heard it Through the Grapevine" selected before shooting even began?*

CL: *There were two songs actually in the script: "I Heard it Through the Grapevine" and "Too Hard to Beg," which was the song that they played when they were doing the dishes.*

"I Heard it through the Grapevine" is about heartbreak. However, the lyrics, which are about a man finding out that his woman is cheating on him, don't literally refer to what's happening on screen. Also, the editor cleverly places the song's lyrics in a way that doesn't directly comment on what the audience is seeing. Only occasionally do they reflect what the characters are feeling, as in the scene of Michael, frantic, being comforted by his wife (*Frame grab #7*, when the words say, "I'm just about to lose my mind, honey, honey") and as Meg walks to the window and stares out sadly (*Frame grab #9*, when the words that play over her are "these tears I can't hold inside").

BO: *Did you shorten the song at all, the recording of "I Heard it Through the Grapevine"?*

CL: *No, you know with rock 'n' roll, if it's a popular song you can't cut into it. It's just very, very hard, because people really know and that becomes terribly distracting, especially in an opening sequence when the song is literally the score. It's like "Row, Row, Row Your Boat." If something's missing, the audience unfortunately has a reaction — what's wrong? — as opposed to getting inside of it, so no, I didn't cut into it.*

BO: *Did that make it harder to work with?*

CL: *No, in a way, it's a little bit like poetry. It becomes a challenge; if you're writing a sonnet it has to be a certain form.*

BO: *But there's a domino effect, isn't there? You time the music and picture out a certain way, it feels right, you're cutting along and then just when you can't make it work at a certain point.*

CL: *You have to say I committed myself to this idea all the way down, but it didn't work so I'll back up, chuck it and start something else.*

BO: *Or you only back up to a certain point.*

CL: *Or back to the point where it's starting to go haywire. A lot of times when I get really, really stuck and feel, the hell with it, I just put in on the bench and I come back and do it tomorrow, just move on....*

BO: *Do you find that you have to do that more when you're working with a song that you can't tamper with?*

CL: *Yeah, to a large extent, because you have limitations, and any time you have limitations and you're trying to dominate them, you just get frustrated.*

BO: *Do you remember being frustrated with this opening sequence?*

CL: *I know I felt that the first time I showed it to Larry, I felt that I had it pretty well figured out and he liked it.... When he sat down, he wanted me to try a lot of things and I got very frustrated and as I recall we kind of went back to what I had originally. There are a few things that are different, but that's kind of what editing is, you try a lot of things and some things work and some things don't, but you have to commit yourself to it.*

BO: *The timing of the music with the picture seemed so fluid.*

CL: *You want a moment to occur on a certain beat because it's strong — or not to occur on a beat — many times you want it to be unpredictable.*

BO: *Can you explain how you cut the montage to the song: was it based more on content or visuals?*

CL: *I think it was less intellectual and more one of image size and movement.*

BO: *Can you elaborate?*

CL: *Well, if there was a move and there was a rise in the music it would make sense to have that matched with the music.... When there's a change in stanza or when the instrumental break starts in the case of "I Heard it Through the Grapevine," it has an upbeat and downbeat.* [She sings the instrumental intro:] *"Oh, buh buh buh buh" and there's a little bit of intro so you would include that with the cuff coming down.* [Frame grab #4]

frame grab 4

BO: *The way that intro is used to present the man's calf* [Frame grab #3] *and then it repeats itself and is used even more emphatically to present the cuff coming down just as the movie's title is superimposed* [Frame grab #4], *well, it's such a significant editing moment. It sets off the whole momentum for the montage. Did the director tell you, "This is what I want?"*

CL: *Larry had several observations on what he thought should come first and last, you know the cuff coming down, having* [the title] The Big Chill *come on* [Frame grab #4]. *He didn't know exactly how to execute it, but it was an idea he had. You know these things evolve in such a way, it's kind of tough to say. I know it was a direction he had on the set, and when I saw the shot, I said, "Well, this is so great, it has to be used in the most effective way."*

Clearly, there is no set pattern in the way the sequence is cut to the rhythm of the song. The downbeat is very close to the cut when she introduces both the song and the man's calf. She not only uses the downbeat within that shot again as the movie's title is introduced, but keeps the momentum going by cutting on the downbeat in the subsequent shot of Karen's hands turning the coffee cup. The first word that plays over that shot — "bet" — also happens to be a very percussive word, which emphasizes that strong beat. And the following shot, where the camera pulls back on Karen (the "out" frame is *Frame grab #5*), does not come in on the downbeat; it's a "soft cut." The next cut of the dead man's shirt being buttoned (*Frame grab #6*) is again a soft cut. The following shot of Michael comes in as a soft cut, followed by two cuts that come in on a downbeat: a shot of his hands and then a shot of him being comforted by his wife (the "out" frame of that shot is *Frame grab #7*). The cuts continue to be unpredictable yet fluid for the rest of the montage.

BO: *The montage feels so naturally linked to the music because you have visual movement going all the time, especially in the transitions. Even if it's subtle, you never just let it sit. It's part of….*

CL: *It's part of momentum and I think a large part of film that has obviously been discovered by the MTV generation is that film is very kinetic.*

BO: *You create that perfect balance between letting it almost sit and then moving on. You don't come to a complete….*

CL: *You do a California stop, you sort of nudge the break but you keep on going.*

BO: *Even with something as subtle as the tear flowing down Sarah's face* [Frame grab #2], *which sets off both the emotion and the first musical notes of the song. You cut out of that shot just as it flows.*

CL: *…you don't want it to go too long*[49]

After the tear on Sarah's cheek flows (the "out" frame is *Frame grab #2*), the shot of Karen's coffee cup begins and ends with the cup being turned. In the next shot of Karen, the "in" frame is on a camera pull back and the "out" frame (*Frame grab #5*) happens the moment the camera stops and Karen leans in on her elbows.

The rest of the shots cut in and out on some kind of camera motion and/or body motion. Even the dead body shots transition in and out with motion. For instance, *Frame grab #6* (the "in" frame of the shot) starts with a hand-buttoning motion and ends only one frame after the hand leaves the shot. *Frame grab #8* (also the "in" frame of the shot) begins with a hand-buckling motion and again ends one frame after the hands leave the screen.

The most "musical" section occurs when Chloe is doing stretching exercises and once again, the editor cuts in and out on peak movement. For example, *Frame grab #13* (the "out" frame) cuts out just as her leg has stretched all the way upward. The next shot starts with *Frame grab #14* showing that same position, in this case a closer shot of her foot pointed up. Then the camera follows her foot down, and when it barely comes together with the other foot, the editor cuts (the "out" frame of that same shot is *Frame grab #15*). The next shot ends when she's turned away and her legs have just joined together again (*Frame grab #16*). Because the editor has timed Chloe's moves and the cuts so well to the rhythm of the song, she seems to be almost dancing to the music.

As music editor Peric says, "*Carol Littleton has such a wonderful sense of tempo and rhythm you feel you're in that song and the titles fall and the cuts fall as if the song was composed for that sequence…. It seems to us that it flows, but Carol made it flow…. That's the beauty about editing, when the editor can tell a story without ever showing their work.*"[50]

BO [to Littleton]: *How much do you think your background as a musician adds to your effectiveness as an editor, particularly in a sequence like this?*

CL: *I think when you're a musician, you learn that you're not a metronome. You need to be expressive with the line, the line of the song, the line of the melody, the line of the rhythm whatever it happens to be. It's not even something that you know, it's something you can feel and I think I was just reacting to that…. It's all about rhythm and choices, many times unconscious… but if I stop and think about it and look at it, well, I know I came about doing that because it's musical, but I may not be thinking of it at the time, to tell you the truth.*

THE FLASHBACK

BO: *In this movie, you fought for an editorial choice that had far-reaching implications.*

CL: *There was a scene at the end of the movie that was a total flashback to Ann Arbor in 1969.*[51]

†LK: *One of the first ideas for* The Big Chill *that I had was that the movie would end with a flashback to this same group of guys in college on Thanksgiving Day. You would see the life they had been talking about up until then in the movie and you would see Alex who has been missing from the whole movie. The suicide. You would actually see him and what part he played in this group. You would get to compare their memories that you'd been hearing about for the first hour and forty-five minutes of the movie with the reality that you would see in the flashback…. It was a wonderful sort of crystallization of everything we'd been talking about.*[52]

CL: *The whole movie was a realization of where they are now, to flash back and realize that they were really the same people, but they'd just gotten older. But we already knew that, it permeates the whole thing. I felt very strongly that an audience, the minute that we dropped the flashback, we had it where it was supposed to be…. We had it [the flashback] throughout the film, we cut it all kinds of [ways]. We spent more time on the flashback trying to integrate it here, there, everywhere and finally I encouraged Larry that we needed to look at it without it, just to see and he really didn't like it. Having the flashback there makes it so specific to a specific time. All the arguments aside, you make it so specific, it's only going to work for this audience who's this age and you're going to cut everybody out of this experience.*[53]

And ultimately….

†LK: *We discovered that [the flashback] totally confused the mood. We had already accrued in the movie all the benefits of that flashback without actually having to see it…. I wanted to tell a very specific story about people of my generation. I had no thought of how popular it would be or how many people would relate to it. When a film gets an enormous response like [The Big Chill] did, when not only my generation but older people, younger people related to it in a powerful way, you're thrilled because that's your highest hope, for something that you told, something so specific that it can be universal for people. It doesn't always happen and in that case it did, and I was very surprised and very delighted.*[54]

COMPARING MOVIES

BO: *What would you say was the difference between cutting* The Big Chill *and* Body Heat?

CL: *I think* The Big Chill *was more difficult than* Body Heat. *They were both a lot of fun, very challenging for me.*

BO: The Big Chill *is very talky with not much plot.*

CL: *This movie is a set piece when you think about it. It's a play…*

When I was cutting Body Heat *I was very aware of the style of film noir, and I wanted it to match that. It's not very cutty, it's in long, long pieces. It's not like this at all in* [The Big Chill]. *One film* [Body Heat] *is linear in its overall structure, it's architecture, and* The Big Chill *is totally circular; and I think if we talk about editing in an abstract way* The Big Chill *is a really difficult film to do, I'm sure a really difficult film for Larry to write, because each character that's introduced into a scene leads us to another character that leads us to another scene…. And while it's very talky, it's very alive, you're not even very aware of the fact that it's just a stage…. You are never aware of the curtain closing, the curtain opening, the curtain closing. It just had to be very fluid from one to the next and the next, building its own kind of steam, have its own momentum. I think the sleight-of-hand in editing has to be in a way more elegant because you don't want to draw attention to it. What you're doing has to be imperceptible.*[55]

CHAPTER 14

MAKING MAGIC

Now that you've read all about it, the only way you can really learn how to edit is to get in there and cut a scene. You can watch forever, but until you wrestle with the film, you won't know how to make the countless decisions every editor must face: Where do I start that cut, where do I end it? What do I cut to and where do I start that cut? There is no real preparation for all this except on-the-job training. With any luck, you would have a talented, experienced editor take a look at your work and ask you why you made the choices you did: Why did you cut there? What's better about cutting there than cutting here? The master editor might also give you a few words of wisdom before sending you on your way.

Over time you will develop wisdom through your own experience, and you can be sure of one thing: You will be a better editor five years from now than you are today. The beauty of learning all these tricks and techniques is that once you start cutting and putting them into practice, they'll become second nature to you. Veteran editors get to the point where they've seen just about every kind of challenge and know how to handle it.

There are intangibles to editing that can't be written about or even taught, those qualities that set you apart as an editor and an artist. Experience will give you the confidence — and nerve — to make the most of your talent and to take that extra step that goes beyond everyone's expectations. There are many amazing surprises in the cutting room, things that shouldn't work, but do. Some of the most dazzling moments in movies happened because an editor took a chance and broke a few rules. Editing can also be mysterious. There are times an editor makes an amazing cut that even he can't fully explain.

Movies are the most elaborate, problem-plagued, expensive form of entertainment there is, and whether a movie's a hit or miss — well, let's just say the buck stops in the cutting room. It's where the mistakes are felt the most, and it's the last place to fix them. All you, the editor, can do is help the director make the best of what he's got. In that process you'll discover that flexibility and empathy are as important for an editor as knowledge and talent.

Audiences today are very tough to please. They have a lower threshold for boredom and a higher threshold for excitement than ever. But there's one reality that's timeless: If the movie seizes the audience's heart and imagination, then you the editor have done your job. You really have made movie magic.

CONTACT SHEET: *12 ANGRY MEN*

frame grab 1-01

frame grab 1-02

frame grab 1-03

frame grab 1-04

frame grab 1-05

frame grab 1-06

frame grab 1-07

frame grab 1-08

frame grab 1-09

frame grab 1-10

frame grab 1-11

frame grab 1-12

frame grab 1-13

frame grab 1-14

frame grab 1-15

frame grab 1-16

frame grab 2-01

frame grab 2-02

frame grab 2-03

frame grab 2-04

frame grab 2-05

frame grab 2-06

frame grab 2-07

frame grab 2-08

frame grab 2-09

frame grab 2-10

frame grab 2-11

frame grab 2-12

frame grab 2-13

frame grab 2-14

frame grab 2-15

frame grab 2-16

frame grab 2-17

CONTACT SHEET: *THE GRADUATE*

frame grab 1-01

frame grab 1-02

frame grab 1-03

frame grab 1-04

frame grab 1-05

frame grab 1-06

frame grab 1-07

frame grab 1-08

frame grab 1-09

frame grab 1-10

frame grab 1-11

frame grab 1-12

frame grab 1-13

frame grab 1-14

frame grab 2-01

frame grab 2-02

frame grab 2-03

frame grab 2-04

frame grab 2-05

frame grab 2-06

frame grab 2-07

frame grab 2-08

frame grab 2-9

frame grab 2-10

frame grab 2-11

frame grab 2-12

CONTACT SHEET: *REAR WINDOW*

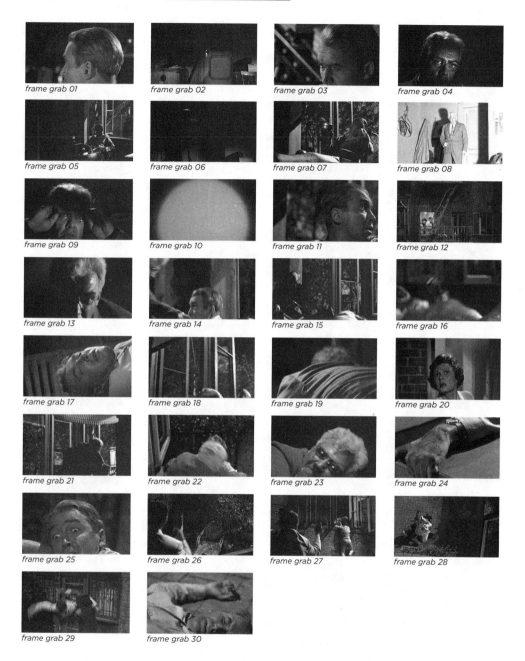

frame grab 01

frame grab 02

frame grab 03

frame grab 04

frame grab 05

frame grab 06

frame grab 07

frame grab 08

frame grab 09

frame grab 10

frame grab 11

frame grab 12

frame grab 13

frame grab 14

frame grab 15

frame grab 16

frame grab 17

frame grab 18

frame grab 19

frame grab 20

frame grab 21

frame grab 22

frame grab 23

frame grab 24

frame grab 25

frame grab 26

frame grab 27

frame grab 28

frame grab 29

frame grab 30

CONTACT SHEET: *CHINATOWN*

frame grab 1-01

frame grab 1-02

frame grab 1-03

frame grab 1-04

frame grab 1-05

frame grab 1-06

frame grab 1-07

frame grab 1-08

frame grab 1-09

frame grab 1-10

frame grab 1-11

frame grab 1-12

frame grab 1-13

frame grab 2-01

frame grab 2-02

frame grab 2-03

frame grab 2-04

frame grab 2-05

frame grab 2-06

frame grab 2-07

frame grab 2-08

frame grab 2-09

frame grab 2-10

frame grab 2-11

frame grab 2-12

frame grab 2-13

frame grab 2-14

frame grab 2-15

frame grab 2-16

frame grab 2-17

frame grab 2-18

frame grab 2-19

frame grab 2-20

frame grab 2-21

frame grab 2-22

CONTACT SHEET: *BUTCH CASSIDY AND THE SUNDANCE KID*

frame grab 1-01

frame grab 1-02

frame grab 1-03

frame grab 1-04

frame grab 1-05

frame grab 1-06

frame grab 1-07

frame grab 1-08

frame grab 1-09

frame grab 2-01

frame grab 2-02

frame grab 2-03

frame grab 2-04

frame grab 2-05

frame grab 2-06

frame grab 2-07

frame grab 2-08

frame grab 2-09

frame grab 2-10

frame grab 2-11

frame grab 2-12

frame grab 2-13

frame grab 2-14

frame grab 2-15

frame grab 2-16

frame grab 2-17

frame grab 2-18

CONTACT SHEET: *THE FRENCH CONNECTION*

frame grab 01

frame grab 02

frame grab 03

frame grab 04

frame grab 05

frame grab 06

frame grab 07

frame grab 08

frame grab 09

frame grab 10

frame grab 11

frame grab 12

frame grab 13

frame grab 14

frame grab 15

frame grab 16

frame grab 17

frame grab 18

frame grab 19

frame grab 20

frame grab 21

frame grab 22

frame grab 23

frame grab 24

frame grab 25

frame grab 26

CONTACT SHEET: *BODY HEAT*

frame grab 01

frame grab 02

frame grab 03

frame grab 04

frame grab 05

frame grab 06

frame grab 07

frame grab 08

frame grab 09

frame grab 10

frame grab 11

frame grab 12

frame grab 13

frame grab 14

frame grab 15

frame grab 16

frame grab 17

frame grab 18

frame grab 19

frame grab 20

frame grab 21

frame grab 22

frame grab 23

frame grab 24

frame grab 25

frame grab 26

frame grab 27

frame grab 28

frame grab 29

frame grab 30

frame grab 31

CONTACT SHEET: *A HARD DAY'S NIGHT*

frame grab 01

frame grab 02

frame grab 03

frame grab 04

frame grab 05

frame grab 06

frame grab 07

frame grab 08

frame grab 09

frame grab 10

frame grab 11

frame grab 12

frame grab 13

frame grab 14

frame grab 15

frame grab 16

frame grab 17

frame grab 18

frame grab 19

frame grab 20

CONTACT SHEET: *THE BIG CHILL*

frame grab 01   frame grab 02   frame grab 03   frame grab 04

frame grab 05   frame grab 06   frame grab 07   frame grab 08

frame grab 09   frame grab 10   frame grab 11   frame grab 12

frame grab 13   frame grab 14   frame grab 15   frame grab 16

frame grab 17   frame grab 18   frame grab 19   frame grab 20

frame grab 21

ACKNOWLEDGMENTS

Thank you, Michael Wiese, for always believing that I would write the definitive book on film editing. Ken Lee, for your guidance as the taskmaster throughout. Linda Norlen, for your knowing, collaborative nature during the painstaking editing process. Gina Mansfield, for your brilliant and enthusiastic job on such a visually challenging book. Cathy Linder and Karol Kamin, for your astute comments and willingness to plow through my opus. Tom Swartwout, for your help as my ultimate film editor resource, and for making sure that what I wrote always rang true. Suzana Peric and Carol Littleton, for your invaluable insights and contributions to my book. Thank you to my mother, for your endless support, and to my father, who gave me my enthusiasm for life and film editing. Thank you to my daughters Molly, for always being my cheerleader during the book's long evolution, and Danielle, for your diligent and very savvy advice. Which leads me to Sam. Thank you for 23 years and for everything you gave me: love, inspiration, and — especially — our daughters.

NOTES

1. O'Steen, *Cut to the Chase*, xv.
2. Lumet, *Making Movies*, 81.
3. Littleton, interview with author.
4. Ibid.
5. O'Steen, *Cut to the Chase*, 131–132.
6. Lumet, *Making Movies*, 14.
7. Lumet, *Making Movies*, 161–162.
8. O'Steen, *Cut to the Chase*, 60.
9. Ibid., x.
10. Ibid., 63.
11. La Valley, *Focus on Hitchcock*, 25.
12. Ibid., 40.
13. Hitchcock, interview from *Rear Window* DVD.
14. La Valley, *Focus on Hitchcock*, 24.
15. Ibid., 43.
16. O'Steen, *Cut to the Chase*, 13.
17. Hitchcock, interview from *Rear Window* DVD.
18. Gottlieb, *Alfred Hitchcock: Interviews*, 132.
19. Hitchcock, interview from *Rear Window* DVD.
20. Gottlieb, *Alfred Hitchcock: Interviews*, 100.
21. Polanski, *Roman*, 346.
22. Ibid., 349.
23. O'Steen, *Cut to the Chase*, 73–74.
24. Ibid., 124.
25. Ibid., 198.
26. Richard C. Meyer assumed the role of editor of *Butch Cassidy and the Sundance Kid* after the departure of John C. Howard, the original editor.
27. Friedkin, interview from *The French Connection* DVD.
28. Ibid.
29. Ibid.
30. Ibid.
31. Ibid.
32. Littleton, interview with author.

33.   Littleton, interview from *Body Heat* DVD.

34.   Kasdan, interview from *Body Heat* DVD.

35.   Littleton, interview with author.

36.   Ibid.

37.   Peric, interview with author.

38.   Lester, interview from *A Hard Day's Night* DVD.

39.   Peric, interview with author.

40.   Ibid.

41.   Ibid.

42.   Ibid.

43.   Littleton, interview with author.

44.   Littleton, interview from *The Big Chill* DVD.

45.   Kasdan, interview from *The Big Chill* DVD.

46.   Littleton, interview with author.

47.   Ibid.

48.   Kasdan, interview from *The Big Chill* DVD.

49.   Littleton, interview with author.

50.   Peric, interview with author.

51.   Littleton, interview with author.

52.   Kasdan, interview from *The Big Chill* DVD.

53.   Littleton, interview with author.

54.   Kasdan, interview from *The Big Chill* DVD.

55.   Littleton, interview with author.

GLOSSARY

A list of movie terminology used in this book

ACTION CUT: Using body motion as a bridge when cutting to a change in camera angles. Also used to show continuity of movement when a subject exits or enters a frame.

BLOCKED OUT: The way a camera and actors are positioned.

CAMERA CUT: To preconceive the exact choice and sequence of shots.

CAMERA LENSES:

Depth of field: The range of sharp focus that is affected by the length of the lens.

Field of view: Area covered by a lens.

Telephoto: Very long lens that causes images to seem closer to the camera and to each other; often used to take close shots of distant objects.

Wide angle: Less than normal length lens that has a large field of view and a greater depth of field; often used to encompass much information in a confined location.

CAMERA MOVES:

Crane: A move from a wheeled platform with a boom on which the camera is mounted, which can raise and lower itself to many levels and swivel to many angles.

Crab dolly: A move from a wheeled platform with a mounted camera and steering control, which has a combination of moves in nearly any direction.

Dolly: A move from a wheeled platform or on tracks that move forward or backward.

Pan: The camera moves left to right.

Steadicam: A handheld but stable camera.

Swish pan: Like a basic pan but very fast with blurs between its beginning and end points.

Tilt: The camera moves up and down.

Zoom: The camera lens moves in or out with no loss of focus.

CGI: Computer-generated imagery.

COVERAGE: Camera angles and setups necessary for a scene.

CROSS-CUTTING: Intercutting between the main elements of a scene to establish parallel action and eventually build to a climax.

CUTAWAY: An edit also known as "cutting to the kitchen sink," that is, to something that is not related to the action within the frame but is somehow connected to the scene, such as a secondary action or observer.

DAILIES: Film shot the previous day that is shown on film, tape, or computer for the director, cast, and crew.

DUTCH ANGLE: A shot used to portray psychological unease or tension by tilting the camera at an angle.

FINAL MIX: Separate tracks of dialogue, music, and sound effects that are equalized and combined into one track by technicians on a soundstage.

FIRST CUT (OR ROUGH CUT): The stage of production when the editor puts the movie into the first complete chronology of scenes before fine-tuning begins.

FRAME GRAB: Individual frame taken from a movie.

"IN" FRAME: The first frame of a shot.

INSERT: A close shot of an object or a specific piece of action.

INTERCUTTING: Edits that cut back and forth.

JUMP CUT: A visual discontinuity created from one shot to the next or by removing a section of film from the beginning, middle, or end of a shot.

KINESTHESIS: The physical reaction of an audience responding with small muscle movements that mirror what they're watching.

LIFT: A section of film removed from an edited movie.

LINED SCRIPT: The shooting script that an editor uses, which has lines down each page to show what part of a scene is covered by each camera angle, along with detailed notation about each of the different takes.

MASTER SHOT: The all-inclusive shot that establishes characters and their setting.

MATCHED CUT: An edit in which the action of the previous shot matches up perfectly with the subsequent shot.

MONTAGE: A sequence of shots, usually without dialogue, which compresses the narrative.

MOVEMENTS IN MOVIEMAKING:

Cinema verité: A movement that blossomed in post World War II Europe, a precursor to the modern documentary; using handheld cameras and portable sound equipment, filmmakers had the freedom to observe and record real people in real situations.

Film noir: A style of movie popular in a cynical postwar America: moody stories of crime and passion, in which the dark subject matter was reflected in the visual style.

German expressionism: Movies of the 1920s and 1930s that were highly stylized, using oblique angles, deep shadows, distorted perspective, and claustrophobic composition, all of which had a powerful influence on the film noir movement.

Neorealism: A film movement originating in Italy in the 1940s that used a documentary approach to convey political ideas, with on-location cinematography, minimal script, and often nonprofessional actors. In allowing editors the freedom to let the story take shape in the cutting room, neorealism influenced the New Wave movement.

New Wave: A revolutionary movement founded by a group of French film critics and students who became directors themselves. They considered logical and conventional storytelling unnecessary, and their style of editing, in particular, broke the rules: using pans, tracking shots, zooms, and jump cuts to fracture time and space and make the audience aware that they were being manipulated by editing.

Wide-screen projection: A technique of moviemaking using a wider lens developed in the 1950s; well suited for grand scale "spectaculars," because it could encompass more information and show greater contrast between foreground and background action.

MOVIOLA: The first projection device used by editors to view the film while cutting.

MUSIC:

Downbeat: The prominent first beat of a measure.

Hard cut: An edit made on a downbeat, thereby calling attention to itself.

Playback: Pre-recorded music that accompanies any singers, musicians, and dancers performing in a movie.

Score: Music written by a composer specifically for a movie.

Scoring: A session in which musicians perform a composer's work along with the projected film on a sound stage.

Soft cut: An edit that comes either between beats or on a beat other than the first.

Source: A sequence of music or song taken from a definable source that accompanies a scene or is heard in the background (coming from a radio or CD player, for instance).

OBJECTIVE VIEWPOINT: The audience is on the outside looking in and sees what happens before the actor does.

OPTICALS (*The basics*)

Dissolve: A transition device in which one shot gradually fades out at the same time the next shot fades in, so that at midpoint each shot is equally superimposed over the other.

Double framing: Repeating frames two or three times.

Fade: A transition in which the outgoing shot gradually disappears into blackness or washes out to a white screen, which is called a "fade-out"; a "fade-in" is the reverse.

Freeze frame: Repeated printing of a frame.

Skip framing: Eliminating every second or third frame.

Wipe: A transition in which a dividing line sweeps across the screen and wipes out the shot to reveal an entirely new shot.

"OUT" FRAME: The last frame of a shot.

OUTTAKE: A take not selected by the director.

OVERLAPPING DIALOGUE: Carrying the dialogue from one shot over to the beginning of the next.

OVER-THE-SHOULDER SHOT: Shooting past an actor's shoulder or part of his head to another actor.

PICKUP SHOT: A portion of a take that is shot to supplement the shooting of the same angle.

POSTPRODUCTION: The time period after a movie is shot.

POV: Point of view.

PREVISUALIZATION: Digital graphics that are used to create a rough version of a sequence, often with digital counterparts to actual actors that can be used for editing before a director films the final version of a movie.

PRINCIPAL PHOTOGRAPHY: Shooting that involves the entire cast and original crew.

REVERSE ANGLE: A shot that is the opposite perspective of a shot already taken.

SECOND UNIT PHOTOGRAPHY: Shooting by a secondary crew that doesn't require the director or principal actors.

SEQUENCE: A series of scenes connected by story, time, or place.

SHOT SIZE (*Overview of shot sizes, from closest to longest distance*):
    Tight close-up: Head with part of chin and top of head cropped off.
    Close-up: Head.

Close shot: Head to shoulders or breast.

Medium close shot: Head to waist.

Medium shot/ medium full shot: Head to knees.

Full shot: Whole body.

Medium long shot: Middle distance showing small group and some geography.

Long Shot: Full geography.

SLATE NUMBERS: The system for identifying each take during filming.

SOUND:

Foley: Sound recorded in sync with the onscreen action (such as footsteps).

Looping (or ADR): Post-synchronized sound where dialogue is replaced by recording it on a soundstage in sync with the original picture.

Post-synchronized: Sound recorded after shooting.

Synchronized: Sound recorded during shooting.

Voice over: Recorded narration that embellishes what's on screen.

Wild track: Sound that's not in sync with the specific action, usually ambient sounds such as crowd noise.

SOUND DESIGNER: Crew member responsible for the postproduction effects.

SPOTTING SESSION: The step in production when the sound and music editors run the movie with the director and film editor to decide what needs to be changed and added.

STAGE LINE: An imaginary line that cuts through the middle of a shot; if the camera crosses it, the viewpoint will be reversed and the audience will become disoriented.

STOCK SHOT: Pre-existing film from a library.

STORYBOARD: Shots sketched in sequence as a blueprint for coverage.

SUBJECTIVE VIEWPOINT: The audience sees what the actor does and they react together.

TAKE: Unit of film shot from the same angle.

TEMP DUB OR SCRATCH MIX: More sound and music added beyond what the editor did in his first cut but preceding the final mix.

TWO SHOT: Two actors within a frame.

WIPING THE FRAME: Cutting to a shot in which something or someone moves across the screen, often in front of the subject, filling the screen.

WRAP: To finish shooting.

BIBLIOGRAPHY
& OTHER REFERENCES

Gottlieb, Sidney, ed. *Alfred Hitchcock: Interviews*. (Conversations with Filmmakers Series.) Jackson, Mississippi: University Press of Mississippi, 2003.

La Valley, Albert J., ed. *Focus on Hitchcock*. (Film Focus series.) Englewood Cliffs, New Jersey: Prentice-Hall, Inc., 1972.

Littleton, Carol, interviewed by Bobbie O'Steen. New York, December 2007.

Lumet, Sidney. *Making Movies*. New York: Alfred A. Knopf, Inc., 1995.

O'Steen, Sam as told to Bobbie O'Steen, ed. *Cut to the Chase: Forty-Five Years of Editing America's Favorite Movies*. Studio City, California: Michael Wiese Productions, 2001.

Peric, Suzana, interviewed by Bobbie O'Steen. New York, December 2007.

Polanski, Roman. *Roman*. New York, William Morrow and Company, Inc., 1984.

VIDEOGRAPHY

The author acknowledges the copyright owners of the following DVD supplements from which quotations have been used in this book for purposes of commentary, criticism, and scholarship under the Fair Use Doctrine.

Bouzereau, Laurent, writer, director, producer. "The Big Chill: A Reunion," retrospective documentary from *The Big Chill*, 15th Anniversary Collector's Edition DVD. Directed by Lawrence Kasdan. Culver City, California: Columbia/Tristar Home Video, 1998.

Bouzereau, Laurent, producer. "Body Heat: The Post-production," DVD Café/ Blue Collar Productions, from *Body Heat*, deluxe edition DVD. Directed by Lawrence Kasdan. Burbank, California: Warner Home Video, Inc., 2006.

Bouzereau, Laurent, writer, director, producer. "Rear Window Ethics: Remembering and Restoring a Hitchcock Classic." *Rear Window*, Collector's Edition DVD. Directed by Alfred Hitchcock. Universal City, California: Universal Studios Home Video, 2001.

Friedkin, William. Commentary track. *The French Connection*, Collector's Edition DVD. Directed by William Friedkin. Los Angeles, California: Twentieth Century Fox Home Entertainment, 2005.

Lester, Richard, director and Walter Shenson, producer. "The Production Will Be Second to None," "The Principal Filmmakers," and "Look at My Direction." Supplemental material, Disc 2. *A Hard Day's Night*, the Miramax Collector's Series DVD. Directed by Richard Lester. Burbank, California: Buena Vista Home Entertainment, 1964.

SCREENPLAY EXCERPTS AND FRAME GRABS

The author acknowledges the copyright owners of the following motion pictures from which single frames and screenplay excerpts have been used in this book for purposes of commentary, criticism, and scholarship under the Fair Use Doctrine.

A Hard Day's Night, the Miramax Collector's Series DVD. Directed by Richard Lester. Burbank, California: Buena Vista Home Entertainment, 1964. All Rights Reserved.

Body Heat, deluxe edition DVD. Directed by Lawrence Kasdan. Burbank, California: Warner Home Video, Inc., 2006. All Rights Reserved.

Butch Cassidy and the Sundance Kid. Directed by George Roy Hill. Beverly Hills, California: Twentieth Century Fox Entertainment, 1969. All Rights Reserved.

Chinatown. Directed by Roman Polanski. Hollywood, California: Paramount Home Entertainment, 1974. All Rights Reserved.

The Big Chill, 15th Anniversary Collector's Edition DVD. Directed by Lawrence Kasdan. Culver City, California: Columbia/Tristar Home Video, 1998. All Rights Reserved.

The French Connection, Collector's Edition DVD. Directed by William Friedkin. Los Angeles, California: Twentieth Century Fox Home Entertainment, 2005. All Rights Reserved.

The Graduate. Directed by Mike Nichols. Santa Monica, California: Metro Goldwyn Mayer Home Entertainment, 1969. All Rights Reserved.

Rear Window, Collector's Edition DVD. Directed by Alfred Hitchcock. Universal City, California: Universal Studios Home Video, 2001. All Rights Reserved.

Twelve Angry Men. Decades Collection DVD. Directed by Sidney Lumet. Beverly Hills, California: Twentieth Century Fox Entertainment, 1957. All Rights Reserved.

SONGS

"Can't Buy Me Love," Words and Music by John Lennon and Paul McCartney. © 1964 Sony/ATV Music Publishing LLC. All rights administered by Sony/ATV Music Publishing LLC, 8 Music Square West, Nashville, Tennessee 37203. All rights reserved. Used by permission.

"I Heard It Through The Grapevine," Words and Music by Norman J. Whitfield and Barrett Strong. © 1966 (Renewed 1994) Jobete Music Co., Inc. All Rights Controlled and Administered by EMI Blackwood Music, Inc. on behalf of Stone Age Music (A Division of Jobete Music Co., Inc.) All Rights Reserved. International Copyright Secured. Used by Permission.

"Raindrops Keep Fallin' On My Head," from *Butch Cassidy and the Sundance Kid*, Lyric by Hal David, Music by Burt Bacharach. Copyright © 1969 (Renewed) Casa David, New Hidden Valley Music and WB Music Corp. International Copyright Secured. All Rights Reserved. Used by permission of Alfred Publishing Co., Inc.

ABOUT THE AUTHOR

BOBBIE O'STEEN is a writer based in New York City. She developed her passion for movies at an early age, watching her father, film editor Richard Meyer (*Butch Cassidy and the Sundance Kid, God's Little Acre, Winning*). Before pursuing film herself, she earned a degree in anthropology at Stanford University and worked with such luminaries as Ray Bradbury and Howard Fast, adapting their novels into screenplays. Shortly after, she joined the ranks of editors, receiving an Emmy nomination for the television movie *Best Little Girl in the World* and assisting on feature films such as *Straight Time* and *Hurricane*. In 2002, she wrote a critically acclaimed book on her collaborator and husband of 23 years, legendary film editor Sam O'Steen. Since then, Bobbie has been interviewed extensively about O'Steen's career, notably for the DVD editions of *Who's Afraid of Virginia Woolf?* and *The Graduate*.

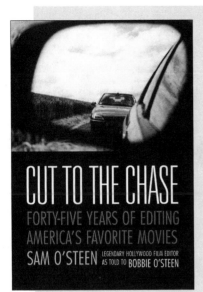

CUT TO THE CHASE
FORTY-FIVE YEARS OF EDITING
AMERICA'S FAVORITE MOVIES

SAM O'STEEN AS TOLD TO BOBBIE O'STEEN

Eclectic and unpredictable films such as *The Graduate*, *Cool Hand Luke*, *Chinatown*, and *Who's Afraid of Virginia Woolf?* ushered in what many historians and movie buffs call The Golden Age of Cinema. As diverse as these films are, they have one thing in common: They were all edited by one man, Sam O'Steen.

Sam O'Steen was a world-renowned editor whose talent, smarts, and desire to get the truth out of the film propelled him to an amazing level of success. He helped shape many of the most influential movies in motion-picture history.

This groundbreaking book takes the reader behind the closed doors of the editing room where Sam O'Steen controlled the fate of many celebrated films. Sam's absorbing stories — from on and off the set — are spiced with anecdotes about producers, directors, and such stars as Frank Sinatra, Elizabeth Taylor, Jack Nicholson, Meryl Streep, and Harrison Ford.

"Cut to the Chase *is a kick! So lively and loaded with gossip and gusto and straight talk about the hard choices in editing. A brilliant book, irreverent and interesting; the careful reticence, not wanting to impose himself on a director's vision while inwardly knowing better, is pure Sam!"*
— Meryl Streep

"*Everything I know about film editing I learned from Sam O'Steen.*"
— Roman Polanski, Director, *Rosemary's Baby, Chinatown, Frantic*

"*Sam was listening to the currents that flow underneath human events.*"
— Mike Nichols, Director, *Who's Afraid of Virginia Woolf?,*
The Graduate, Catch-22

"*Sam O'Steen was an American master and this book tells you where and how.*"
— Robert Benton, Writer/Director, *Kramer vs. Kramer, Places in the*
Heart, Nadine

BOBBIE O'STEEN is a writer with a background in story and film editing. As a film editor, she received an Emmy nomination for *Best Little Girl in the World.*

$24.95 · 250 PAGES · ORDER NUMBER 19RLS · ISBN: 9780941188371

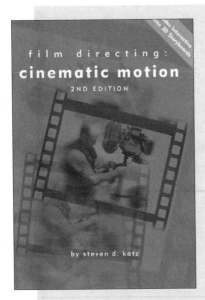

SETTING UP YOUR SCENES
THE INNER WORKINGS
OF GREAT FILMS

RICHARD D. PEPPERMAN

Every great filmmaker has films which inspired him or her to greater and greater heights. Here, for the first time, is an awe-inspiring guide that takes you into the inner workings of classic scenes, revealing the aspects that make them great and the reasons they have served as inspirations.

An invaluable resource for screenwriter, cinematographer, actor, director, and editor, Pepperman's book uses examples from six decades of international films to illustrate what happens when story, character, dialogue, text, subtext, and set-ups come together to create cinematic magic.

With over 400 photos of selected movie clips laid out beautifully in a widescreen format, this book shows you how to emulate the masters and achieve your dreams.

"Setting Up Your Scenes *is both visually stunning and very useful for students of cinema. Its design, layout, and content make the book unique and irresistible.*"
    – Amresh Sinha, New York University/The School of Visual Arts

"*Pepperman has written a book which should form the basis for an intelligent discussion about the basic building blocks of great scenes across a wide variety of films. Armed with the information in this book, teachers, students, filmmakers, and film lovers can begin to understand how good editing and scene construction can bring out the best storytelling to create a better film.*"
    – Norman Hollyn, Associate Professor and Editing Track Head,
      School of Cinema-Television at the University of Southern California

"*Pepperman dissects some very infamous scenes from some very famous movies – providing us with the most breathtaking black and white stills – in order to highlight the importance of the interplay between dialogue, subtext, and shot selection in great filmmaking.*"
    – Lily Sadri, Writer, Screenwriter, *Fixing Fairchild*,
      Contributor to *www.absolutewrite.com*

RICHARD D. PEPPERMAN has been a film editor for more than 40 years and a teacher for more than 30. He is the author of *The Eye Is Quicker*.

$24.95 · 245 PAGES · ORDER NUMBER 42RLS · ISBN: 1932907084

FILM & VIDEO BOOKS

TO RECEIVE A FREE MWP NEWSLETTER, CLICK ON WWW.MWP.COM TO REGISTER

SCREENWRITING | WRITING

And the Best Screenplay Goes to... | Dr. Linda Seger | $26.95

Archetypes for Writers | Jennifer Van Bergen | $22.95

Cinematic Storytelling | Jennifer Van Sijll | $24.95

Could It Be a Movie? | Christina Hamlett | $26.95

Creating Characters | Marisa D'Vari | $26.95

Crime Writer's Reference Guide, The | Martin Roth | $20.95

Deep Cinema | Mary Trainor-Brigham | $19.95

Elephant Bucks | Sheldon Bull | $24.95

Fast, Cheap & Written That Way | John Gaspard | $26.95

Hollywood Standard, The | Christopher Riley | $18.95

I Could've Written a Better Movie than That! | Derek Rydall | $26.95

Inner Drives | Pamela Jaye Smith | $26.95

Joe Leydon's Guide to Essential Movies You Must See | Joe Leydon | $24.95

Moral Premise, The | Stanley D. Williams, Ph.D. | $24.95

Myth and the Movies | Stuart Voytilla | $26.95

Power of the Dark Side, The | Pamela Jaye Smith | $22.95

Psychology for Screenwriters | William Indick, Ph.D. | $26.95

Rewrite | Paul Chitlik | $16.95

Romancing the A-List | Christopher Keane | $18.95

Save the Cat! | Blake Snyder | $19.95

Save the Cat! Goes to the Movies | Blake Snyder | $24.95

Screenwriting 101 | Neill D. Hicks | $16.95

Screenwriting for Teens | Christina Hamlett | $18.95

Script-Selling Game, The | Kathie Fong Yoneda | $16.95

Stealing Fire From the Gods, 2nd Edition | James Bonnet | $26.95

Way of Story, The | Catherine Ann Jones | $22.95

What Are You Laughing At? | Brad Schreiber | $19.95

Writer's Journey, – 3rd Edition, The | Christopher Vogler | $26.95

Writer's Partner, The | Martin Roth | $24.95

Writing the Action Adventure Film | Neill D. Hicks | $14.95

Writing the Comedy Film | Stuart Voytilla & Scott Petri | $14.95

Writing the Killer Treatment | Michael Halperin | $14.95

Writing the Second Act | Michael Halperin | $19.95

Writing the Thriller Film | Neill D. Hicks | $14.95

Writing the TV Drama Series – 2nd Edition | Pamela Douglas | $26.95

Your Screenplay Sucks! | William M. Akers | $19.95

FILMMAKING

Film School | Richard D. Pepperman | $24.95

Power of Film, The | Howard Suber | $27.95

PITCHING

Perfect Pitch – 2nd Edition, The | Ken Rotcop | $19.95

Selling Your Story in 60 Seconds | Michael Hauge | $12.95

SHORTS

Filmmaking for Teens | Troy Lanier & Clay Nichols | $18.95

Ultimate Filmmaker's Guide to Short Films, The | Kim Adelman | $16.95

BUDGET | PRODUCTION MGMT

Film & Video Budgets, 4th Updated Edition | Deke Simon & Michael Wiese | $26.95

Film Production Management 101 | Deborah S. Patz | $39.95

DIRECTING | VISUALIZATION

Animation Unleashed | Ellen Besen | $26.95

Citizen Kane Crash Course in Cinematography | David Worth | $19.95

Directing Actors | Judith Weston | $26.95

Directing Feature Films | Mark Travis | $26.95

Fast, Cheap & Under Control | John Gaspard | $26.95

Film Directing: Cinematic Motion, 2nd Edition | Steven D. Katz | $27.95

Film Directing: Shot by Shot | Steven D. Katz | $27.95

Film Director's Intuition, The | Judith Weston | $26.95

First Time Director | Gil Bettman | $27.95

From Word to Image | Marcie Begleiter | $26.95

I'll Be in My Trailer! | John Badham & Craig Modderno | $26.95

Master Shots | Christopher Kenworthy | $24.95

Setting Up Your Scenes | Richard D. Pepperman | $24.95

Setting Up Your Shots, 2nd Edition | Jeremy Vineyard | $22.95

Working Director, The | Charles Wilkinson | $22.95

DIGITAL | DOCUMENTARY | SPECIAL

Digital Filmmaking 101, 2nd Edition | Dale Newton & John Gaspard | $26.95

Digital Moviemaking 3.0 | Scott Billups | $24.95

Digital Video Secrets | Tony Levelle | $26.95

Greenscreen Made Easy | Jeremy Hanke & Michele Yamazaki | $19.95

Producing with Passion | Dorothy Fadiman & Tony Levelle | $22.95

Special Effects | Michael Slone | $31.95

EDITING

Cut by Cut | Gael Chandler | $35.95

Cut to the Chase | Bobbie O'Steen | $24.95

Eye is Quicker, The | Richard D. Pepperman | $27.95

Invisible Cut, The | Bobbie O'Steen | $28.95

SOUND | DVD | CAREER

Complete DVD Book, The | Chris Gore & Paul J. Salamoff | $26.95

Costume Design 101 | Richard La Motte | $19.95

Hitting Your Mark – 2nd Edition | Steve Carlson | $22.95

Sound Design | David Sonnenschein | $19.95

Sound Effects Bible, The | Ric Viers | $26.95

Storyboarding 101 | James Fraioli | $19.95

There's No Business Like Soul Business | Derek Rydall | $22.95

FINANCE | MARKETING | FUNDING

Art of Film Funding, The | Carole Lee Dean | $26.95

Complete Independent Movie Marketing Handbook, The | Mark Steven Bosko | $39.95

Independent Film and Videomakers Guide – 2nd Edition, The | Michael Wiese | $29.95

Independent Film Distribution | Phil Hall | $26.95

Shaking the Money Tree, 2nd Edition | Morrie Warshawski | $26.95

OUR FILMS

Dolphin Adventures: DVD | Michael Wiese and Hardy Jones | $24.95

On the Edge of a Dream | Michael Wiese | $16.95

Sacred Sites of the Dalai Lamas– DVD, The | Documentary by Michael Wiese | $24.95

Hardware Wars: DVD | Written and Directed by Ernie Fosselius | $14.95

To Order go to *www.mwp.com* or Call 1-800-833-5738